The Boston Region
1810-1850
A Study of Urbanization

Studies in
American History and Culture, No. 10

Robert Berkhofer, Series Editor
Director of American Culture Programs
and Richard Hudson Research Professor of History
The University of Michigan

Other Titles in This Series

The Boston Region
1810-1850
A Study of Urbanization

by
Francis X. Blouin, Jr.

RESEARCH PRESS

Produced and distributed by
UMI Research Press
an imprint of
University Microfilms International
Ann Arbor, Michigan 48106

Library of Congress Cataloging in Publication Data

Blouin, Francis X
   The Boston region, 1810-1850.

   (Studies in American history and culture ; no. 10)
   Bibliography: p.
   Includes index.
   1. Boston region, Mass.—Economic conditions. 2. Cities
and towns—Massachusetts—Boston region—Growth—
History. 3. Urbanization—Massachusetts—Boston region—
History.   I. Title. II. Series.

HC108.B65B56   330.9744'603   79-28080
ISBN 0-8357-1077-7

To Mother and Dad
Suzanne, MaryEllen and John

CONTENTS

MAPS

FIGURES

ix

TABLES

ABBREVIATIONS

BA   A number of citations appear in the footnotes as **BA** followed by a number. These citations refer to specific manuscript collections in the Baker Library, Harvard University. The collections consulted for this study are listed numerically in the bibliography.

MHS   Massachusetts Historical Society

MSL   Massachusetts State Library

MVT   Merrimack Valley Textile Museum

PREFACE

Many studies have appeared in recent years which examine the process of urbanization within the context of a particular city. While those studies imply that the example of one city can be applied reasonably to others, few historians have seriously attempted to investigate the process of urbanization in the context of groups or systems of cities. Many historians and particularly geographers have offered models of one sort or another which attempt to explain the process of national or regional urban growth, but few studies exist which try to apply these theoretical concepts to a specific area or region at a specific point in time. Few studies attempt to study the mechanisms by which this process takes place over time. This study examines the history of a region surrounding Boston, Massachusetts, from 1810 to 1850. It is not a history of Boston but is rather a historical analysis of an interdependent system of 219 cities and towns in which Boston was the focal central place.

The thrust of the study is to suggest through the use of a variety of sources that urbanization within the individual cities and towns of the region was not an independent process. Rather the pace and progress of urbanization in one area both depended on and affected the level of urbanization elsewhere in the region. This dynamic view of the process rests very much though not entirely on the expanding manufacturing base of the regional economy. Thus the study stresses various changing and expanding economic activities in the region and stresses the nature of various linkages operative in the region over time. The period 1810 to 1850 was chosen since it was a critical time period for the region as the economic base shifted from commercial to manufacturing activity. This shift significantly affected the spread of economic activity and the development of linkages in the region. Sources for the period are adequate but not nicely systematic. Thus it is possible only to suggest rather than to prove the applicability of theoretical models and concepts to the Boston case.

Chapter I in an abstract way examines theoretical concepts developed by historians, geographers, and economists relevant to a regional study. The chapter does not set forth a systematic model but rather a set of concepts and assumptions drawn from geography and economic theory which form the essential questions addressed to the historical sources. Chapter II and chapter III discuss the structure of the Boston region and the nature of the spread of economic activity over time and space. The final three chapters discuss linkages which suggest the extent and nature of economic interdependence among the cities and towns of the Boston region.

The staffs of a number of libraries and archives were helpful in locating material of relevance to this study. Mr. Robert W. Lovett, Mrs. Eleanor C. Bishop, and Mr. Kenneth Carpenter of the Baker Library, Harvard University, were particularly helpful. Also helpful were the staffs of the Wilson Library of the University of Minnesota; the State Libraries of Massachusetts and New Hampshire; the Massachusetts State Archives; the Merrimack Valley Textile Museum; Houghton and Widener Libraries of Harvard University; and the Hatcher and Clements Libraries of the University of Michigan. I would also like to acknowledge MIT Press' 1966 publication of Allan Pred's book, *The Spatial Dynamics of Urban Industrial Growth, 1800-1914,* from which I obtained Figure I-1 on page 5. Numerous colleagues at the Universities of Minnesota and Michigan offered encouragement and suggestions, particularly the staff of the Bentley Historical Library. Robert Berkhofer, Maris Vinovskis and Glenn Porter read the manuscript and offered many helpful critical comments. Professors John R. Howe, George D. Green, and John Modell of the Department of History of the University of Minnesota jointly directed the dissertation phase of this project offering three important and different perspectives on the study. Mrs. Martha M. Folk, Ms. Julia Young and Mrs. Dorothy Foster prepared the final copy. To my parents who always emphasized the value of knowledge and inquiry I am particularly grateful.

Francis X. Blouin, Jr.
Ann Arbor, Michigan 1979

I

URBAN GROWTH ON A REGIONAL SCALE

Over the past few years, urban history has not only emerged as a discipline but gradually has developed a multiplicity of subfields. The field itself emerged in the 1960's as something new and quite apart from traditional social history, of which the history of cities had always been an important part. The new urban history was to focus on the systematic study of cities and their populations. Its method would involve the careful application of social science theory to the data available on the physical city and urban populations.

With the publication of the works of Stephan Thernstrom, the practitioners of the new urban history plunged into considerations of the problems and extent of social mobility in the urban setting. With the publication of the Yale papers in 1969 the whole question of mobility became nearly synonymous with the new urban history.[1] Efforts in this direction have contributed enormously to understanding urban populations. The works of Peter Knights, Richard Sennett, Stuart Blumin, Joan Scott and others have ingeniously sought to chart population movements and demographic changes in Boston, Chicago, Philadelphia and Charmeaux.[2] Though methodological problems abound, a multitude of mobility studies has appeared on nearly every major American city and several foreign cities. The mobility question has certainly arrived, but this approach does not exhaust the valid possibilities for the study of urban history.

Even in the 1960's Sam B. Warner was trying to steer urban history in other directions. Warner was interested more in the total city, the physical city and the question of planning and priorities in the evolution of urban places.[3] Warner offered comprehensive themes in urban history through which he attempted to explain not only cities in America but the whole character of urban life and structures in America. This too was part of the new urban history, but it rested on a much less structured methodology and a less standardized body of evidence than did the mobility studies. His work has not been widely imitated.

A third direction, even less popular than Warner's, has involved the study of urban structures. A group of historians, geographers and economists have explored the city not so much as a crowded population center, but rather as an economic unit among other units. This group, by far the least influential in charting the course of the new urban history, is concerned with the structure and growth of urban America—the inner dynamics of urbanization in the economic sense over time and space. Individuals such as Allan Pred and Eric Lampard most notably have offered models for the process of urban and industrial growth from the perspectives of the spatial diffusion of population and economic activity. In their work they have isolated many of the key variables in the growth process.[4]

It is to this third relatively unsung but important subdivision of urban history that this study is addressed. The study examines the history of urban development in the Boston region (later defined) from 1810 to 1850. It focuses not on the character of the urban populations but rather on the process of urbanization through which cities emerge to sustain large numbers of people in small amounts of space. When the population of a region urbanizes, one assumes that there is a greater concentration of population at specific points in the geography and that the population is increasingly engaged in nonagricultural pursuits. This study seeks to examine the process by which selected areas become so urbanized.

The chapters which follow examine urbanization on a regional scale, which is to say that in order to understand the process of urbanization one must look at economic activity in whole regions. This is not to suggest a simple city-hinterland model but rather to suggest a structured interdependent system of cities operative in the region. In such a regional system, the economies of each work to the mutual advantage of each other over time. This study examines a specific region over a specific period of time, noting its economic characteristics, the location of specialized activity, and the urban hierarchy which structures the system. More importantly, however, it seeks to delineate the infrastructure within the region—the mechanisms or linkages which facilitate this mutual dependence.

Within this context it is impossible to isolate one or two towns or cities for study. To understand the process of urbanization in a particular city or town, that is to understand how increasingly larger numbers of people can come to occupy and cope with a given small amount of space, the economic activity of a particular city or town must be set in its regional context and its relationship to the economic activities of other places in the region must be understood. So, this study examines cities and towns, large and small, expanding and declining, established and new, coastal and inland, and attempts to delineate particular aspects of the process of urbanization in the particular region.

Urbanization—what the process is and what causes the process—is clearly a very big question. Volumes have been written about urbanization in the context of one particular town. To raise the question to a regional scale makes it an even larger and more complicated undertaking. This study does not answer the question in all its dimensions but does try to break down the process into various elements and isolate important factors at work in this historical process out of a belief that the regional perspective on the process of urbanization is an important one and one to date generally neglected by urban historians. In determining the spread of economic activity in the region and analyzing the linkages which facilitate the movement of the product of that activity within the region and beyond, the interdependent nature of the region emerges, which interdependence is really a precondition for urban development in the component cities and towns.

The writings of many geographers, economists and historians have contributed insights which together offer a body of logical observations and principles regarding the process of urbanization. This chapter draws from that body of literature a cluster of related propositions about the process of urbanization. The rest of the study demonstrates the utility of these propositions for describing and explaining aspects of urban development in the Boston region. Because of lack of data for the period, this study does not attempt to "test" the model statistically. I wish rather to explicate and then embody it and in so doing to tie together and to clarify relevant aspects of the region and later apply these observations specifically in the New England area and specifically in the early nineteenth century.

Cities are economic units within national economies. Wilbur Thompson has explored in detail the applicability of economic analysis to the city. In his much discussed study of urban economies he shows that the growth of viable urban economies involves much the same process as that of national economies. By applying an export base model of urban growth Thompson argues that the growth of urban economies depends on the *"Stage of Export Specialization* in which the local economy is the lengthened shadow of a single dominant industry."[5] As the dominant industry develops, this will encourage new products to move in, causing further expansion of local activity when the local economy "fills out in range and quality of both business and consumer services."[6] Cities thus import and export goods and services and must in the process achieve a diversified economy to survive. My study, in discussing the city as an economic entity, relies on the Thompson application of the export base model to the growth of urban economies.

If we then consider cities to have growth patterns which are based on the viability of the export base, what are the dynamics involved in the growth process? Allan Pred, in his classic study of the spatial dynamics of urban industrial growth, offers a model particularly applicable to the nineteenth century. Thompson also offers a model, but his present-oriented study with its discussion of the social sciences offers a more complicated analysis than this study requires. Pred, on the other hand, is interested specifically in the evolution of urban places based on the presence of manufacturing. Pred suggests that until 1840 urbanization in America was based on the development of the mercantile sector. Mercantile services provided the export base. As the wholesale-trading complex grew, more earnings were pumped into the local economy allowing for expansion of tertiary activity such as construction, and retail trade.[7] Only in the 1840's and 50's does Pred see a shift in the economic base of urban growth to the industrial sector.

The Pred model offers a simple statement of the essential process of growth within an urban place. The multiplier effect represents the economic inputs, such as capital investment, into the urban area generated either by internal market activity or by import. This stimulus generates either a new plant or firm which in turn stimulates local tertiary activities such as construction and sales of materials. Upon completion of the physical structure housing the new economic unit either by construction or renovation, and upon necessary expansion of the public utility and transportation sectors, an urban place can more readily welcome another established economic unit as part of its economic base. This new plant or other activity will in turn stimulate the local economy as its jobs channel funds into retail activities, etc. (i.e. the secondary multiplier effect). This process, Pred argues, raises the urban place to a new local or regional threshold. Pred's concept of new levels or thresholds is important to his model; it is also important to my study, which attempts to broaden Pred's definition.[8]

For Pred's analysis the new threshold, attained in the process of expansion of the economic base, refers to an expansion of the urban market through increased population and concurrent purchasing power. As this market increases, its threshold rises at each point in this step by step process. Manufacturers make their decisions on location with these changing urban markets in mind. For example, in a growing nineteenth-century city it might have been logical at some point for an entrepreneur to establish a brewery for the local market at a sufficient scale to compete with imports from other locations. The immediate effect of this threshold for the local economy is to increase the likelihood of attracting yet other industry, new or enlarged, which would further expand the economic base of the city and thus begin the cycle once again.[9] Pred's model is not one of simple repetitive cycles but rather suggests that as cities grow, based on an expansion of economic activity, the structure of urban activities changes and the relationship of the many sorts of human and economic activities to each other changes as the growth process takes place. Pred also adds, as a major and debatable thrust to his model, that large industrial cities have an enhanced likelihood of spawning new inventions because their populations are more attuned to developments in various industries. New inventions, of course, inspire new industries and this enhances the dynamics of his model. Pred is conscious of other stimulants, as well, such as comparative

Figure I-1

The Circular and Cumulative Process of Industrialization and Urban Size Growth.

Source: Allan R. Pred, *The Spatial Dynamics of U.S. Urban-Industrial Growth, 1800-1914* (Cambridge, Mass., MIT Press, 1966), p. 25.

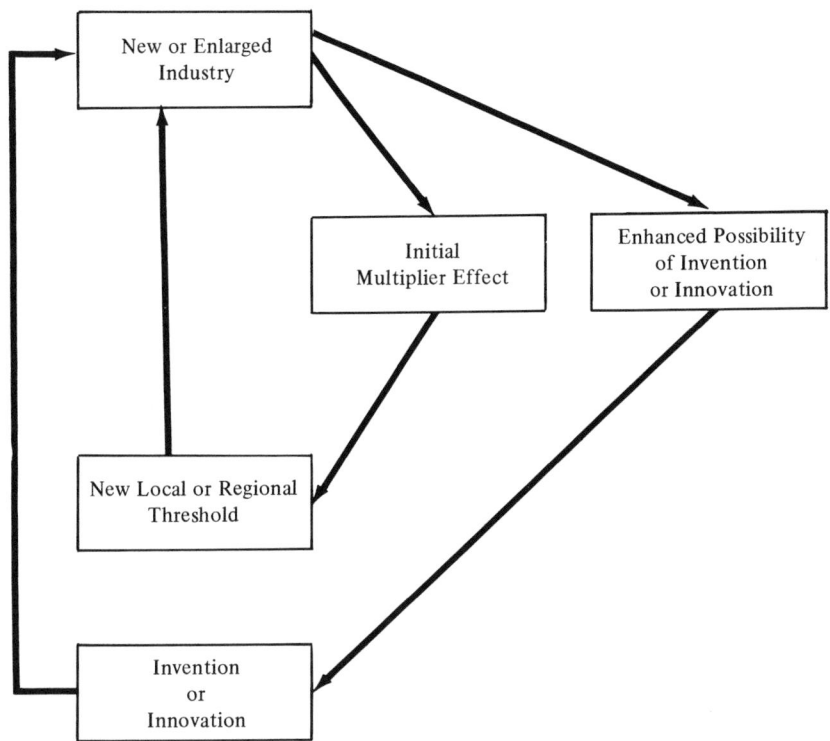

wage rates, agglomerative economies and entrepreneurial inputs. These variables aside, the figure (I-1) represents the essential variables of his model.[10]

Pred's model has emerged as a classic interpretation of urban industrial growth. The dynamics in the model suggest urban industrial growth as an ongoing process—one could reverse the arrows and see the dynamics of urban decline or stagnation. The model very neatly recognizes the relevance of urbanization to industrialization without blending the two. For an analysis of regional economic growth, it is of course less useful, yet the concepts within the model remain helpful. Pred, in his discussion of relative city size, alludes to the whole question of urban systems, but he chooses here not to explore the relevance of his model to this wider set of problems.[11]

An important question avoided in the Pred model is that of urban location. The economic activity described in Pred's model takes place within the context of space as well as time. An urban economy, while self-contained in the sense of Thompson's work, exists within larger economies and its growth or decline affects and is affected by economic conditions in other cities and towns and the spaces which surround it, and is affected in such a way as to permit "predictions" about critical inputs exogenous to Pred's single city growth models.

Of prime relevance at this point is the large body of literature contributed by economists and geographers on location theory. These scholars, in their awareness of space and location as a factor in economic development, were among the first to recognize the importance of the region as an economic unit and to recognize the economic role of cities within a region. Men such as A. Lösch, W. Christaller, W. Isard, and B.J.L. Berry have attempted to explain the spatial distribution of economic activity within a given region. Since regions generally encompass many cities and towns, they argue that in an economic sense cities influence an area wider than their political boundaries and cities are in turn influenced by the conditions of the surrounding hinterland.

Basically, location theorists see urban growth as a function of regional economic growth. Regional growth depends on access to both supply and demand. The economic growth and development of a region will depend on what kind of access at competitive cost a point in space has "to the inputs of production and its access at competitive costs to markets for the outputs of this production."[12] Inputs include labor supply, capital, resources, intermediate supply inputs, etc. Outputs include various categories of final or intermediate products. However, access to outputs and inputs, though the basis for location theory, is a broad concept, of which different aspects have been emphasized by various authors.

August Lösch has emphasized the role of markets in determining the spatial distribution of economic activity. The Lösch model starts very much in the abstract with a flat undifferentiated plane upon which resources and population are distributed randomly. He then considers one firm located on the plane producing product X. Proceeding with normal microeconomic analysis, he poses a theoretical product demand curve.

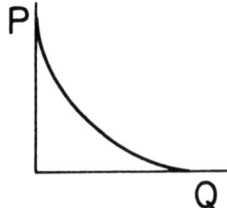

In order to include the spatial variable, he adds a third dimension to the curve:

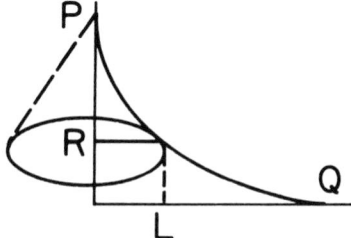

when P = R and Q = L then $\pi 2L$ is the area or circle of demand. Lösch then adjusts the cone for varying freight and transport charges which are spatial variables affecting costs, and these may in turn affect price within the particular cone of demand.

Once the particular firm has established its cone of demand then it logically follows that similar firms will arise filling in the entire plane so as to absorb total plane demand:

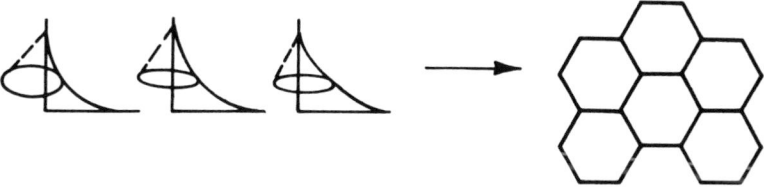

Lösch thus suggests a hexagonal pattern for trading areas of firms, as the hexagons cover the entire plane.[13] This process results in one hexagon for every center of production or consumption. The total of these hexagons results in "systematic arrangements of the various commodities. The plane formerly deprived of all spatial inequalities becomes highly crowded with networks of economic areas."[14]

Though Lösch appears to have isolated key variables in the location process, the exact nature of the process remains vague. Approaching location theory from a market perspective, Lösch's analysis fails to answer some important questions. In showing the importance of market demand, he suggests that inherent in this process of spatial development is the formation of cities and towns—central places. For Lösch, however, these central places are a result and not a cause of what he considers the more important process of market area development. He does not see the region as a rigidly defined unit, but rather as containing a system of various overlapping hexagonal areas of different sizes solely determined by the market or demand cone for individual firms or industries.

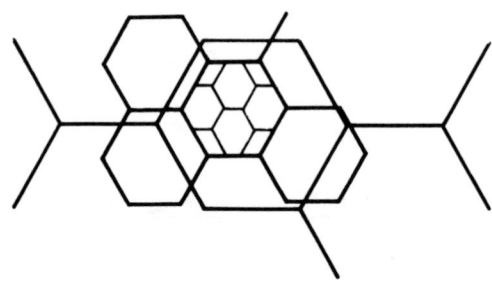

The Lösch model rests on the assumption that a region is self contained. All economic activity for its population is located within its boundaries. Lösch's sector analysis of regional development neglects the role of imports and exports to the region which Thompson would consider key variables in the developmental process.[15] Lösch further de-emphasizes the role of cities. As Eric Lampard has shown, "the size and distribution of Löschian cities depends on how many particular goods and services of what size markets coincide at any individual central place."[16] Lösch's analysis cannot explain a hierarchy of urban places. Rather the location of central places become strictly a variable dependent on his shifting hexagonal market system.

Lösch's de-emphasis of urban hierarchies was in large measure a reaction to the very rigid hierarchical system suggested by Walter Christaller four years earlier. The Christaller model proposes seven orders of central places serving as distribution centers for certain goods and services which would be determined by the demand of the regional population. Christaller's hexagonal network is much more organized than Lösch's, in fact, organized to an unrealistic degree. For Christaller, each subarea is located within a larger one so goods within a market area the size of A would be distributed at central place A. Within market area A there might be three or four areas of size B each with a central place B at which goods with a B size market area might be distributed. This same process would hold for production as well.

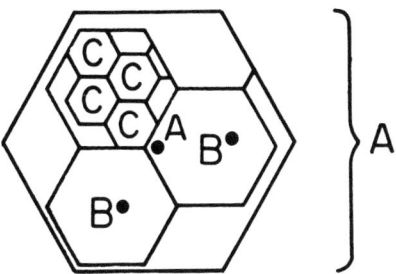

Christaller's process of market development begins with one large center which, through population growth and economic development, is split up into increasingly smaller sectors, resulting in a hierarchy of production and distribution centers.[17]

As Lampard points out, this model is not a system of cities as he uses the term but rather a "taxonomic ordering of their different functions" in order to explain the "numbers, sizes and spatial distribution of cities."[18] Nevertheless, the presence and importance of central places is evident in Christaller. But in Lösch's more sophisticated attempt to describe the nature and function of the hexagonal markets, the function of central places becomes a rather passive one. Christaller's model has a greater sense of the dynamics of growth. The works of Lösch and Christaller best state classic location theory. Lösch, beginning with his undifferentiated plane, looks at spatial differentiation from the bottom up while Christaller, beginning with his one single central point of distribution, looks at the process from the top down.

More recently, Brian J.L. Berry attempted to synthesize these two views. Rather than attempting to explain the spatial differentiation of the entire economy, he chose to analyze specifically the geography of market centers and retail distribution. Berry maintained that

> the geography of retail and service business displays irregularities over space and through time, that central place theory constitutes a deductive base from which to understand these regularities and that the convergence of theoretical postulates and empirical regularities provides substance to marketing geography and to certain aspects of city and regional planning.[19]

Berry's empirical analysis revealed no orderly system of hexagonal markets in Christaller's sense but rather a much less easily drawn system of overlapping market areas like those of Lösch. However, within this market network, Berry found a distinct hierarchy of central places. His hierarchy was one of distribution centers based on the supply and demand of specific categories of retail goods.

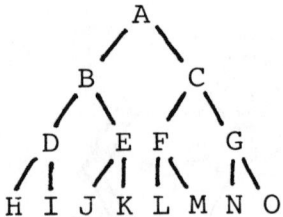

Products flow up and down the hierarchy of centers which would actually be the cities and towns of a region. "A" would be the largest regional city, B, C, etc. All retail functions of D would be contained in B and all functions of B plus additional functions (more specialized) would be contained in A. The spatial distribution of these centers is determined largely by the transportation network, and the extent of demand for a particular retail product.[20]

Unlike Christaller and Lösch, Berry tests his model. In the American Midwest in the 1960's he indeed finds a retail hierarchy in operation. The location of various distribution centers of goods depends to a great degree on the extent of demand for that good. Location, always shifting and changing, depends also on the historical fact of existing transportation sources. The railroad played a key role in the location of various distribution centers in the Midwest.[21]

Berry's study follows neatly from the pioneering works of Lösch and Christaller, but his approach is much narrower. Berry is strictly concerned with the retail sector and his conclusions hold valid only for that particular sector of the economy. It is not clear whether the manufacturing, financial and other sectors of the economy locate according to the same principles. Also, within the retail sector Berry assumes perfect competition. He does not consider the market power of individual firms in affecting individual consumer demand decisions, which becomes important with the growth of nation-wide firms in the late nineteenth century. Under more realistic assumptions, the process of location of a firm can be a very complex one. The Pred model discusses this type of decision only when generated within a city for the urban market. But clearly these decisions also are a component of his initial multipliers and have great bearing on the course of development of an urban place.

Classical location theory has isolated many of the variables which are part of the process of regional economic development. From the demand side it has shown the importance of markets in determining the spatial location of production and distribution activity. It further suggests that producers and distributors can operate more efficiently within central places, thus offering an economic and spatial rationale for the growth of cities within a region. Yet classical theory as set forth by Christaller and Lösch, and narrowly refined by Berry remains vague for purposes of understanding the urbanization process.

Walter Isard and Martin Beckmann, operating somewhat apart from the classical framework, have offered highly quantitative investigations of the variable components of location theory and answer many questions left unanswered by the classic school. Isard sees the real problem of location theory not as one of why things are located where they are, but as one of efficient use of resources through optimum location decisions.[22] Isard sees regions as comprising a hierarchy of strategic nodal sites or central places. This multi-nucleated pattern is webbed by transport networks. For Isard, the region is a dynamic organism dependent on three important factors: (1) cost relations of various economic activities, (2) consumer preferences, (3) transport technology. The interaction of these variables changes over time, causing continual shifts in the spatial distribution of economic activity.[23] Isard's approach is sensitive to the individual economic activites of a region without neglecting the regional economy as a whole. He is able to combine the ideas of both Lösch and Christaller in a model much broader and more encompassing than Berry's.

Isard sees economic activity as taking place in a "time space continuum."[24] Within this continuum the forces of deglomeration and inequality of resource endowment press society into a spatial framework. The process of deglomeration is a function of relative costs, consumer preference and the law of diminishing returns. It is much like Christaller's division of a market area, but less orderly. Expansion of the hinterland, increasing population, and new markets all create demand for new outputs, access to which induces new firms at new locations or in existing market centers. There is also inducement for the relocation of existing firms. Unlike Lösch and more precisely than Berry and Christaller, Isard assumes the inequality of resource endowments.[25] Thus location decisions of the firm must consider access to inputs of resources, capital and labor as well as access to outputs. For Isard, a key input in determining all location decisions is cost of transport. The transport input includes the level of transport technology at a given time and the transport rates. He suggests that reduced transport rates have tended to "transform a scattered ubiquitous pattern of production into an increasingly concentrated one, and to effect progressive differentiation and selection between sites with superior and inferior resources and trade routes."[26]

Isard's model is far more complex than the classical model and more thorough, more extensive and less mechanical. He is aware of the complexities involved in individual location decisions as well as the implication of these decisions for the economy as a whole. His input-output model basically pertains to one industry or firm but it is further elaborated to account for a competitive economy. Location decisions of an individual firm or industry must take into account the degree of dispensability of the product (the substitution effect), geographic occurrence (sources of the commodity), and mobility (ease of transport). These factors limit the location possibilities of individual firms because of the competitive nature of the economy within which decisions ultimately must be made.[27]

Isard's work greatly refines and expands the framework of the classical school. He is concerned not only with markets but also with the supply side and the competitive economy. He seems to capture best the complexities of location decisions and the efficient usage of space. However, as in Lösch's model, central places (cities and towns) are a dependent rather than an independent variable. Urban economies can in fact upset logical location decisions by exerting agglomerative pressure on individual industries or firms. Isard finds that "the accumulated fixed investments of an urban mass in conjunction with its vested social institutions entail major geographic immobilities and rigidities and, for the most part, tend to preclude urban relocation. Cities attract or repel units of production in accordance with the urbanization economies or diseconomies relevant to each unit of production."[28] Thus Isard does not argue that concentration of activity is necessarily economically efficient.

Martin Beckmann has offered a model of location decisions which is basically similar to Isard's but not as well developed. Beckmann does, however, emphasize the positive role of central places in efficient distribution of economic activity. Using Christaller's flow approach in analyzing the hierarchy of central places, Beckmann makes a much stronger argument for central place hierarchies as the efficient spatial distribution of economic resources. Rather than using Christaller's seven orders of central places, Beckmann distinguishes four orders of places categorized in terms of types of products exported to other centers.[29] The Beckmann scale of central places seems complementary to Isard. While Isard would not deny the importance of the role of central places in the distribution of goods, Beckmann stresses cities and towns as having a more positive role.

The analysis offered by location theory seems at the heart of any consideration of regional development. The broad spatial area covered by a particular region facilitates a variety of economic activity. The spatial distribution of these activities and the reasons behind such a distribution provide the key to understanding the economic development of a region as a whole as well as the central places within the region. The classical school and its more recent interpreters stress in varying degrees the importance of markets, transportation, inputs, outputs, competition and central places in the process of spatial differentiation. They also find the process an integral part of the larger process of economic development on the regional and national level.

Though location theory isolates key spatial variables in the process of economic growth, it remains unconcerned with the details of the process of industrialization and urbanization as it affects particular cities. Location theory and the Pred model are not mutually exclusive. Location theory emphasizes more strongly the complexity of the spatial distribution of economic activity. With a greater sense of the complex pattern of locations of economic activity, the Pred model can be applied to regions as well as to specific urban places. Given a hypothetical urban hierarchy, a new industry established in towns D, E, and F, might well have been financed through resources in A. The secondary multiplier effects of the industry will not only be felt in D, E, and F, but the profitability of the new firms in the towns will yield a return on investment to A.

Most location theorists begin with an undifferentiated plane, and even the Pred model as a body of theory attempts to be universal. However, in reality areas have evolved over time to become substantially differentiated in terms of perceived resource endowments, access to which would weigh significantly in location decisions thereafter. The areas have also become spatially differentiated in political and social as well as economic developments. Though enlightening about the process of location, location theory lacks sensitivity to the broader historical processes of urbanization and industrialization.

A number of scholars have taken off from location theory for broader considerations of either industrial development or urban development. For any historical study such departures seem vital so that the more theoretical models might be elaborated and refined and therefore better fitted to a specific historical context. In the forefront of this kind of approach is the massive study by Perloff, Dunn, Lampard and Muth. Perloff et al. recognized the central importance of location theory in the process of regional development but they also included other kinds of considerations.

For Perloff et al., location factors are only some of the many factors influencing the character of regional economic development. They also emphasize factors influencing the volume and composition of regional economic activity. In order to determine these factors they take a comparative approach, comparing one region to another or to the national economy. They are concerned with a region's relative growth, and its comparative ability to hold and attract economic activities.[30] A region's comparative position is largely dependent on the presence of necessary factors of production, on changes in taste (consumer demand) and on government policy. Any change in the interaction of these variables within a region can have drastic effects on the state of the regional economy. Similar shifts on the national level can work to favor one region while working to the disadvantage of another.[31]

To these factors Perloff et al. add the variables suggested by location theory with particular emphasis on access to inputs and outputs.[32] The entire analysis works within the context of a loosely defined model of industrial growth. They are concerned with the internal evolution of the industrial base within the region. In their sector analysis they are particularly concerned about the role of government, the entrepreneur and the process of increasing specialization and economies of scale. The Perloff *et al.* study sets the principles of location theory within the larger historical context of U.S. industrial growth and development. Location theory becomes an important part but not the whole source of explanation regarding regional development since broader historical considerations such as the westward movement of the labor force need be considered.[33]

Eric Lampard also takes off from location theory in seeking to explain the process of urbanization in two important articles. Lampard uses the principles of location theory to explain the existence of urban hierarchies in the nation. For Lampard the economic activities of urban localities are at the root of the process of urban growth. Building on Thompson's work he suggests that if growth is conceived as a supply function, then one must look to urban places where changing investment activities and the mix of slow and fast growing industries directly affect the aggregate supply curve. The aggregate investment and production patterns of various localities form the basis upon which economic growth is measured. Lampard emphasizes the spatial diffusion of this pattern and then suggests a system at work which ties the varied economic units together, stressing his familiar theme of specialization. In abandoning the rather static view of central places of the classical location theorists, Lampard makes the systems of cities a dynamic component of the process of urban growth. He finds that, "The specialization of city and country and the resulting interdependence of small towns, cities and metropolises are . . . manifestations of the same pervasive specialization—differentiation—reintegration tendency that yields increasing returns (decreasing costs) to scale."[34] While the evolution of a region over time may not be as smooth as Lampard suggests, his recognition of interdependence of cities and towns adds a whole new dynamic to the process of urbanization which the Pred model lacks in its focus on a single urban place.

Lampard finds that the principles of location theory are useful in explaining this tendency toward specialization. He emphasizes the role of organization of production and distribution through specialized economic units within a spatial framework. He stresses the role of the transportation input in achieving space economy within his system of cities. But Lampard carries the analysis further in emphasizing that urbanization has contributed "to the progressive unfolding of the industrial system."[35] Drawing upon the work of the Chicago School and more recently upon the work of Otis D. Duncan, Lampard suggests that cities exert influences over the patterned activities of populations which in turn affect the total economic system in the broadest sense or, in

Duncan's terminology, the "eco-system."[36] Thus population becomes a factor in a dynamic way in the evolution of the systems of cities. He concludes that cities contribute to the whole system by (a) lowering fertility rates, (b) transferring relatively unspecialized low productivity, extractive occupations to more productive manufacturing and service sectors, and (c) forming a new urban middle class, all of which not only builds on the principles of location theory but also fits location theorists' models into the larger framework of the process of urbanization, suggesting that systems of cities, hierarchical arrangements of central places, play an active role in the process of economic development and demographic change.[37]

Both the Lampard and Perloff studies accomplish two things. They show the relevance of location theory to the study of the process of regional economic growth and urbanization. They also place these processes within a historical framework applying economic and geographical theory to specific historical problems.

Lampard and the location theorists suggest that to understand the process of urban growth one must be sensitive to the economic activities outside the political boundaries which normally constitute the definition of an urban place. Each central urban place has a hinterland composed of towns, rural areas, and in some instances, small cities. Rather than being scattered points on a map, these places interact economically with one another in very important ways.

Location theory serves to explain the spread and to some extent the specialization of economic activity from point to point on a map. It provides a model for the spread and differentiation of natural and human resources and the need for various types of economic activity to have access to those resources. However, in a world of specialized economic activity coordination becomes vital. Each point in space must be linked in some way to the other to permit efficient exchange of specialized goods and services. Location theory also suggests various linkages which tie together the spatially diffused specialized economic units of regions or of whole nations. Lampard goes a bit further and suggests a whole system through which the economic activities of various places are linked.

Though Lampard, Pred, Berry and others are talking about a dynamic process that takes place over time, neither they nor others for that matter have attempted to apply these principles to a specific cluster of cities or a region in a specific period of time. The theorists have discussed forces at work which mold the urban economic environment but how are these forces manifest in urban institutions? How are these forces reflected in the decisions of individuals? To what extent do individuals perceive the process at work? To what extent do specific characteristics of specific regions at specific points in time limit the process of urbanization?

A few recent studies have begun to look beyond the experience of a single town or city to the larger regional context of local experience and have considered some of these questions. In an analysis of the transformation from rural town to small city of Kingston, New York, Stuart Blumin discussed forces external to local activity which led to this transformation. He particularly emphasized the impact of the canal on the extractive industry and commercial services of the town. Essentially Blumin has set Kingston in its regional context though it remains a study of a singular town. Since he does focus on a single town, Blumin is able to assess the impact of this change on the population and institutions of the town.[38]

In a study of the economic growth of the Philadelphia region during the period 1810-1850, Diane Lindstrom has argued the importance of demand within the region to the process of economic growth. Lindstrom has very effectively argued against the Callender-Schmidt-North model which stressed the role of demand external to the region. Lindstrom through analysis of regional commodity flows clearly shows the extent of local demand for regional products and the effect of this consumption on local economies. Her eastern demand model, however, emphasizes behavior of the regional economy at the aggregate level within the context of trends in the Northeast and devotes little attention to the institutional structure and variation within the region and among the various cities and towns of the Philadelphia region.[39]

Roberta Miller in her study of the Syracuse region chooses a city-hinterland model. She emphasizes the impact of change brought on the upper New York region by the Erie Canal and later by the railroads. Miller concentrates on hinterland-central places flows: population from hinterland to city, consumer goods and trade services from city to hinterland, agricultural production from hinterland to city. In so doing she provides a sense of a changing city-hinterland relationship based on the changing structure of economic activity in central places.[40]

My study of the Boston region attempts to apply the various questions of location theory and the Lampardian ideas of systems of cities and city regions to the history of this early industrial region. The Boston region in the early nineteenth century, 1810-1850, was undergoing great changes. During those years the regional economy expanded and shifted from a primarily commercial port oriented region to a region of more mixed economic activity. Many of the ports were still active in 1850, but during the period inland manufacturing expanded significantly. This study emphasizes the region as an interdependent system of cities and towns and is based on traditional sources: government documents, business records, personal papers and contemporary printed sources. Systematic data over time for the period do not exist in sufficient quantity to permit accurate measurement of the various dimensions of the process of urbanization on a regional scale.[41] Quantitative sources along with literary and other sources are used together to suggest the nature and complexity of the evolution of the system of cities in the Boston region over a specific period of time.

Three questions form the basis of this study.

(1) What were the boundaries of this particular region?

The term "region" presents both a conceptual and a definitional problem. According to Perloff and Dunn, the term is "generally used to describe a group of geographically contiguous areas which have certain complementary characteristics or which are tied by extensive interareal activity or flows."[42] For my study the key concept in the Perloff-Dunn definition is "interareal activity or flows." If regional boundaries are drawn among the myriad of cities and towns (units) in America, some criterion must be established to determine the place of each geographical unit in a regional system. Geographers are fond of using the concept of flows. The concept of flows can best be examined by expanding from the Pred model of one geographical unit—a city or a town. The initial multiplier has already been suggested and could come from a source outside the unit. It could be an investment by institutions or individuals in another town. It could be a branch of an economic activity already established in another town. New construction might require some expertise not available locally; thus a contractor would be forced to call for services based elsewhere. Likewise the new or enlarged industry would have to acquire raw materials not available within the town and ship its products to ultimate markets. If one could determine the source of all investment, the source of raw materials, the source of non-local services and the destination of final products and follow the distribution patterns of these local imports and exports, certain relationships would emerge, which would permit one, empirically, to delineate an urban region. Sources for the period do suggest clear limits if not boundaries to the economic region influenced by Boston.

(2) What was the spatial distribution of various activities through the region and what was the extent of specialization of those activities in various cities and towns of the region?

Any hierarchy of cities at work in the Boston region during the period would emerge in a region characterized by towns which specialized in specific activities, products of which were either exchanged within the region or exported from it. Location theory would suggest that these patterns when aggregated would reveal a city placed within an urban hierarchy. Cities low in the hierarchy would be to a large extent dependent on specialized services available in larger, more diversified cities above. By the same token, larger cities further up the hierarchy would depend on the productivity of smaller units down the line to generate demand for its more specialized services. This hierarchical relationship would rest on a continuous flow of goods and services through the hierarchy creating an interdependence of all units within the hierarchy. The space so hierarchically structured can be said to be the region of the urban place at the top of the hierarchy *or* can be said to be a regional area where the hierarchy is not quite so symmetrical.

(3) What sorts of linkages existed to connect the various locations and activities together? Did the linkages operate within the framework of a system of cities?

These questions concerning linkage form the heart of my study. If there is indeed a region, and if there is indeed a hierarchy of cities, the extent and direction of the linkages which connect the various economic elements of the region will determine the extent to which the regional economic activity depends on and at the same time fosters a system of cities. These linkages form the infrastructure of the system. The linkages are the basic elements of a working system. As these linkages shift direction, are replaced or are abandoned, the nature of the system of cities which constitute the region change significantly. These linkages structure the region. The nature and extent of these linkages influence the location decisions and thus affect the economic base of the cities and towns in the region, which in large part determines the level of urbanization in each of the cities and towns of the region.

Consider the textile industry which was one of the most important economic activities in the Boston region at the time. In 1813, Francis Cabot Lowell's Boston Manufacturing Company, a textile firm, was incorporated. Its success encouraged emulation and extension. With the assistance of Nathan Appleton, Lowell began to search for new sites for the expansion of his highly successful enterprise. Most appealing was the small town of East Chelmsford located on the fast moving Merrimack River. The abundance of water power at that site was thought to be a most suitable power source for the mechanized looms which efficient textile production had come to require. Lowell began to build what would soon become the largest factory town in New England. In 1824 the town was appropriately renamed Lowell. By 1825 it had a population of 1,500 with 11,000 spindles in operation. By 1835, the population reached 15,000 with 120,000 spindles in operation.[43] This is an example of exceptionally rapid growth.

However, to understand patterns of growth in Lowell, it seems imperative to understand the relationship of each town to the others and the extent to which the cities and towns of the Boston region, as defined in the following chapter, were linked together hierarchically. Thus this study of the Boston region focuses on the concept of linkages, as the basic elements of an infrastructure through which the economic activity of one town supports that of another. Linkages are manifest in transportation networks, credit networks, and in the exchanges and distribution (i.e., flows) of goods and services through the region. Linkages hold the region together.

In the process of this dynamic interaction of local economies, each city and town experiences varying degrees of growth (or decline). In Pred's terminology, each city and town would achieve various thresholds and enter its own dynamic cycle of growth. From the regional perspective of this study, the demands external to the local economy will be emphasized rather than internal "city demand" in stimulating local economies to the point where new thresholds or new levels of urbanization are achieved.[44] Thus new industry can appear at some location within a region to respond to greater regional, national or world demands. The location decision within the region will depend on availability of and access to specific resources. If this can be achieved at competitive prices, then a decision will be made to locate a new industry or expand an existing industry within the region in a specific town. This decision will not only have a stimulative effect on the town but will have a stimulative effect on other cities and towns in the hierarchy.

This was precisely the case with Lowell and the textile industry. The location of the industry there had an obvious effect on the growth of Lowell. However, the growth of Lowell also had an important effect on the city of Boston which was at the top of the regional hierarchy. The growth of the textile industry in Lowell placed greater demands for services in Boston; thus the level of urbanization in both cities increased. My study attempts to define the Boston region, examine the distribution of economic activity within the region, and suggest the pattern of linkages which would reflect the interdependence of the 219 cities and towns of the region.

II

THE REGION, 1810-1850

One of the most difficult problems of any regional study is defining the extent of the region chosen for study. Despite the fact that regions appear to be an operational unit in both pre-industrial and industrial economies, their boundaries are difficult to determine. This chapter attempts to establish a sense of the boundaries of the Boston region, 1810-1850, by looking at complementary characteristics of the various towns of the region and using various secondary sources with primary observations which suggest the direction of the flow of goods and services through the region.

The concept of flows of goods and services suggests movement. To the extent that such movement of goods and services follows a particular geographic pattern, one could say that a dependent relationship exists between the point of origin and certain intermediate points and in some cases the final destination. For example, if a manufacturer in city A always ships his goods to larger city B, then one could assume that he is dependent upon some service in city B. If all manufacturers in city A ship to B, then one could assume that the relationship between A and B is a dependent one and that A is very likely a part of the hinterland of B.

Once the boundaries of the region are determined through analysis of the flows of goods and services the number of component cities and towns can be determined. Their rank ordering, if rank ordered according to population or other criteria, should suggest a hierarchical structure among the various elements of the region. If a structure does emerge, the question follows: is there a system of cities at work within the region?

In studying aspects of the evolution of the Boston regional economy, my study is primarily concerned with the region as an economic entity. Therefore, the flows of goods and services become particularly important in determining the regional boundaries. Likewise, the rank ordering of cities and towns according to the relative presence of retail and financial institutions become very important criteria and the central thrust of this chapter. Region is, however, a more complicated notion and a precise all encompassing definition is virtually impossible to achieve. The economic aspect of regions is but one of the multi-dimensional facets of regions. One could conceive of a region defined by political preference, ideology, language, or voting characteristics, all suggestive of flows of one sort or another, and thus boundaries.

When considering the various dimensions of regional activity, the problem of establishing fixed boundaries becomes more difficult. Each dimension of regional activity might well suggest a different boundary. The region of cultural influence of the primary city in the region might be quite different from the region of economic influence of that same city. Within the context of economic regions there are subcategories which might lead to differing conceptions of a region. The financial influence of one city toward another might be somewhat different than the industrial or commercial influence of the same city. When considering the economic influence of one city toward another, one is essentially measuring flows of capital, goods, services, or business decisions. To draw a single sharp line between one economic region and another is a near impossible task.[1]

Regions can of course vary in size. Douglass North, in his analysis of economic growth in the United States 1790-1860, delineates three large regions based on characteristic extra-regional flows. These were roughly defined as the East, West and South.[2] The Boston region is a segment of North's eastern region. In considering Boston as an economic region it is particularly important to be aware of regions operating at many levels. In the Boston case for example, though one could argue that the Boston region was an entity in itself, one could also argue that it was a part of the larger New York region, particularly in the area of finance and other services. From the period of my study into the twentieth century, Boston becomes increasingly subordinate to New York. However, for the early nineteenth century, Boston and New York might be more accurately considered rivals.[3]

The Boston region, where does it begin? Where does it end? Any new world map printed after 1640 is likely to designate a point on the Atlantic coastline "Boston." A closer look might reveal political boundaries which, though changing over time, delineate a spatial area called the town, later (1822) the city of Boston. Even observers in the mid-nineteenth century noted that Boston had a peculiar function in relation to other cities and towns in New England. Writing in 1856, Oliver Bacon noted:

> New York, undoubtedly was built by her commerce, and no other city like her will ever appear on the American Continent. Boston is the New York of New England, with more established institutions, more Americanism in her constitution. Cincinnati claims to be the center of the United States; not the geographical center, but the center of influence and force, about which, when all distributary forces shall be removed, other cities shall revolve, and to which they shall be tributary.[4]

He suggested that the influence of the city stretched beyond its political boundaries, but he begged the question of how far it stretched and what kind of influence it exerted.

For purposes of definition of the region, my study shall focus even more narrowly on the flow of goods and services from, to and through Boston. Even this relatively one dimensional approach is difficult to rely on because complex and diverse regional and sub-regional flows of different goods make unique and sharp boundaries difficult to determine. The boundaries established for Boston in my study will be flexible enough to account for economic change during the years 1810-1850. But even with this flexibility there were certain peculiarities in the New England area of the early nineteenth century that complicate the process of definition. These difficulties arose from circumstances both within and outside the regional limits as defined in this chapter.

The Boston region 1810-1850 can generally be considered as a nine county area comprising 219 cities and towns. In my study the terms city and town are used but are not meant to suggest any qualitative difference. In 1810 there were no "cities" in the region. Boston, the first town to officially change named status, did so in 1822 after considerable debate. The typology in Appendix III suggests more urbanized and less urbanized places which is for purposes of this study a more meaningful distinction for the period. The town system of government was so ingrained in New England that towns were reluctant to become "cities" even though perhaps by all other measures the area was so urbanized that the term city was surely more appropriate.[5] Included in the Boston region are eight counties in Massachusetts: Suffolk, Essex, Middlesex, Worcester (part), Norfolk, Bristol, Plymouth, Barnstable and one county, Rockingham, in New Hampshire. This nine county area will form the basis for what will be considered the Boston economic region (see maps II-1 and II-2).

Through the early nineteenth century Boston served this nine county area in many ways, which will be discussed in chapters 4 through 6. Most importantly the city was a great commercial service center for its region. The port of Boston was an active one throughout the period. The city was also a banking, wholesaling and manufacturing center. Most of the towns in the region depended on Boston for one or another service. Thus the nine county area generally surrounds this dominant urban central place.[6]

To the east, the region was bordered by the ocean which linked, via the coasting trade, the ports in the region to each other as well as to those outside. Many of the prominent ports of the region are legend: Plymouth, Salem, Newburyport, and Portsmouth. The arm of Cape Cod (Barnstable County) created somewhat of an obstacle for intraregional coastal transport to the southernmost ports of New Bedford. Fall River, and Wareham, thus causing them to fall partly, though not entirely, within the regional orbits of Providence or New York.

To the south, the region was bordered in part again by the ocean and to the southwest, by the Providence region. Like Boston, Providence was a commercial service center to its region which clearly included all of Rhode Island.[7]

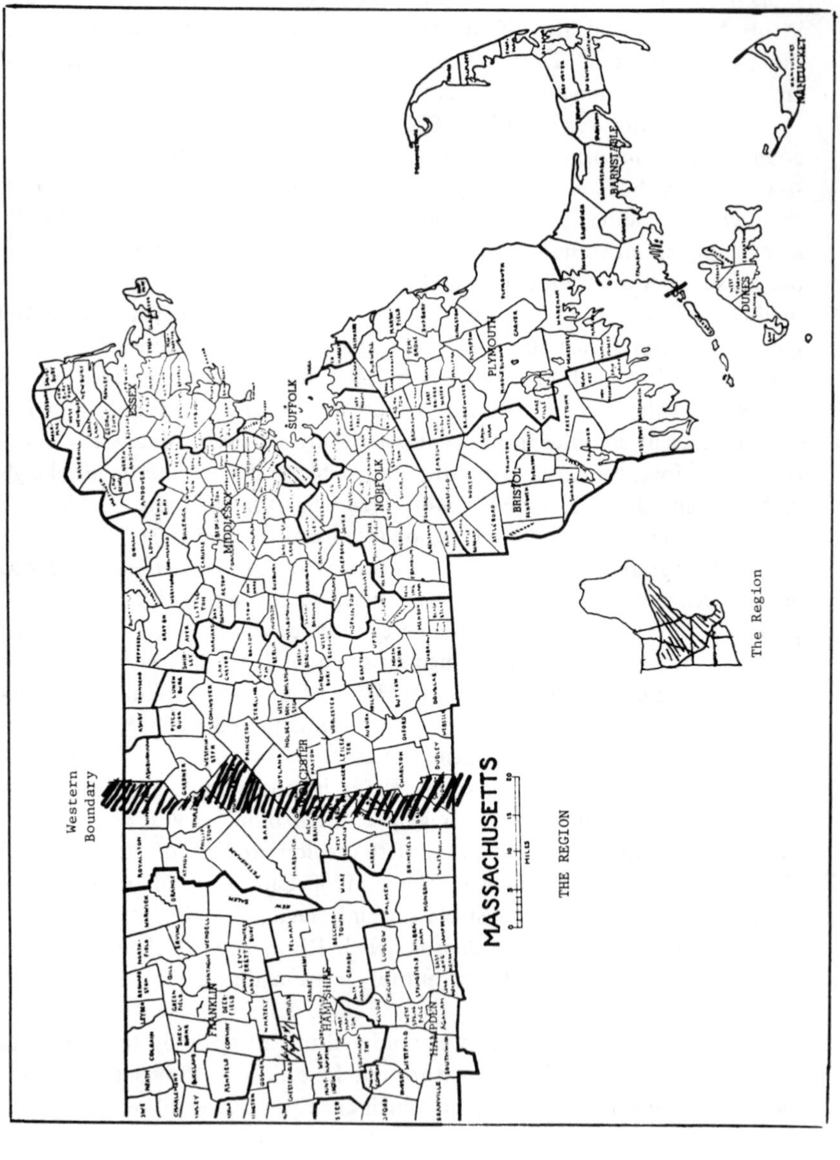

Map II-1. The Region

Map II-2. Rockingham County, New Hampshire

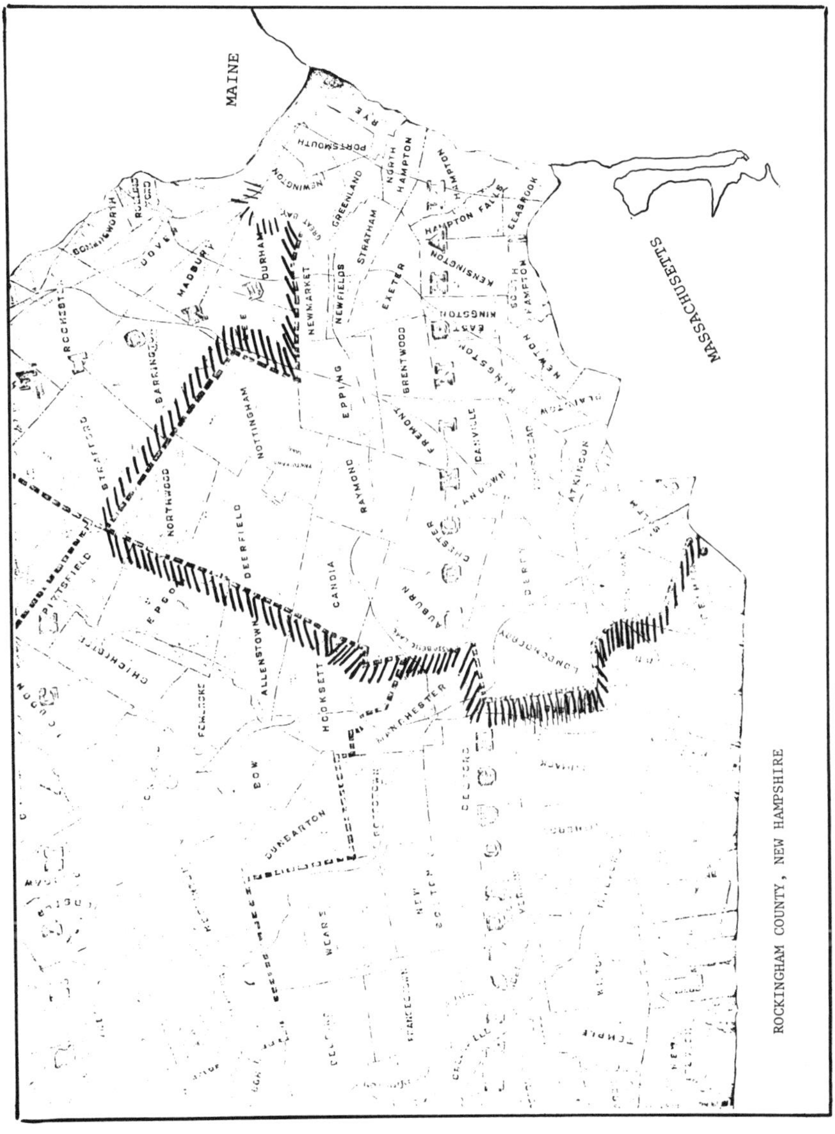

However, it would be an error to presume that the Boston and Providence regions were neatly separated by state boundaries. This problem will be discussed further.

As shown in map II-1, the western boundary of the region was marked by the eastern edge of the Connecticut River basin. The line through Worcester County has been drawn to so indicate. At that point the influence of New York City and Hartford become important. For the period of this study this influence should be considered as competitive rather than complementary to that of Boston, particularly after the opening of the Erie Canal in 1825 and before the start of service on the Western Railroad in 1841.[8]

The northern boundary is a more difficult one to determine. The only urban centers to the north equal to Boston in size and importance were in Canada. Unlike the southern and western areas surrounding the Boston region, this northern area during the early nineteenth century was very thinly settled and served by smaller towns. From a cursory view of population data between 1810 and 1850, it appears that towns in this northern area remained generally stagnant and the rural areas sparsely populated.[9] These towns all may have in fact been dependent on Boston in one way or another. Exceptions to this general observation would be the clusters of towns dependent on the many seaports in Maine, the most important of which was Portland. Manchester and Nashua, New Hampshire were important industrial towns which mushroomed during this period and had stronger ties to the larger and more established cities in the region. As political rather than economic centers, Concord, New Hampshire, Augusta, Maine and Montpelier, Vermont served a larger territory within the Boston region.[10]

Generally, however, the area to the north of Boston remained an area of small towns during the period under study. Rockingham County in New Hampshire was typical of this kind of area and thus was included in the region for detailed study. However, the northern boundary should really be seen as fading all the way up to the Canadian border. As the region industrialized and the transportation network improved over time, the influence of Boston gradually became more intense in this northern area. This is discussed further in chapter 4.

This general outline emerges from an analysis of the patterns of flows of goods both raw and finished across the region. Flows of goods are difficult to determine, but the McLane Report of 1833 does give some indication of the origin of raw materials and the destination of final products for the various towns in the region. The report, compiled in the early 1830's by the Secretary of the Treasury, Louis McLane, was to be a detailed report relative to manufactures in the United States. All states were surveyed to some degree, but nearly one third of the two volume report pertains to manufacturing in Massachusetts providing data at the firm level.[11] Unfortunately, the report does not trace the flow of goods in detail. An ideal source would trace the flow of goods in exact amounts listing each port or place where goods might be handled. McLane reports, for example, that Plymouth and New Bedford cordage makers used large amounts of Russian and Manila hemp. Scattered iron workers used a good deal of English iron. Lynn shoemakers used local as well as foreign hides. The textile industry brought in southern cotton. McLane also reports exports. Lynn shoes were sent all over the United States. Textiles were consumed locally, shipped to Boston and beyond. By examining this report town by town, particularly for towns on fringe areas, a sense of such flows can be gained, then projected chronologically forward and backward with appropriate modifications.

Since many kinds of goods did indeed flow through the region, regional boundaries suggest that a good percentage of these goods flowed through the Port of Boston—the gateway. Boston usually was the first step for goods brought into the region and the last step for goods to be exported from the region. An ideal concept or flow pattern of a coastal region would have Boston as a funnel for all flows in and out of an otherwise self-contained region. The flows, or more specifically linkages, were, however, more complicated than this ideal funnel pattern would suggest. Externally, at the extremes of the region, there was considerable overlap. To the west in towns such as Chester, Monson, Rowe and Springfield, nearly all manufactured goods listed in the McLane report went to Hartford or to New York City, suggesting that they were shipped along the Connecticut River and handled by commercial houses in those cities. However, some would often go to ports in Massachusetts as well. In Williamsburgh in 1833, Wells and Bodman's annual satinet production was "all sold in Boston."[12] Yet Williamsburgh is considerably west of the Connecticut River. It is not clear whether these goods went to Hartford and then on to Boston by water or straight to Boston via overland transport. Nevertheless, it seems wise to be aware of regional overlap in flows of goods in the west.

Portland, Maine, presents a peculiar problem in the north, involving both regional independence and international regional overlap. Between 1810 and 1830, with the exception of textile and paper exports, the Portland region was largely self-contained. Most of its output was consumed within the Maine area.[13] Toward 1850 Boston began to exert more influence over the area. As the Boston region increasingly industrialized, there was greater demand for raw materials which Maine could provide. As Maine gradually industrialized, there was more dependence upon Boston as a source of finance capital.

However, Maine was not entirely within Boston's orbit. Portland was half a day nearer Europe than Boston and two days nearer than New York. The Canadians, particularly in Montreal, were interested in the port since it was located on nearly a straight line between Montreal and Europe. In the late 1840's and 1850's Canadians negotiated a Portland-Montreal Railroad which would bring the Portland and northern New Hampshire-Vermont areas into the Montreal hinterland to the extent that international arrangements would permit.[14]

For purposes of my study, the Portland area will be considered self-contained and apart from the Boston region.

Portland and the area west of Boston illustrate many problems of regional fringe overlap. Providence is quite another story. Providence, only fifty miles from Boston, was an active port throughout the eighteenth century. Mercantile activity there built substantial fortunes which needed constant re-investment. In the early nineteenth century, the ports of Providence and especially Newport began to decline considerably. Providence entrepreneurs such as Samuel Slater very early began large scale investments in manufacturing throughout the area. This activity spilled over the Rhode Island boundary into Massachusetts in the area south of Worcester and in the southeast area of Bristol county. Because of the proximity of these two areas to both Boston and Providence, it is difficult to determine to what region they belong.

Worcester, for example, which will be one of the principal areas studied, is located nearly equi-distant from Boston and Providence. During the early nineteenth century there were repeated moves on the part of each city to gain better access and exclusive economic control over Worcester. The central Massachusetts town was important to both cities as a center for inland manufacturing. At the beginning of the nineteenth century the people of Providence wished to construct a canal to link Worcester to the Blackstone River. The Massachusetts legislature, yielding to local interests in Boston and Worcester who were fearful of the loss of Worcester to Providence, refused to charter the measure. Finally in 1822 the two states were able to reach an agreement on usage of the canal, after a Worcester citizens committee clearly pointed out that Worcester was interested in better access to both Providence and Boston. Construction was begun in 1823 by a corporation financed two thirds by Rhode Island investors and one third by Massachusetts investors. However, the canal proved an unsuccessful link due to freezing water in the winter and long delays in warm weather. Ten years later, when the Railroad became a practical means of transportation, one of the first routes chartered was the Boston and Worcester. When Providence later proposed a Providence and Worcester line, there was again considerable objection in Massachusetts. The Railroad was built in 1847 much to the satisfaction of Providence men. In fact it was often said that of the "two unions between Worcester and Providence, the first was weak as water, the last is strong as iron."[15] The arguments and controversies leading up to the completion of the iron link were indicative of the rivalry between the two seaport centers over influence in the interior town.

There is similar regional overlap in the Taunton-Fall River area. Throughout the early nineteenth century Fall River was generally in the Providence region. The Fall River-Pawtucket boundary was in constant flux and contention between the states of Massachusetts and Rhode Island. The problem was settled in 1899. However, the town did serve New Bedford in some capacities such as supplying iron.[16] Taunton was another early manufacturing center which served and was served by both Boston and Providence. It was a short trip by river to Providence and a short overland trip to Boston. Like Worcester, Taunton was caught in the middle whereas Fall River, though eventually located in Massachusetts, was much closer to Providence.[17]

The existence and nature of the Providence, New York and Montreal regions make precise definition of the limits of the Boston region difficult to judge, even when considering only flows of goods. Mindful of these problems at the perimeters of the Boston region, the somewhat arbitrary definition of the Boston region as previously described will be maintained throughout my study.

Certain other problems remain to be resolved. The fact that the Boston region was bounded on the east by the open sea presents difficulties of analysis and definition and is the key to the internal problem, particularly from the standpoint of flows of goods in the early nineteenth century. An open coast provided leaks in the ideal flow pattern. Goods did not necessarily have to flow through Boston, the region's central city, to get into or out of the region. The exports of Salem, New Bedford and Portsmouth (New Hampshire) make this clear.

All three of these cities built up a considerable mature maritime economy during the years prior to the War of 1812. As a result, many local merchants had direct foreign connections which proved helpful in establishing new trade routes. More importantly, they had capital to invest in new ventures in their respective areas. Salem in the 1830's and 40's imported many South American hides for the tanning and shoe industries in Essex County. New Bedford, with its whaling fortunes, served as a port for the southern towns of Bristol and Plymouth counties. Portsmouth was likewise important to Rockingham County and other points in New Hampshire and Maine. As the nineteenth century progressed and as manufacturing developed, these ports became increasingly important as links in the coasting trade. Some of the vessels involved went to Boston, but others bypassed Boston altogether, lending a certain independence of activity to these subregions, since shipowners or captains controlled the flows of goods.[18]

The existence of these semi-dependent subregions within the Boston region might be contrasted with other inland regions such as Pittsburgh, Pennsylvania. Pittsburgh was located at the fork of the Allegheny and Monongahela Rivers. Goods naturally and literally flowed through Pittsburgh. St. Louis was a natural location for a central urban place since it was located near the Missouri, Illinois and the Mississippi with all their tributaries. At a later period the same would be true of the rail centers like Chicago which became large central places as transport centers, located at the forks of various rail systems. The coastline of the Boston region provided a number of potential harbors. Those of Salem, New Bedford and Portsmouth were ports of entry into the region for some goods and did maintain trade linkages to world ports. These served as central places for their subregions and were at some points in time quite independent of Boston. A river system by contrast supports only one central place at key intersections of waterways.[19]

Having generally defined the region, what did the region look like during the period? The dates chosen to provide glimpses are the census years, 1810, 1830, and 1850. Because of the superiority of the McLane report (1833), relative to the census information on manufacturing gathered in 1830, the information on manufacturing in 1830 is taken from the McLane report. The overview in this chapter will generally be concerned with towns within the region. (Chapter 3 will go into further detail on specific industries and attempt to explain location factors behind the spread of industry throughout the region.)

Within a region as large as Boston, structural relationships among the cities and towns should, according to the theoretical literature, emerge in a hierachical form with larger central places serving and being served by surrounding smaller places. This structural scheme would emerge from repeated patterns of flows of goods and services through the region. What was the extent to which such a hierarchy existed in the region? Degree of participation in particular service activities indicate places where demand for services (commercial, retail and other) was concentrated. These central service, distribution and transfer centers formed the structure of the regional hierarchy. The presence of certain institutions in a given place indicates the relative position of that place in the hierarchy. Commercial and financial services distinguish the prominent towns in the hierarchy. However, manufacturing is important, too. Many of the important central places in the hierarchy attracted a number of manufacturing firms. However, during the period 1810 to 1850, the service sector remained very much concentrated in the principal cities of the hierarchy while manufacturing spread increasingly throughout the region.

Consider the region in 1810. The 1807 embargo on all foreign trade was not one of the more popular acts of the Jefferson administration. Its effects on the previously flourishing Massachusetts maritime economy were disastrous. Though a good deal of shipping was revived after the War, the maritime sector was never as dominant.[20] Despite the economic changes, the composition of the region in 1810 generally reflected the dominance of the maritime sector.

A list of the twenty most populous towns in the region, as shown in Table II-1, reveals that the most populous towns were generally on the coast, i.e., 80 percent of the twenty. All but four, Taunton, Rehoboth, Middleborough, and Bridgewater, were located along the Atlantic. Bridgewater, Middleborough, and Rehoboth ranked high because of their comparatively large areas.[21] From the employment statistics of the 1820 census it seems reasonable to assume that these three towns were agricultural areas with low population density. Why Taunton ranked so high is less clear. It was the only non-coastal

Table II-1
The Twenty Most Populous Towns Ranked in the Region, 1810

Rank	Town	Population
1	Boston	33,250
2	Salem	12,613
3	Newburyport	7,634
4	Portsmouth	6,934
5	Gloucester	5,943
6	Marblehead	5,900
7	New Bedford	5,651
8	Newbury	5,176
9	Bridgewater	5,157
10	Charlestown	4,959
11	Rehoboth	4,866
12	Beverly	4,608
13	Middleborough	4,400
14	Plymouth	4,228
15	Lynn	4,087
16	Taunton	3,907
17	Roxbury	3,669
18	Barnstable	3,646
19	Ipswich	3,569
20	Dartmouth	3,219

Source: Census of 1810 (U.S.).

town in Bristol County to experience a growth rate of over 15 percent (1810-1820). That rate was third to New Bedford and Fall River. Taunton was one of the early industrial towns and is typical of a town in the Boston-Providence regional overlap. In general though, towns in 1810 closest to the sea constituted the major population centers.

Proceeding down the list to rank 20-40 (see Appendix I which ranks all towns of population 2,000 or more), 50 percent had a coastal location. Of all towns with a population of 2,000 or more only two were in Worcester County (the portion under study) and two were in Middlesex County (Cambridge and Charlestown), both inland counties. Generally speaking, there were very few population centers away from the coast in 1810.

Central places tend to be centers of information and news flow, and the publishing industry has traditionally located in large urban places. From the point of view of sources of news information, Boston was far and above the leader, publishing eight newspapers in 1810. Of secondary importance were Newburyport, Salem, and Worcester, each publishing two papers. Worcester as a publishing center far exceeds its rank as a population center. This suggests that already by 1810 Worcester was somewhat established as an urban center for the remote interior of Massachusetts.[22] Publishing one paper each were New Bedford, as might be expected, and also Leominster and Haverhill. Neither town was an important center and the presence of a news publication in these two towns varies from the predicted pattern.

Aggregate banking figures provide another indicator of the regional hierarchy. According to the Abstract of Banks for 1810 (which does not include Rockingham County), Boston with its three large banks had five times the capital assets of its closest rival Salem, which had two banks. Of the six other towns with reportable assets only Worcester was not on the coast. This again is an indication of Worcester's predominance in the interior.[23]

Based on the few indices available for the region in 1810, it then appears that Boston, Salem, Newburyport, Portsmouth, New Bedford and Gloucester constituted the principal population centers of the region in 1810, with Worcester close behind. The extent to which these population centers constituted an integrated network of central places is difficult to ascertain, especially since all the towns were coastal.

Another means of assessing the hierarchical relationships among the cities and towns, particularly in the hinterland, would be to examine actual patterns of flows of goods. While exact rankings differentiate function and size levels of the various urban places, the patterns of flows of goods would suggest linkages among the cities and towns. Actual patterns of flows of goods are difficult to determine for the period since the 1810 census of manufactures was aggregated on a county rather than a town level. Despite the problem of the aggregate data, a pattern of specialization in economic activity is apparent. This specialization

Table II-2
Bank Assets and the Number of Banks Ranked by Town in the Region 1810*

Rank	Town	Assets	No. of Banks
1	Boston	$4,600,000	3
2	Salem	500,000	2
3	Newburyport	550,000	1
4	Beverly	160,000	1
5	New Bedford	150,000	1
6	Worcester	150,000	1
7	Plymouth	100,000	1
8	Marblehead	100,000	1
9	Gloucester	100,000	1

* Excludes Rockingham County
Source: Abstract of Banks for the Commonwealth of Massachusetts.

Table II-3
The Twenty Most Populous Towns Ranked in the Region, 1830

Rank	Town	Population
1	Boston	61,392
2	Salem	13,895
3	Charlestown	8,783
4	Portsmouth	8,025
5	New Bedford	7,592
6	Gloucester	7,510
7	Lowell	6,474
8	Newburyport	6,375
9	Lynn	6,138
10	Cambridge	6,072
11	Taunton	6,042
12	Roxbury	5,247
13	Marblehead	5,149
14	Middleborough	5,008
15	Plymouth	4,758
16	Andover	4,530
17	Danvers	4,228
18	Worcester	4,173
19	Fall River	4,158
20	Dorchester	4,074

Source: Census of 1830 (U.S.).

required a network of central places to facilitate the exchange of materials, services and farm products.

Rockingham was the most industrialized of the New Hampshire counties with considerable production in ropewalks, distilled spirits, nails and leather. Shipping these industrial products probably constituted a significant part of the mercantile activity of Portsmouth.[24]

Massachusetts counties in the region reported a great deal more manufacturing activity. Worcester County was an active textile area. Notable but less active in textiles were Bristol and Middlesex counties. Middlesex was active in brickmaking, Essex in leather and shoes, Suffolk in musical instruments, Bristol in tack and nail. Manufacturing was scattered and it is difficult to determine to what extent such activity was concentrated in population centers.[25]

In 1810 it appears that any hierarchical network between cities was at best very primitive. Obviously there must have been some network of market centers exchanging manufactured and agricultural products, especially in areas beyond a reasonable journey to one of the coastal centers such as Boston or Salem. No such hierarchy clearly emerges, although the position of Worcester suggests beginnings.[26]

Better sources for 1830 offer a more complete picture. of what the regional hierarchy had become by that time. The New England economy had revived its foreign trade after the misfortunes of the War of 1812 and had experienced in the 1820's a decade of substantial internal growth. The cities and towns throughout the region were dotted with mills of various sizes, which attested to the considerable growth of the manufacturing sector of the regional economy during the twenty year period. The mills do not tell the entire story since much additional manufacturing activity still took place in the home and in small shops scattered throughout the area.[27]

Though a number of mills were established in the region during the twenty year period (62 in the region) the town ranking was remarkably similar to the listing for 1810.[28] Seventy percent were coastal towns with Boston and Salem dominant. The appearance of Lowell and Worcester, and the improved ranking of Taunton, are an indication of the gradual shift to manufacturing based activity in the interior. Still, population centers in 1830 continued to be concentrated in coastal areas.

Post offices served a number of functions in 1830. Without telegraph and subsequent communications technology, letters assumed a central role in facilitating communication. The ranking of postal receipts would suggest a ranking of places with which residents of the region were inclined to communicate. For 1830, town by town postal receipts are available. For gross receipts the rankings were quite different from the population rankings though the composition of the list was similar to the population list.[29]

Table II-4
Gross Postal and Per Capita Postal Receipts Per Town
Ranked One through Twenty in the Region, 1830

Rank	Town	Gross Receipts	Population Rank	Population Town	Per Capita Receipts
1	Boston	$52,916	1	61,392	$ .86
2	Salem	5,355	2	13,895	.38
3	New Bedford	3,328	5	7,592	.43
4	Newburyport	2,188	8	6,395	.34
5	Portsmouth	1,555	4	8,025	.19
6	Lowell	1,464	7	6,474	.22
7	Worcester	1,332	18	4,173	.31
8	Andover	1,234	16	4,530	.27
9	Charlestown	1,161	3	8,783	.13
10	Taunton	1,034	11	6,042	.17
11	Lynn	883	9	6,138	.14
12	Cambridge	641	10	6,072	.10
13	Haverhill	620	23	3,896	.15
14	Exeter	558	37	2,753	.20
15	Marblehead	531	13	5,149	.10
16	Gloucester	515	6	7,510	.06
17	Leicester	484	*	1,782	.27
18	Roxbury	475	12	5,247	.09
19	Newton	367	46	2,376	.15
20	Dedham	362	31	3,179	.11

* Population below 2,000.

Source: 21st Congress, 2nd Session, Net Amount of Postage accruing at each Post Office for the year ending March 31, 1830 Communicated to the House of Representatives, in *American State Papers,* Post Office, Feb. 28, 1831.

Worcester ranked seventh here as compared to ranking eighteenth in population, which is further indication of its distinctive importance as an urban center for the hinterland. Its per capita usage was fifth. The relatively high receipts for Worcester suggest an increasingly important role in the government and commerce of the hinterland relative to the size of the city. Lowell also ranked high. Lowell has often been portrayed as an instant mill town of enormous proportions, but as will be seen, Lowell became an instant city housing a variety of economic activity only partially related to the textile industry. Interestingly and logically, Boston, Salem, New Bedford, Newburyport, and Portsmouth had high aggregate receipts, and per capita usage which would be expected from commercial ports and mercantile centers.

The number and capital of banks had increased considerably between 1810 and 1830 (see Appendix II) both in coastal towns and in the hinterland. Especially notable is the appearance of banks in Fall River, Taunton, Lowell and the rise of Worcester. These interior towns, in addition to the numerous coastal towns, boasted a significant number of banks with impressive amounts of capital.[30]

The 1830 aggregate valuation of economic activity within the Commonwealth offers a different perspective on the economic contours of the region. For each town the number of shops and shops with houses was enumerated. This index gives an interesting glimpse into the amount of small nonagricultural activity taking place within the various towns. Shops could be commercial or manufacturing concerns or both.[31] In this category only 55 percent of the towns were coastal. Major ports such as Boston, Salem, Newburyport and New Bedford again appear, which suggests that these cities were indeed diversified, i.e., not strictly maritime but housing a fair share of the retail and manufacturing sectors as well. Pepperell, Weymouth and Woburn appear only in this category which indicates that those towns' populations were very much involved in small scale manufacturing such as shoes. Also Lynn, though a coastal town, had an inordinate number of shops relative to population size, which indicates that it was essentially a shoe town rather than a port town.[32]

Shops are an elusive category. The vagueness of the term makes any interpretation largely conjectural. The McLane report for 1833 is a more precise measure of non-agricultural activity, particularly regarding manufacturing. For 1833, the number of individual firms with annual production of $100,000 was tabulated for each city and ranked. The process was somewhat frustrated because the McLane report did not list individual firms for Boston or Salem. Appendix III offers a typology of towns in the region and shows towns with major manufacturing concerns as defined above. Though no specific information was available for Boston and Salem, the aggregate totals of all manufacturing suggest that those cities also contained a significant amount of manufacturing. To what extent it was concentrated in large firms is less certain. In

Table II-5
The Number of Shops Per Town in the Region Ranked
One through Twenty, 1830*

Rank	Town	No. of Shops
1	Boston	1,306
2	Salem	327
3	Charlestown	214
4	Lynn	209
5	West Newbury	206
6	Woburn	180
7	New Bedford	174
8	Haverhill	163
9	Newburyport	133
10	Hingham	132
11	Roxbury	129
12	Beverly	128
13	Wakefield	128
14	Weymouth	128
15	Worcester	123
16	Danvers	117
17	Upton	110
18	Wenham	110
19	Pepperell	107
20	Dorchester	106

* Excludes Rockingham County.
Source: Valuations for the Commonwealth of Massachusetts for 1830. Mss. in the Massachusetts State Library.

any case these two towns are included in special category: I (see Appendix III).

Category I includes significant non-agricultural areas, largely commercial. New Bedford is difficult to classify because whaling was not considered an industry by McLane, though it was in the 1850 census. Newburyport, Marblehead and Portsmouth were principal non-agricultural commercial centers based on aggregate amounts of industry. All coastal towns had some shipping just as all towns in the region had some manufacturing. For purposes of constructing an urban hierarchy for 1830, these coastal towns are included in a separate category. Categories II and III indicate towns which had a significant number of large firms and their principal products. As can be seen, the textile industry was already composed of large firms, as were the iron and paper industries. This general listing does not correspond as well as others to general population distribution among the towns. This differentiation among the towns by industry will be further explored in the following chapter.[33]

Based on the various rankings of towns, it is difficult to determine clearly a hierarchical arrangement among the towns, particularly when blending the commercial and manufacturing sectors. Unlike the Christallerian model in central place theory, no neat subdivisions emerge within the Boston region. Accurate measurement of an historical hierarchy is further obstructed by lack of complete information on flows of activity. Such difficulties aside, however, certain observations can be made. Clearly, Boston occupied a unique position in the region. In all categories, Boston was well above the second ranked town. Of course, many categories could be conceived of for which Boston would not head the list—an example being textiles. In terms of what might be called urban functions and services, such as banking or nonagricultural employment, Boston occupied the highest place within the hierarchy of the region. Subsequent chapters will explore the relationship further.

Boston was also the seat of government for the state. Though this study does not dwell on political relationships, this fact was an important reason behind the overwhelming dominance of Boston in the region. Boston was the capital and as such was the center of political decision-making. Since news traveled slowly, it would seem that those individuals and firms interested in such news would locate near the source.

Salem, New Bedford and Portsmouth surely belong at the second level in the hierarchy. Each was the commercial seat of a subregion within the larger Boston region. In terms of all indices this contention is further underscored. For Lowell and Worcester to be classified on the same level in 1830 is a bit more venturesome. Clearly both cities were the most rapidly growing of a rapidly expanding hinterland. Unlike the three other cities in the category, Lowell particularly had no tradition of dominance in a subregion. Lowell had been in existence for only four years but, because of its unusually rapid econom-

Figure II-1. Conjectured Hierarchy for the Region for 1830

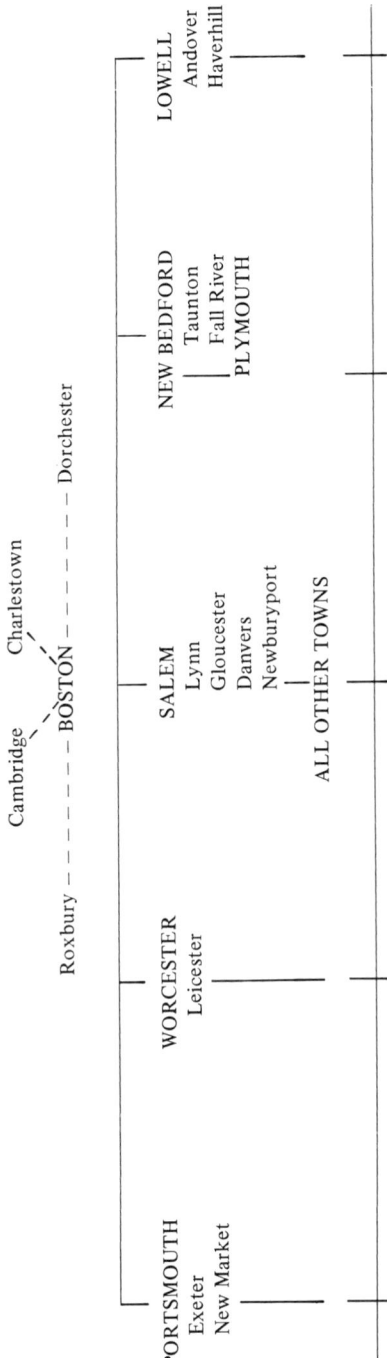

ic growth in a short period of time, the city became an immediate factor in the hierarchy. Worcester was also an emerging center, not as established as the port cities. The town was smaller and less diversified, serving a more isolated sub-region with low order ubiquitous central place functions. Worcester was a hinterland outpost, a county seat, very dependent on the emergence of inland manufacturing and agriculture. Worcester's commercial and financial sectors were no match for the ports.

Further down the hierarchy at Level III it is more difficult to distinguish towns. In the Portsmouth area, Exeter clearly stands above other towns in terms of population and nonagricultural activity to the point of being a rival town to Portsmouth. Surely Exeter must have been of some service to the inland areas. The Salem subregion had a number of very active towns, particularly Lynn and Danvers, which were primarily manufacturing centers. Also Gloucester and Marblehead were very active ports. These port towns such as Gloucester, Beverly, etc. are further problems because of their proximity to the sea which may have given them some commercial independence from Salem, the largest town in their subregion. Newburyport is another special case. It may well be that in 1810 the town was a rival of Salem and thus dominant in the extreme north part of Essex County. The embargo of 1807 hit Newburyport especially hard and the town became a classic example of a town declining in the hierarchy.[34]

In the New Bedford area, Taunton clearly emerges as an interior population center, reflecting the rise of manufacturing activity. Fall River experienced similar growth but should be considered an extension of Providence. Plymouth is a more difficult case. It may have suffered the same fate as Newburyport though at an earlier time since it never was a major commercial port.

In the interior, the hierarchy becomes less clear at Level III. Worcester, Leicester and Mendon appear to be towns on the rise. Generally they had a larger population than neighboring towns and the presence of a bank made each a more potent commercial center. Yet Mendon, like Fall River, was very close to Providence and perhaps should be considered part of that region— certainly in the region overlap. Near Lowell were Andover and Haverhill, which were on the verge of becoming important manufacturing towns. Since Lowell was so new one must be cautious in suggesting patterns of dependence. Obviously, other flow patterns existed before Lowell was created. Andover may have been the center of commercial activity and lost its position almost overnight.[35] The rapid growth of Lowell suggests that rapid changes took place throughout the Essex County area. This would be unlike Worcester which grew more gradually.[36]

By 1830 patterns of development were already quite clearly set within the Boston region. The gradual development of the interior centered around Worcester, Lowell, and the Taunton area. This trend continued through 1850. The 1850 census of manufacturing gives detailed information on the specific

Table II-6
The Twenty Most Populous Towns Ranked by Town, 1850

Rank	Town	Population
1	Boston	136,881
2	Lowell	33,383
3	Salem	20,264
4	Roxbury	18,364
5	Charlestown	17,216
6	Worcester	17,049
7	New Bedford	16,443
8	Cambridge	15,215
9	Lynn	14,257
10	Fall River	11,524
11	Taunton	10,441
12	Portsmouth	9,738
13	Newburyport	9,572
14	Lawrence	8,282
15	Danvers	8,109
16	Dorchester	7,969
17	Gloucester	7,786
18	Andover	6,945
19	Chelsea	6,701
20	Marblehead	6,167

Source: Census of 1850 (U.S.).

industries of the region. The indices for this particular date tend to reinforce the patterns which began to emerge in 1830.

Again it is possible to look at the twenty most populous towns and again Boston topped the list. Lowell overtook Salem and became the second ranked city in the region—a truly remarkable growth. Roxbury and Charlestown by 1850 ceased to be solely rural towns and became quite urbanized, sharing considerably in the growth of Boston. Worcester by 1850 had moved up to rank six which, like Lowell, was a dramatic jump from 1830. This underscores the general pattern of Worcester and Lowell becoming leading hinterland commercial and manufacturing centers, dominant over other towns within their subregions.

Despite the rise of Lowell and Worcester, the majority (70%) of principal population centers still remained on the coast. Newburyport declined still further as expected. Marblehead, Gloucester and New Bedford also experienced some decline, suggesting that any adverse effect from loss in the Maritime sector was felt more heavily in marginal rather than principal ports. The emergence of an inland rail transportation network (as explained more fully in chapter 4) favored the ports of Portsmouth, Salem and especially Boston. These principal ports handled the bulk of materials flowing into and out of the rapidly expanding hinterland. As principal nodes in the rail network these ports could offer commercial and transport services at less cost than other ports. This advantage accounts for the relative decline of the smaller ports along the coast.[37]

Traditional fishing towns such as Dartmouth, Fairhaven, Sandwich, and Barnstable dropped significantly in population over the forty year span. On the other hand, industrial towns such as Waltham (textiles) and Attleboro (jewelry) and others gained considerably. In 1830, 70 percent of the towns ranked by population 20-40 were located on the coast. In twenty years, the interior had developed to such a degree that only 35 percent were so located[38] (see Appendix I).

In terms of banks, Worcester and Lowell again rose in rankings, Worcester from fifth to third and Lowell from eleventh to fifth. Also notable was the rise of Fitchburg from a town with no banks in 1830 to a town with two in 1850. With the exception of Fitchburg, all the towns with two or more banks were included in the towns ranked 1-20 by population. The situation of Fitchburg in 1830 is analogous to that of Worcester in 1810. The town's importance as a banking center was greater than its population size would suggest. In Worcester this differential ranking decreased over time as Worcester's rank in population rose dramatically. This differential for Fitchburg similarly decreased later in the nineteenth century.[39]

For 1850, data on the aggregate number of shops is available through the State Valuation. This data again indicates a great deal of nonagricultural economic activity in the hinterland. Only 40 percent of the twenty towns with

Table II-7

The Number of Shops and Warehouses Per Town in the
Region Ranked One through Twenty, 1830*

Rank	Town	No. of Shops	Town	No. of Warehouses
1	Boston	1,898	Boston	1,726
2	Lynn	586	Newburyport	189
3	Lowell	540	Salem	135½
4	Beverly	447	New Bedford	122
5	Danvers	341	Worcester	120
6	Salem	332	Cambridge	119
7	Sudbury	309	Roxbury	85
8	Abington	308	Gloucester	82
9	Andover	296	Plymouth	73
10	Woburn	279	Marblehead	70½
11	Charlestown	253	Haverhill	69½
12	New Bedford	253	Hingham	62
13	Worcester	252	Lawrence	51
14	Middleborough	250	Somerset	48
15	Randolph	249	Abington	47
16	Roxbury	247	Fitchburg	47**
17	Stoughton	244	Taunton	41
18	Marblehead	235½		
19	Weymouth	239¼		
20	N. Bridgewater	231		

* Excludes Rockingham County.

** The number of towns with warehouses under 40 but above 35 was so large that it seemed best to cut off at 40.

Source: Valuation for the Commonwealth of Massachusetts for 1850. Mss. in the Massachusetts State Library.

the largest number of shops were coastal towns. New to this particular list were Stoughton, Abington, N. Bridgewater, Middleborough, and Randolph, all noncoastal towns located in the southeastern part of the region, indicating a real surge in nonagricultural activity in the Providence-Boston overlap area. Boston continued to dominate this category with three times as many shops as its closest rival, Lynn.[40]

The 1850 valuation also included the category "warehouses" which suggests a different sort of economic activity from "Shops," though no precise definition of the term could be found. It seems likely that these warehouses were used for wholesaling and thus should appear in cities and towns of a higher order in the hierarchy. Table II-7 lists all those towns with forty or more warehouses. Boston dominated the area with 1,726. An enormous gap separated Boston from Newburyport, second on the list, with 189. Newburyport's position on the list is somewhat strange since the town was by all other indices a much smaller and slower growing town than Boston. Of course, whether the valuation included both active and inactive warehouses is not known. Some of this large number may have been relics of more prosperous days in Newburyport. Salem, New Bedford, Gloucester, Plymouth and Marblehead, the more prosperous coastal towns, had a significant number. Interior warehousing facilities were located mainly in Worcester and Fitchburg in the west—further evidence of the emergence of Fitchburg. In the north, Haverhill and Lawrence had a significant number. Notably absent from the list is Lowell which had only two warehouses.[41] Given the concentration of textile production in Lowell it seems that that particular industry was integrated to the extent that warehousing was counted as part of the mill or perhaps some of the warehousing may have been located in Boston.[42] To the south, Taunton and Somerset had a good number of warehouses. Fall River, perhaps for the same reasons as Lowell, had only nine.

From the perspective of communication, Boston clearly dominated the region with 107 periodical publications. Its closest rivals were Lowell with eight and Worcester with seven. Fitchburg had two along with Haverhill and Lawrence. The rest of the towns with two or more were located along the coast[43] (see Table II-8).

The 1850 Census provided detailed information on individual manufactures for all towns. Thus it is possible to rank all cities within the region by total number of large firms (those producing over $100,000 annually). Once again Boston clearly dominated the region with sixty-five large firms. These produced a variety of products: lead, copper machinery, distilled liquor, gas, glass, pickles, etc. (see Appendix III).[44] This aggregate figure may be somewhat deceiving, as in the case of the seven tailoring firms which in 1850 together produced nearly one million dollars worth of ready-made clothing. Most of the actual work was done outside of Boston in the hinterland on contract with a

Table II-8
Towns With Three or More Newspapers and Periodicals Ranked, 1850*

Rank	Town	No. of Periodicals
1	Boston	107
2	Lowell	8
3	Worcester	7
4	Salem	5
5	New Bedford	4
6	Taunton	3
	Gloucester	3
	Newburyport	3

Towns with 2: Lynn, Haverhill, Lawrence, Fall River, Fitchburg, Chelsea, Plymouth, Dedham, Roxbury, Cambridge

* Excludes Rockingham County.
Source: Manuscript Returns for the Census of 1850 (U.S.) in the Massachusetts State
         Library.

Boston firm.[45] Second ranked New Bedford poses a particular problem. Most of the twenty-one firms there were concerned with whale fishery which was not considered "manufacturing" by all census takers. If whaling is considered manufacturing, then New Bedford ranks second, and if not, then it would be third with only eleven large firms (whale oil and textiles).

Other concentrations of major industrial firms were textile and shoe towns of Lowell, Roxbury, Worcester, Fall River, Andover, Lynn, and Salem. Medford ranks high as a shipbuilding center. Portsmouth and Salem, though two of the principal urban centers of the region, had only five large firms, which suggests that their economies rested almost exclusively on commerce rather than manufacturing. Boston and New Bedford achieved a greater balance between commerce and manufacturing.

From the various functional indices for the principal cities of the region, it seems appropriate to hypothesize that in 1850 there was a distinct hierarchy among the principal population centers of the region. Again in 1850 Boston dominates the hierarchy. Boston in 1850 was as active as ever, not only in commerce but also in manufacturing. It also continued to be the cultural, intellectual and certainly the symbolic center of the region. At the second level, Salem, New Bedford, Worcester, Lowell and Portsmouth persisted, all becoming increasingly active in the manufacturing sector of the economy.

At the third level, the coastal subregions remain similar to the 1830 period. Plymouth is a notable exception as 1850 saw further decline in the port town. The more interesting developments occur in the hinterland. Fitchburg, Blackstone and the new town of Clinton emerged as third level centers characterized by rapid population growth, growth in service industries and general development of the nonagricultural sector of their respective local economies. This pattern also fits the older Lowell area. Andover, Haverhill and Lawrence began their rise as principal manufacturing centers, while Lowell remained the center of this part of the region. Far from being strictly a textile city, Lowell was a genuinely diversified economy with firms representing fifty different branches of industry in 1850 as well as an array of financial institutions.[46]

At the base of the regional economy were the approximately 200 small towns which fed the rest of the hierarchy and which in turn were fed through the hierarchical structure of the region. From the point of view of the distribution of economic activity, these towns appear insignificant. But in the dynamics of commodity flows through the region, these towns play a much more visible role.

The story told by these three static pictures of the region in 1810, 1830 and 1850, is the story of the gradual development of the western section of the region with comparative stagnation in the coastal areas. Maps II-3 and II-4 illustrate this development for Massachusetts. During the early years, 1800-1830, most of the towns experiencing growth rates of 15 percent or more

Figure II-2. Conjectured Hierarchy for the Region for 1850

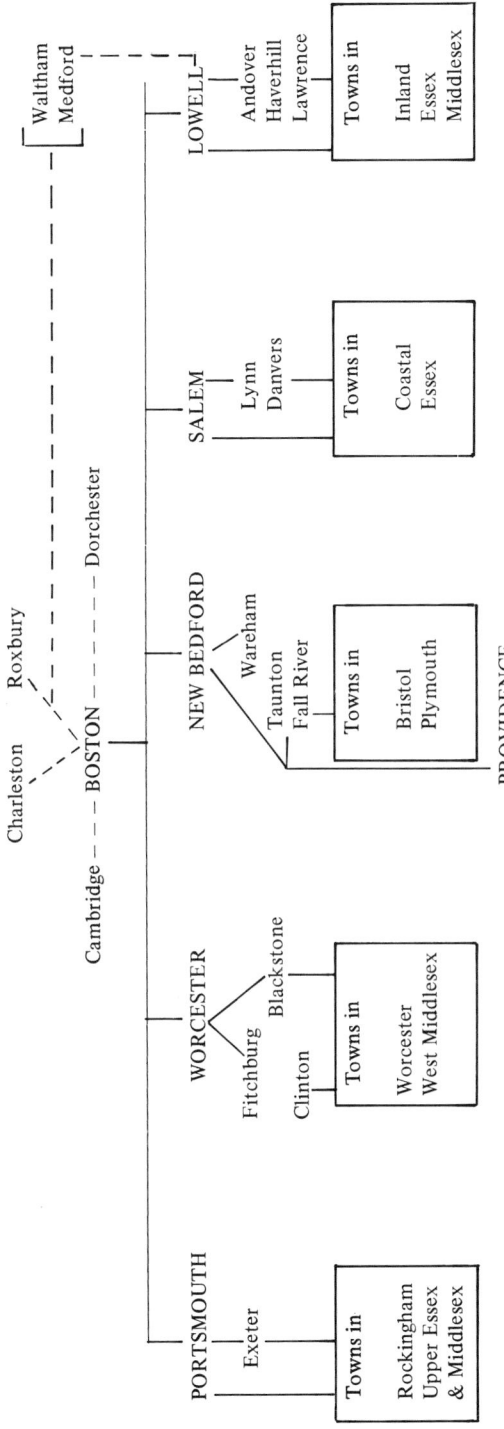

Note: The linkages suggested in this hierarchy are examined in detail in the last three chapters.

were located along the coast. The exception is the cradle of the American textile industry. By and large most inland towns experienced relatively slow population growth. Map II-4 really shows a dramatic change in the population growth of the western part of the region. From 1830-1850 there is considerable growth throughout the region, but especially in the hinterland.[47]

For the overall urban development of the region, the period of decline of marginal coastal towns, of the survival of principal commercial centers, and of the development of the interior was a critical period for the urban growth of the region. By 1810 the beginnings of the urban hierarchy in an industrial setting began to emerge. In 1810 the roots of this network were apparent with the growth of Worcester. By 1830, with the rise of Lowell and the further rise of Worcester, accompanied by the decline of many coastal towns, the new hierarchy begins to appear more clearly. From 1830 on, the hierarchical network in the region is characterized by remarkable stability. As was noted, the conjectured hierarchies for both 1830 and 1850 were similar except at the lowest level. Throughout the early nineteenth century the rank orderings maintained a high degree of stability as well. A number of coastal towns drop out in 1830 along with large inland agricultural towns. By 1830 a set of somewhat changed rankings in relation to 1810 is very similar to the 1850 list. Seventeen towns appeared on both lists. By 1850 the hierarchical relationship between towns had become firmly established at the higher levels. Boston, Salem, Worcester, Lowell and Portsmouth remained even 100 years later among the principal towns of the region.

Geographers have pointed out the remarkable stability of the urban superstructure in the United States, particularly during the last 100 years. New York continues to dominate, with Chicago and Los Angeles, as regional centers. Boston, San Francisco, Philadelphia seem a notch further down. As the country grew, these orderings changed somewhat, particularly with the development of the west. In general, though, the structure has been stable and permanent.[48]

It seems that this phenomenon holds true for smaller regions as well. The dominance of coastal towns in the Colonial-Revolutionary era yielded in the early nineteenth century to a balance between principal coastal towns and interior towns. As the economy continued to expand and grow more complex, some shifts did occur in the regional rankings, for example, the rise of Fitchburg. Yet by 1850 it appears that a stable urban hierarchy had emerged in the region.

The hierarchy was the basic structural framework for the movement of products through the region. Unfortunately, for the early nineteenth century, detailed data does not exist for confirmation of the hierarchies offered in this chapter. In fact, it is doubtful that at any period in time sufficient data exists to trace in detail economic flows through a region the size of this Boston region. Nevertheless, these conjectures serve as a point of reference for subsequent analysis of the regional economy and its relationship to component cities and

Map II-3. Population Stability, 1800–1830

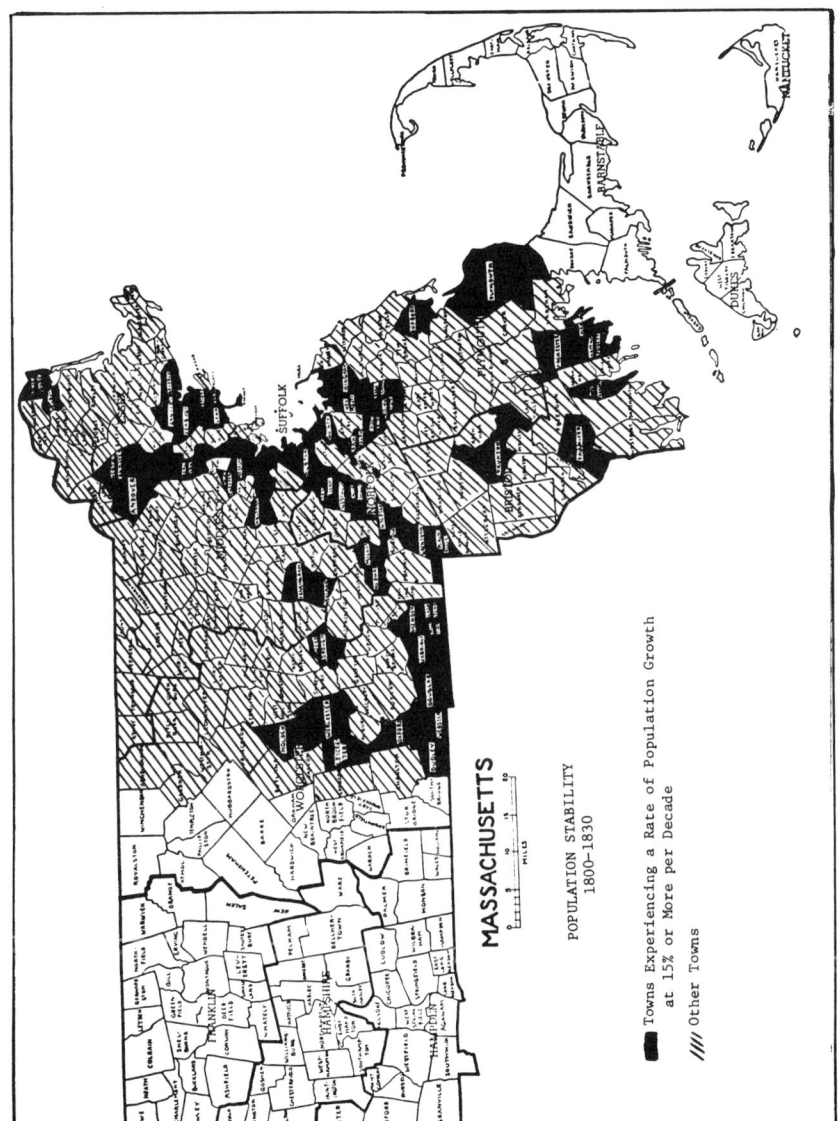

MASSACHUSETTS

POPULATION STABILITY
1800–1830

■ Towns Experiencing a Rate of Population Growth
  at 15% or More per Decade

/// Other Towns

towns. Though the hierarchies at the higher level exhibit some stability, it is important to recall that the hierarchical system of cities suggested in this chapter was not a rigid or fixed system. The relationship of the economic activities of various towns and cities was in constant evolution, in response to changes in transport technology, shifts in resource bases, and in the relationship of the region to the rest of the national and international economy.

It would be a mistake to assume that all economic activity was distributed evenly throughout the structural framework. There was considerable variance among all cities and towns in the relative economic importance of commerce, manufacturing and agriculture. The more important cities in the hierarchy were all extremely active urban economies, yet these economies, though diversified, were not all self-contained. They depended a great deal on the variety of economic activity scattered throughout the smaller towns in the region.

What then was the extent of the spread of economic activity through the region? To what extent did the economic activity of towns and cities in the region become specialized over time? Close study of the Boston region presents an opportunity to look in a detailed way at the spread of industry throughout the region. Relevant theory would suggest that the greater the specialization of activity in the towns of the region the greater the reliance on the linkage elements of the infrastructure of this hierarchically arranged system of cities. At this point location decisions, why an industry chooses to locate at a particular point on the map, become very important. Specialization and diffusion of economic activity in the region suggest the importance of the spatial dimension in understanding urbanization on a regional scale. The relevant literature on location theory suggests the importance of access to resources in the process of national location decisions. Chapter III looks at the importance of regional location decisions in determining the spread of economic activity in the Boston region.

Map II-4. Population Stability, 1830-1850

MASSACHUSETTS

POPULATION STABILITY
1830–1850

MILES

■ Towns Experiencing a Rate of Population Growth
  at 15% or More per Decade

///// Other Towns

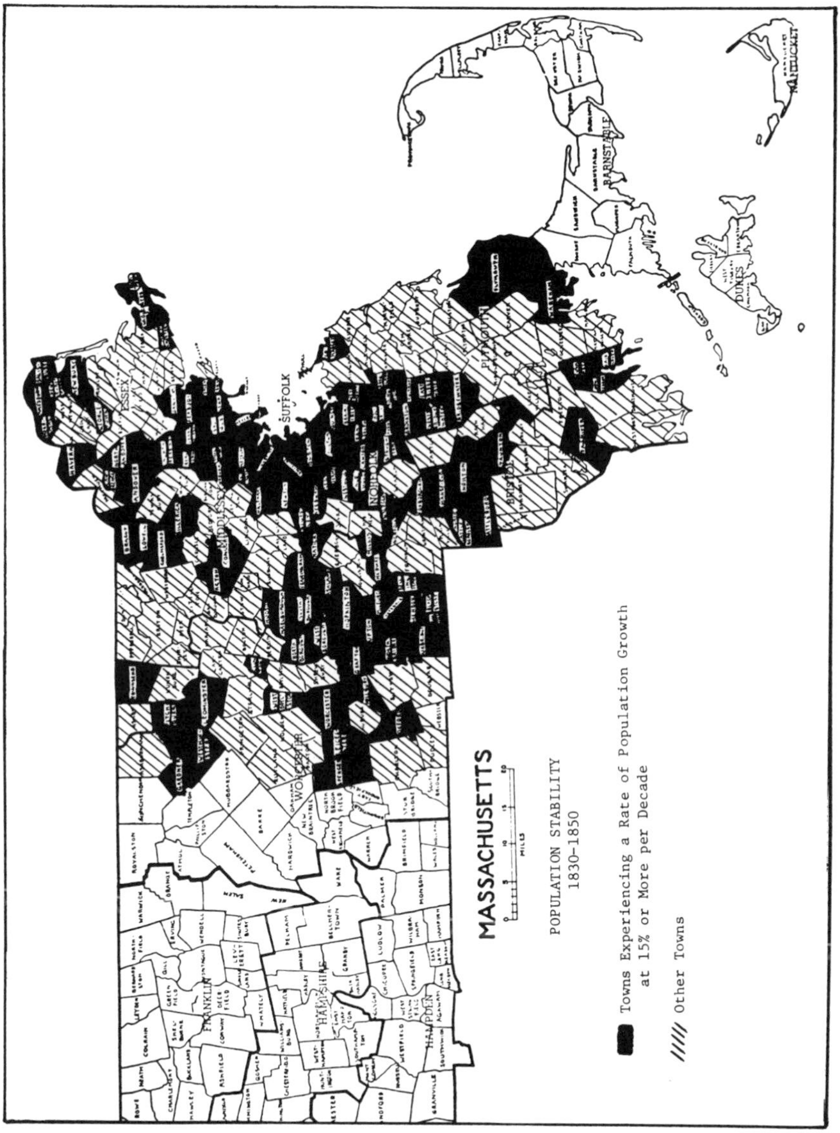

III

MANUFACTURING IN THE REGION, 1810-1850

Despite the substantial stability within the regional hierarchy of aggregate manufacturing economic activity, it is important to note that all sectors of economic activity were not represented in all segments of the hierarchy. Nor did all large towns have large amounts of all segments of the manufacturing economy. Highly aggregated data on manufacturing in the Massachusetts urban hierarchy give a misleading impression of uniformity and stability over time. Beneath the aggregates there can be found considerable spatial differentiation in the industrial base of the regional economy. This chapter examines selected industries in detail and their distribution throughout the region in 1810, 1830 and 1850. Important in the historical process which created the distribution were the location decisions made by individual manufacturing firms based on the need for access to the various resources of the region. As these many separate location decisions were made, the urban network shifted somewhat to accommodate and serve the growing areas of the region. Through the early nineteenth century this shift was gradually away from the coast and toward the interior.

The textile and the boot and shoe industries were chosen for detailed study, since they were the largest industries in the region. Machinery and tanning and currying, which were important support industries for the textile and shoe industries, were also selected. Printing and publishing and the manufacturing of musical instruments were chosen as examples of industries highly concentrated in a few towns of the region.

The McLane report gives detailed aggregate figures for all towns in 1833 and the manuscript census for manufacturing for 1850 gives comparable figures. From these sources, the evolving distribution of specific industries can be determined. The census of 1810 was also used to extend the historical perspective further back in time. However, since it was aggregated at the county level, individual town data could only be surmised. A quick glance at the comparative data indicates that the twenty year period 1830-1850 witnessed a substantial spread in the industrial sector of the regional economy and considerable development of the interior.

Probably the best known and most widely studied industry of the period is the textile industry. It was the first really to organize into the factory system.

In many ways it was a pioneer industry and spread rapidly throughout the region.[1] In 1810 the industry produced approximately $2.3 million in the region, mostly as a cottage labor industry with production concentrated in Middlesex, Worcester and Bristol counties.[2] By 1830 the industry did a volume of $11.5 million in factories and shops spread among eighty-seven towns within the region.[3] By 1850 the comparative rate of growth slowed down somewhat, but output reached $32.1 million spread among ninety-four towns but becoming increasingly concentrated in a few.[4] (Appendix IV lists all towns containing units of production for the textile industry in 1830 and 1850.)

Maps III-1 and III-2 show the location and output of textile mills by town in the region. It is worth noting that production was centered in three areas around Lowell, Worcester and Taunton. There is a notable lack of production along the coast, with the exception of Salisbury at the extreme north. In 1830 there was some textile production in the Plymouth area, but by 1850 much of that production had ceased. Though most of the principal urban areas were along the coast, particularly through 1830, the industry chose to locate inland. Boston, the most populated area, had no textile output listed within its political boundaries even through 1850.

It is well known that the location of this industry was very dependent on the power resources of the inland rivers, especially as the industry moved into the factory stage. The clustering of textile activity in maps III-1 and III-2 reflects the industry's need for access to water resources. The two earliest textile developments were the Blackstone basin, including such towns as Dudley, Webster and Uxbridge, and the Merrimack basin which powered the most important of the textile mills of Lowell, Andover and later Lawrence. Boston, with relatively poor power resources, was not an attractive location. The decision to locate the textile industry inland was the principal factor in pre-1850 interior development. The textile industry and such ancillary industries as textile machinery were the only large industries to settle principally in the interior.

During the course of the early nineteenth century, individual textile firms grew and the number of firms expanded through the region. In 1810 all counties in the region reported some production in textiles, nearly all of which was the work of cottage labor. The McLane report mentioned eighty-seven towns in the region which were active in textile production in 1833. This total had risen to ninety-four in 1850. Though the number of towns engaged in textile activity remained relatively static, due primarily to the lack of distinction between factory and cottage system of production, the scale of production in selected towns changed dramatically as the industry became more capital intensive. In 1810 Worcester County had the highest total production, followed by Bristol, Middlesex and Rockingham, all with similar totals. By 1833, Lowell itself had grown to capture 18 percent of the regional output, followed by Fall River at 7.9 percent and Mendon with 5.7 percent. In 1850 Lowell had grown to a full 31 percent of the regional output, with Fall River remaining almost unchanged at 8.2 percent. Clinton, a new town reflecting mid-century development of the Nashua River basin, followed with 6.4 percent.[5]

The machinery industry was generally confined to fewer towns within the region. The 1810 census contains no figures for a separate machinery industry. In 1833, twenty-nine towns were engaged in machinery production. Boston and Worcester were the major centers accounting for 12 percent each of total production. In 1850, Boston remained the center of machinery production with 31.8 percent of the total. Lowell (12.8%) and Taunton (10.3%) developed considerably, largely due to the expansion of the railroad and the development of the textile industry in their respective river basins (see Appendix V for complete figures). The machinery industry flourished both inland and in coastal locations. Major cities within the network such as Boston, Lowell, Worcester, and Fall River and Fitchburg had machinery firms and all were termini for railroad lines.[6] Unlike the textile industry, the machinery sector was an urban industry apparently requiring easy access to transportation systems to get the product to its ultimate markets both coastal and inland. Also the railroad was a major purchaser of heavy machinery which would suggest further reasons for a central location.

The boot and shoe industry was by far the most widespread form of manufacturing. All counties reported some output in this category. McLane found 141 towns engaged in shoe production and the 1850 census listed 154 such towns. The major centers for shoe production were coastal. Lynn was the leading center for shoe production in 1830 with 12 percent and in 1850 with 16.6 percent of total output. In 1830, the only notable inland clusters of activity in shoes were in the upper Blackstone basin and the eastern Merrimack basin area. Haverhill was second to Lynn to output both in 1833 (5.6%) and 1850 (6.7%). At mid-century principal shoe production towns were generally located along the coast or within easy access to the coast. Certainly the coastal location was advantageous in terms of cheap transporation. Maps III-3 and III-4 illustrate the coastal preference among the principal locations of shoe production. It must be kept in mind that over 50 percent of the towns on the map engaged in some form of shoe production. Those towns mapped were principal centers of shoe production and thus considered most important to the regional economy. The only inland area of note for shoe production was the upper Blackstone valley which in parts was navigable down to Providence through the Blackstone Canal[7] (see Appendix VI for complete figures on the shoe industry).

The factory system was appearing in the larger shoe producing towns by 1850 for a combination of reasons. Generally the larger the producer, the greater was the percentage of output shipped outside the region, which necessitated easy access to a commercial port. Access to tanneries was also an important consideration in the location decision and these were located predominantly

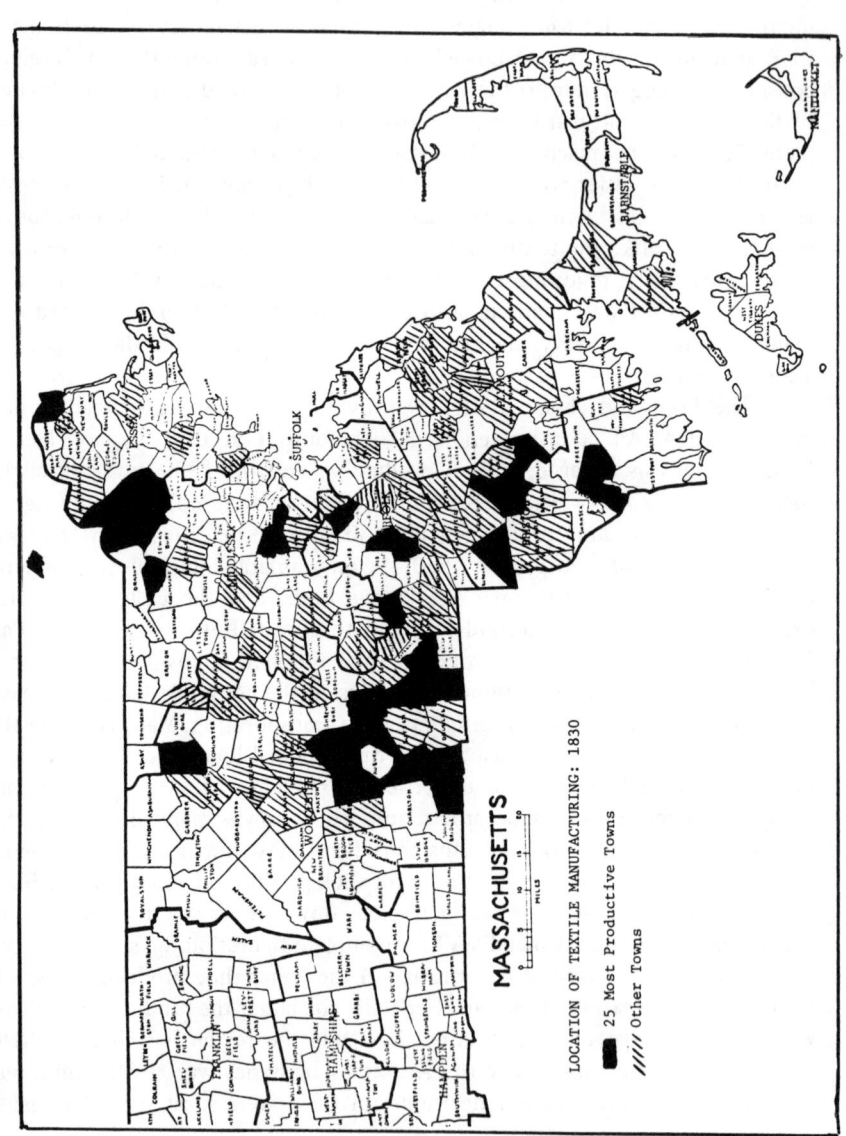

Map III-1. Location of Textile Manufacturing, 1830

Map III-2. Location and Textile Manufacturing, 1850

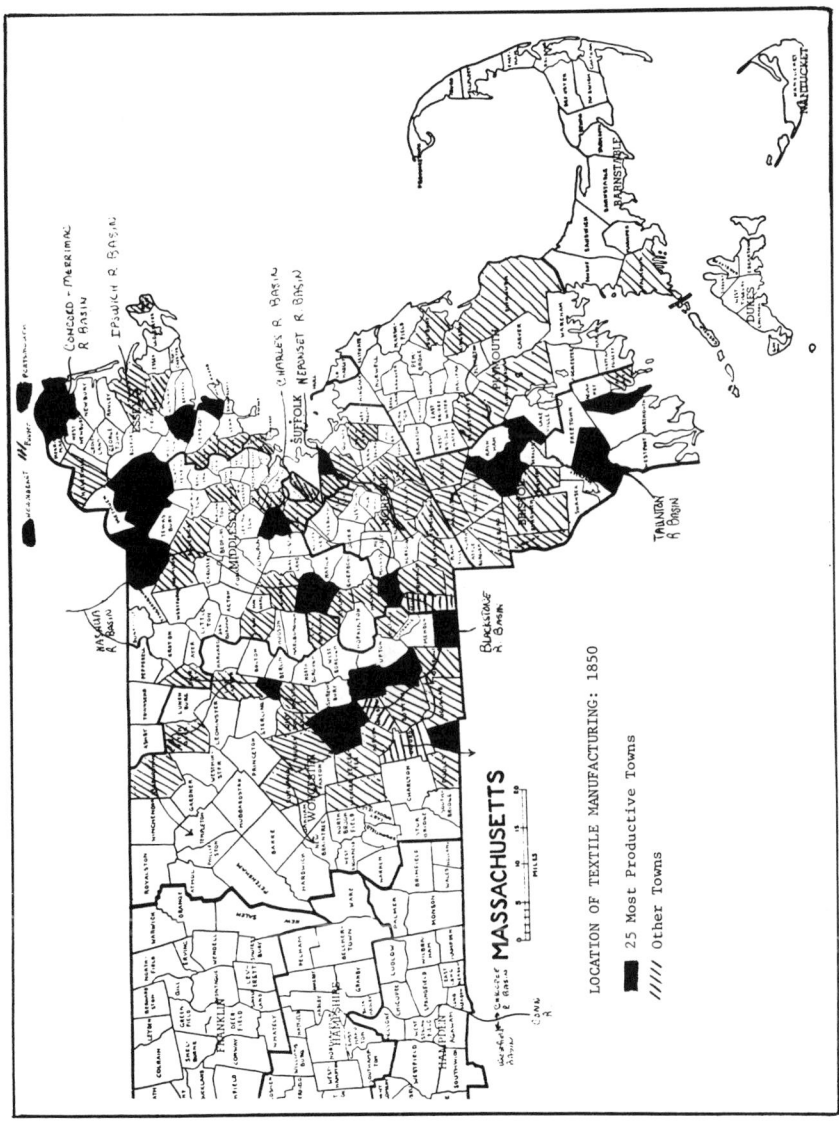

LOCATION OF TEXTILE MANUFACTURING: 1850

■ 25 Most Productive Towns

///// Other Towns

Map III-3. Location of Shoe Production, 1830

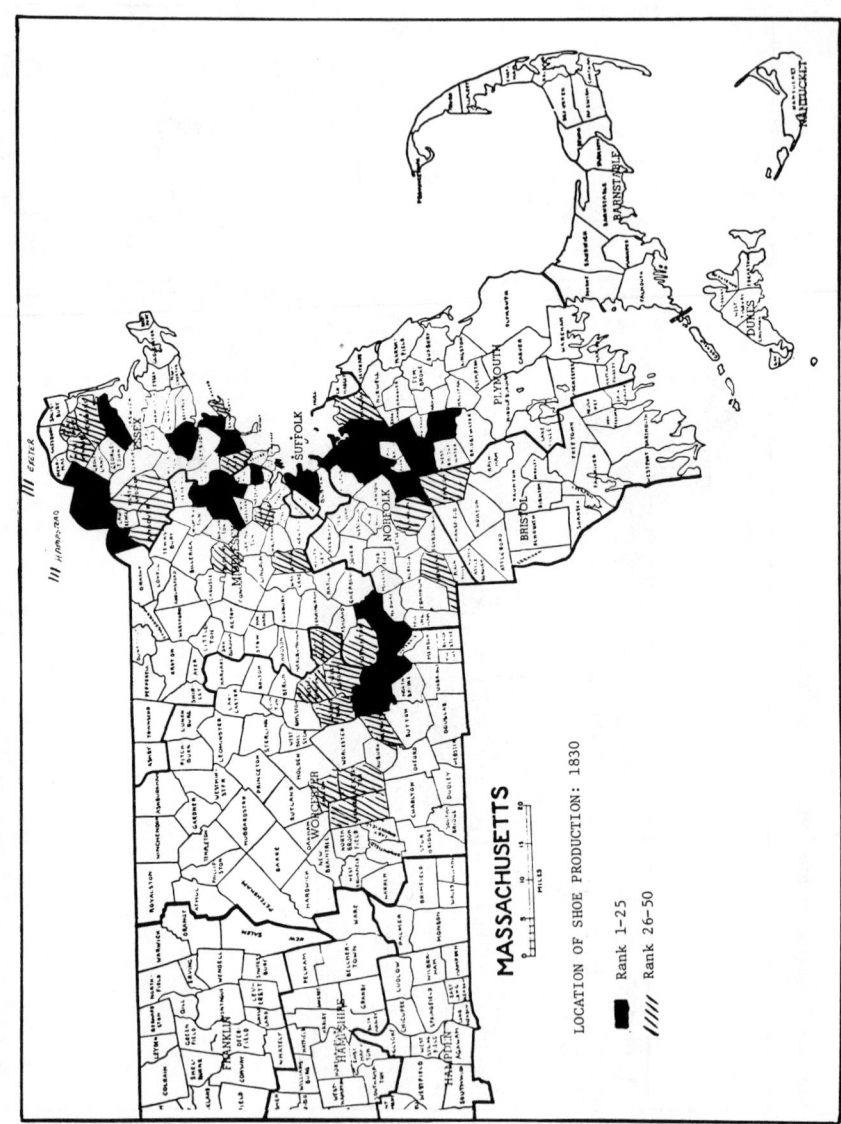

LOCATION OF SHOE PRODUCTION: 1830

■ Rank 1-25

/// Rank 26-50

MASSACHUSETTS

Map III-4. Location of Shoe Production, 1850

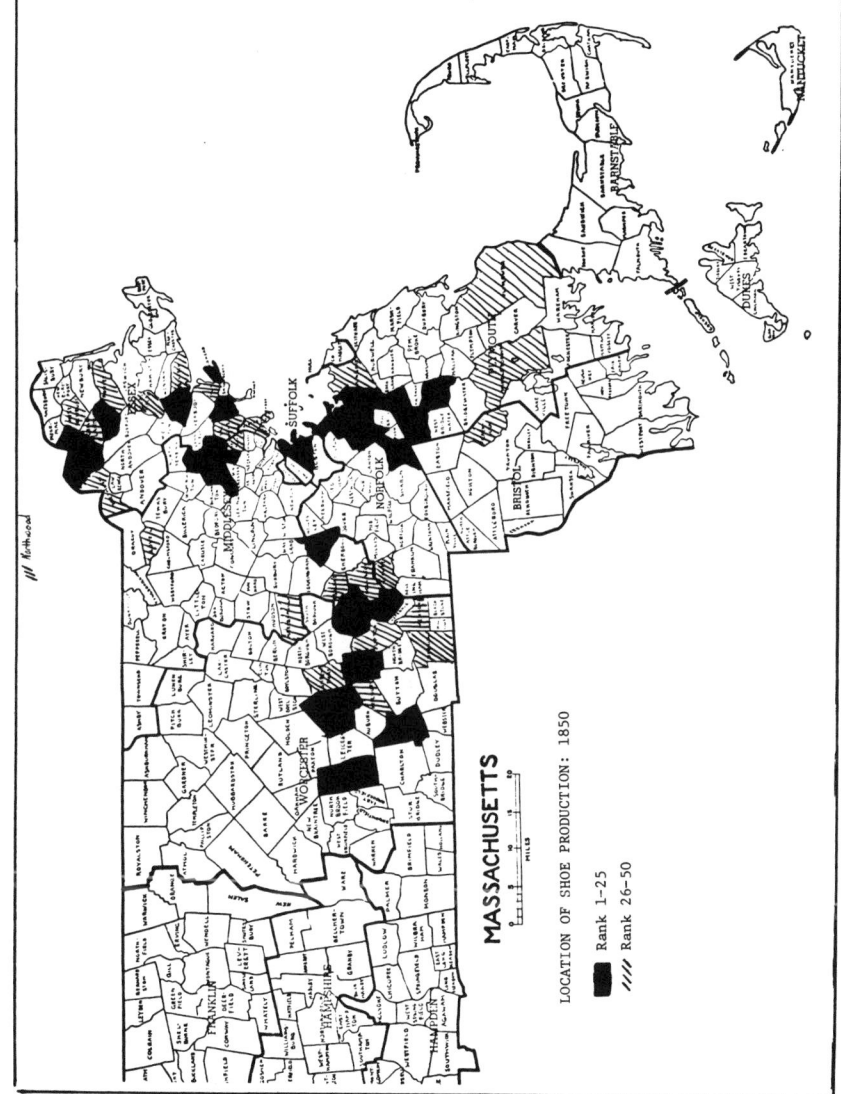

MASSACHUSETTS

LOCATION OF SHOE PRODUCTION: 1850

■ Rank 1–25

//// Rank 26–50

Map III-5. Location of Tanning and Leather Production, 1830

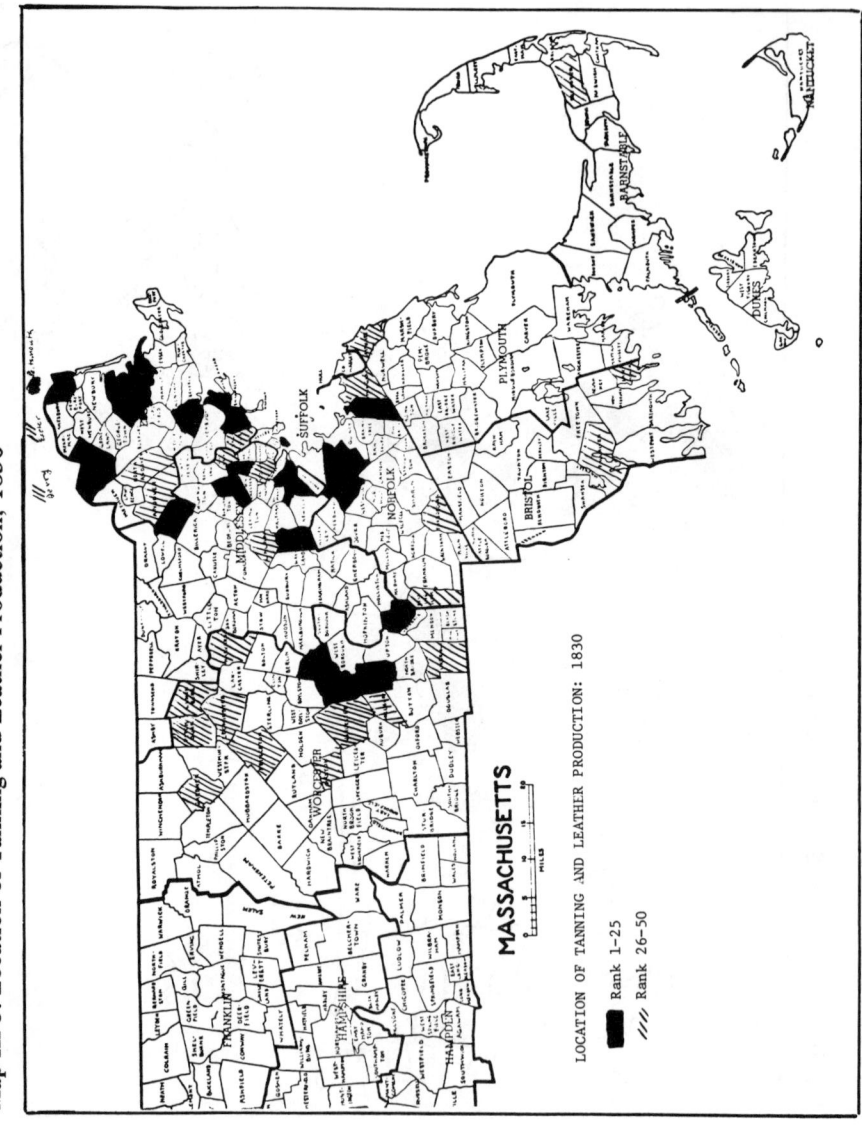

MASSACHUSETTS

LOCATION OF TANNING AND LEATHER PRODUCTION: 1830

■ Rank 1-25

/// Rank 26-50

Map III-6. Location of Tanning and Leather Production, 1850

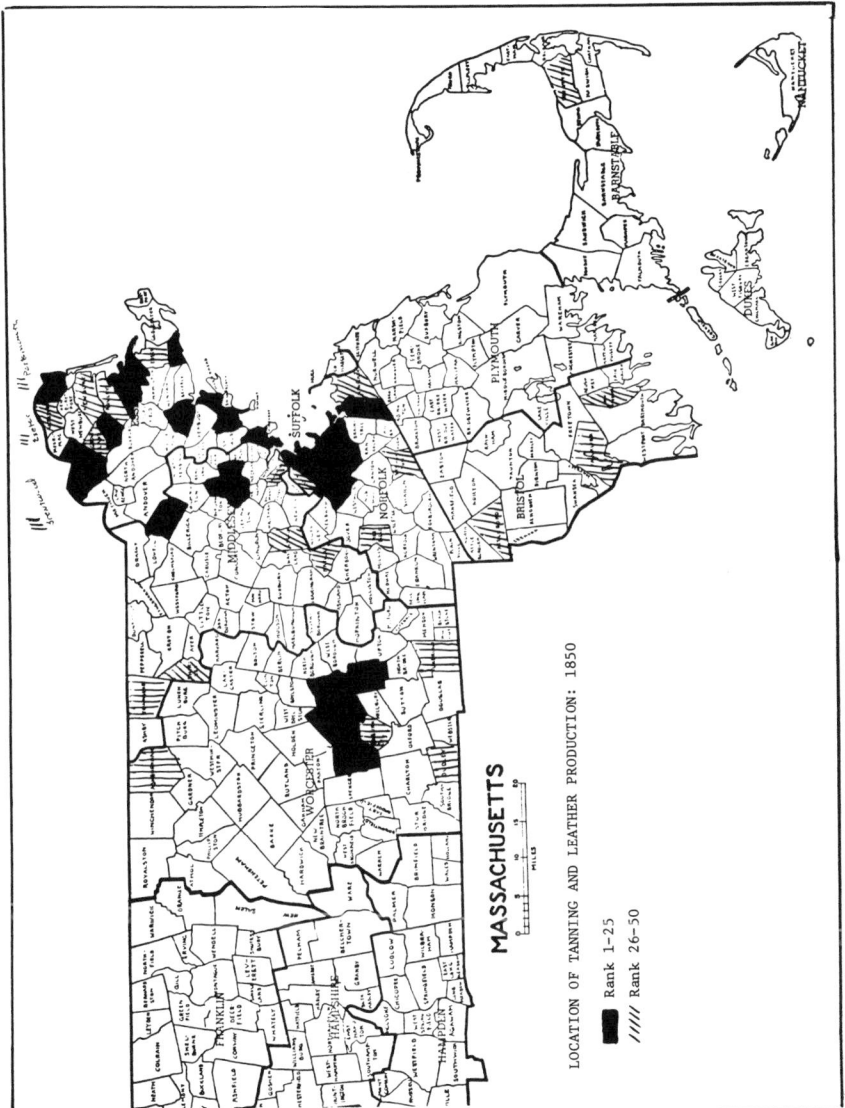

MASSACHUSETTS

LOCATION OF TANNING AND LEATHER PRODUCTION: 1850

■ Rank 1–25

///// Rank 26–50

Map III-7. Location of Tack and Nail Production, 1830

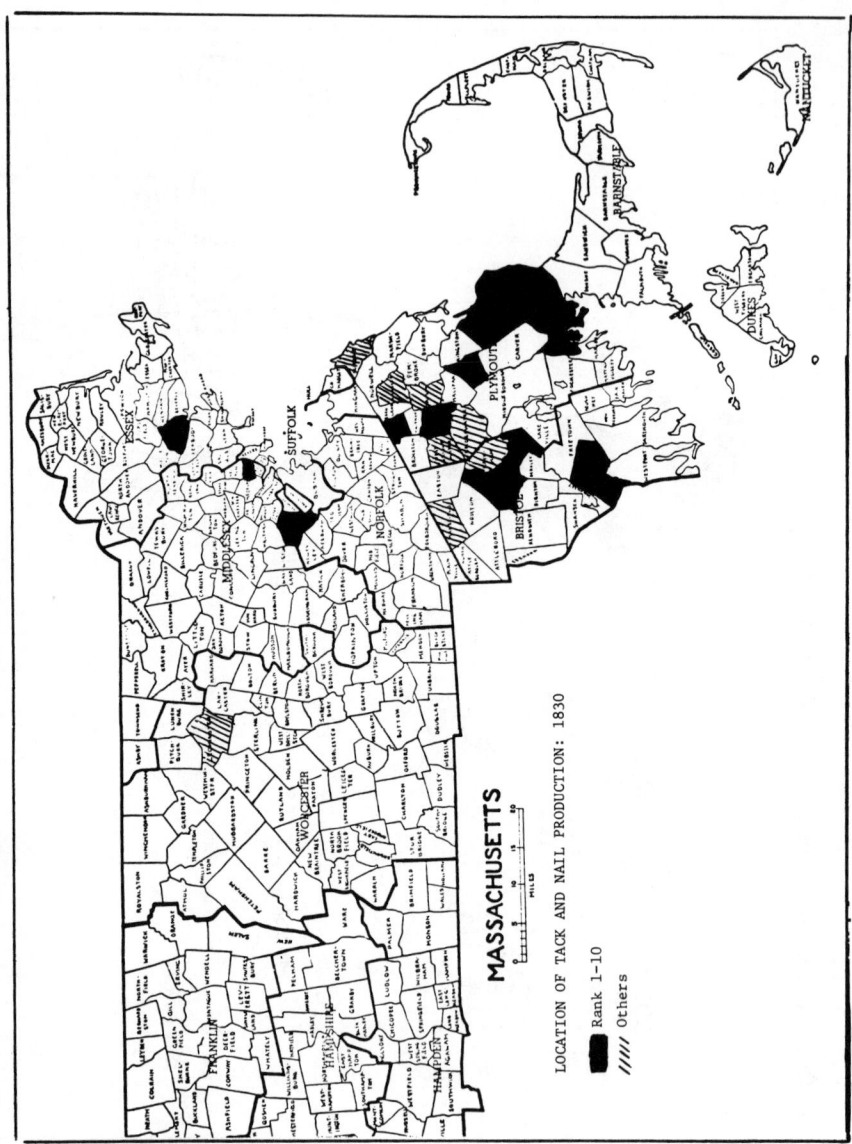

MASSACHUSETTS

LOCATION OF TACK AND NAIL PRODUCTION: 1830

■ Rank 1-10

//// Others

Map III-8. Location of Tack and Nail Production, 1850

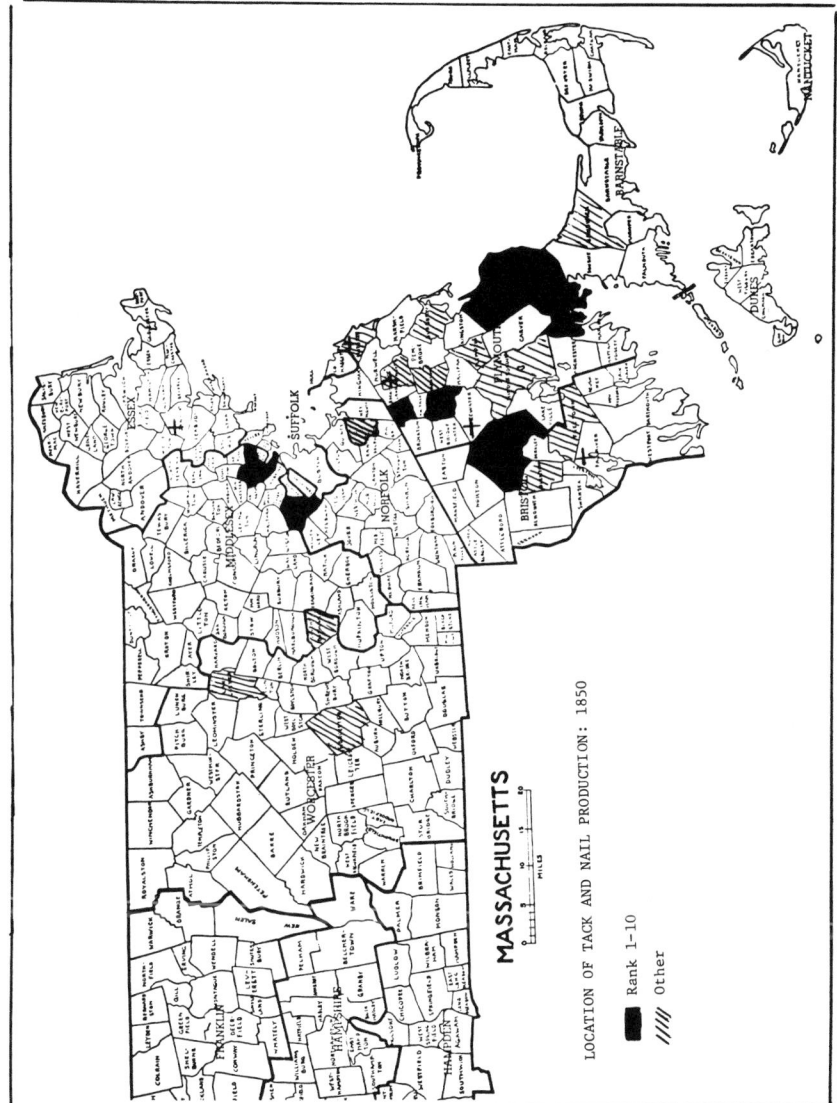

MASSACHUSETTS

LOCATION OF TACK AND NAIL PRODUCTION: 1850

Rank 1-10

//// Other

on the coast. The use of the sewing machine toward 1850 required capital investment. Thus the machine was usually bought by large firms and found only in the larger shops. This cost saving device required the worker to journey to the shop to perform tasks which once could have been performed by hand in the home. This development required a large labor pool relatively close to the factory location.[8]

Serving the boot and shoe industry was the tanning and leather industry. Though the industry was widespread in terms of the number of towns engaged in such activity, most of the production was fairly concentrated in a few towns. In 1810, all counties reported some output in tanning and leather, principally Essex, Middlesex and Worcester. In 1830, Danvers led the 114 towns with 16.5 percent of output. In 1850, Salem led with 26.9 percent and Danvers followed with 15.9 percent. Maps III-5 and III-6 illustrate the coastal trend in the tanning and leather industry. In 1833, most of the production was located along the coast or in towns with easy coastal access. The exception was in the upper Blackstone valley and the Nashua valley, reflecting the location pattern of the boot and shoe industry, an obvious market (see map III-3). The principal deviation was in the upper Nashua river valley where there was an unusually large amount of leather production for the amount of shoes produced. In 1850 (map III-6), the industry became more strongly coastal. Twenty of the twenty-five large output towns had easy access to the coast. The exceptions were Tewksbury and the four towns near Worcester in the upper Blackstone valley. The twenty-five towns accounted for 95 percent of the production in 1830 and 85 percent in 1850. (Note that the composition of the list changed somewhat— see Appendix VII for complete list.)[9]

Robert LeBlanc in a study of the location of manufacturing in New England has suggested that the coastal clustering of tanning and leather firms was due mainly to the need for raw materials. By 1810 the local tanbark resources of the region had been depleted. Hemlock bark required for the process was "imported from Maine, presumably by coasting vessels." Also the large coastal tanneries were "partially dependent on imported hides." LeBlanc concludes that "the juxtaposition of large tanneries and the shoe industry in eastern Massachusetts cannot be construed as a market orientation of the tanning industry . . . location factors acting independently upon each industry brought about their concentration in the same area." He does note, however, that the economies in the proximity of the two industries were real.[10]

Unlike the previously discussed industries, the tack and nail industry was confined to a relatively small number of towns. In 1833, eighteen towns had tack and nail production and all but three of these were located in Plymouth and Bristol counties, an area with a number of iron deposits. In 1850, twenty-three towns engaged in the activity, with seven located outside the two county area (see maps III-7 and III-8). In both periods all such activity was located with easy access to the coast. Wareham from 1825 on was the principal center of nail manufacturing for the region—35 percent of production in 1833 and 40 percent in 1850. Its location seems peculiarly well suited. It was near the iron deposits of the southern section of the region, and had access to Boston for imported iron and long distance transportation. As the industry expanded, it increasingly relied on imported Russian iron. It also had access to the major Massachusetts ports as well as to New York, Connecticut and Rhode Island ports, all without having to sail around Cape Cod which may have been a significant factor, given the weight of nail shipments and the relatively small return for shipment. Perhaps coastal access and access to iron supplies within the region explains the emergence of the area as an important nail center in the early nineteenth century[11] (see Appendix X for the complete list).

The location of other industries primarily followed the obvious sources of key raw materials or access to markets. The shipbuilding industry and related industries such as cordage, etc. were located in such coastal locations as Portsmouth, Boston, Quincy and Medford. The hat industry was located primarily inland where available straw and imported palm leaves would be made into hats of one sort or another by farm families during the winter months. The hat industry, incidentally, sustained an active wire industry in Worcester and other inland towns which grew in response to the need of the hatmakers to bind together their leaves and straw. Chair and furniture making flourished inland near raw forest reserves and the many inland saw mills. All these were generally much smaller industries in terms of total as well as major firm output than those chosen for detailed study.

A general overview of the location of the various industries in the region reveals a pattern which the theoretical literature suggests. Location theory would suggest that the more important factors determining the location of a firm is the access to resources. In making a location decision a firm would be required to assess its relative priorities in terms of access to raw materials, transport facilities, labor, capital, etc. These considerations would be counter-balanced by the need for access to markets. For the manufacturing sector in the early nineteenth century resources were usually a more important consideration.

For the textile industry the need for power was a primary concern. Francis Cabot Lowell personally picked the site of his Lowell mills because of assurances that the currents were the best available in New England for his mills. The McLane report and the 1850 census show that there were textile works scattered all along the region's major rivers and their tributaries. With the mills came ancillary industries such as bleaching and dyeing. Generally these industries would locate close to a mill though there are some instances of these activities locating in towns without mills.

For other industries not so dependent on water power, other considerations played a major role in the decision-making process. Prior to the railroad, water transportation was the cheapest and most effective means of transportation. It is interesting that there were many coastal clusters of major industrial activity which were not centered around Boston, the principal city of the region. The predominance of coastal locations for the largest firms in the region, particularly those engaged in the shoe, nail and leather industries and excepting the textile and machinery firms, seems to suggest that access to the sea was an important factor. By 1850 the railroad became a viable alternative. According to the maps, however, more established industries such as nails, leather and shoes show no real shift in location between 1830 and 1850. Machinery, on the other hand, definitely did shift—perhaps as a new industry it was more flexible and/or more clearly allied to the railroad itself. Though machinery was the only industry to exhibit a definite shift, nearly all industries were spreading or shifting spatially during the period 1830 to 1850. The hinterland shared in a significant portion of this expansion. Railroads were then constructed to move supplies and serve expanding markets. The location maps show, however, that shifts in major concentrations of industries did not occur during the period. Abrupt shifts in location patterns should be considered the exception rather than the norm. An expanding industry can change location by choice of new plant sites while established or slow growth industries would face much more costly relocation decisions.

Traditionally, historians have cited cheap labor as the incentive for firms to move away from the more thickly settled coast. The location maps suggest that entrepreneurs of large firms in the early nineteenth century did not always see labor as a primary consideration in a location decision. Access to water transportation does seem to have been an important consideration both in terms of the need for imported raw materials and of the need to get finished products to their ultimate markets. However, the choice of location surely involved local considerations and other immeasurables which affected the whims of individual entrepreneurs. No doubt tradeoffs were necessary in the ultimate choice of location. A proper location—i.e., economically efficient choice—should have given the perceptive entrepreneur a distinct economic advantage over the competition. The boot and shoe industry was scattered throughout the region. However, the large producers and the large concentrations of large producers were clustered in select locations within the region. This would suggest, though not conclusively prove, that certain locations within the region were economically more efficient than others—or at least allowed for greater capacity in production. It was feasible for an entrepreneur in Lynn or Haverhill to think in terms of $100,000 annual output. However, it seems less likely that a Poplin, Eastham or Sandow shoemaker could think in such grand terms given available alternatives for the early nineteenth century.

At the same time, it is worth noting that not all industry chose to locate in the Boston area. There obviously were some distinct disadvantages when compared to other locations. Most likely land was expensive and power less readily available. Peter Knights' study of the working classes of Boston suggests an extremely high rate of mobility in the labor force. Though he offers no figures on mobility within the region as I have defined it, his findings suggest that labor freely drifted to wherever jobs could be found. Thus, perhaps, the early nineteenth-century entrepreneur would choose a site assuming that workers would come to wherever jobs appeared. Of course wage levels required by the worker and skill levels required by the entrepreneur would affect some location decisions.[12]

The scattered distribution of industrial activity throughout the region resulted from a myriad of locational decisions made by thousands of individual entrepreneurs. The decision-making process seems to have followed some logic though it is difficult to predict location on the basis of the simple variables presented here.

Since economic activity was spread about the region in varying degrees, there was some local specialization in particular industries. Nearly all the towns had a grist mill, blacksmith, and carpenter shop, but very few had a nail factory, wire works or a piano factory. Among towns which engaged in uncommon economic activity, most production was centered in very few towns. During the period many towns in the region became increasingly specialized. For example, in 1830 the ten towns with the largest amount of textile production accounted for 52 percent of total output—in 1850 the figure was 69.4 percent. The twenty-five most productive towns accounted for 77.8 percent in 1830 and 83.2 percent in 1850. In the boot and shoe industry, despite the large numbers of towns reporting some output, the ten most productive towns accounted for 46.7 percent in 1830 and 56.0 percent in 1850. The twenty-five most productive towns accounted for 74.9 percent in 1830 and 76.2 percent in 1850. The tanning and currying industry was even more concentrated. The ten most productive towns in that sector accounted for 61.8 percent in 1830 and 84.2 percent of the total output in 1850. The twenty-five most productive accounted for 81.0 percent in 1830 and 95.7 percent in 1850. As previously discussed, very few towns engaged in tack and nail production. The five most productive towns accounted for 75.5 percent in 1830 and 69.1 percent in 1850. The ten most productive towns accounted for 91.7 percent in 1830 and 92.0 percent in 1850.[13]

Various towns throughout the region acquired an unusually large share of a particular sector. Lowell, obviously due to its power sources, accounted for 18 percent of textile production in 1830 and 31 percent in 1850. Lynn accounted for 12 percent of shoes produced in 1830 and 16.6 percent in 1850. Amesbury had a significant portion of carriage manufacturing. Attleborough had a large concentration of jewelers. Quincy was a granite center. Boston also housed substantial portions of some industries. In 1830, 91.3 percent of the printing and publishing industry was located in Boston. By 1850 that percentage decreased slightly to 89.3 percent.[14] In the manufacturing of musical instruments, Boston also predominated with 99 percent of reported output in 1830 and 91.6 percent in 1850[15] (see Appendices VIII and IX for complete lists).

Throughout the region there were obviously many towns devoted to the specialized production of one or two items in far greater quantity than the particular town could possibly require for its own population. This specialization was of considerable importance to the regional economy in that it implied a flow of goods and services from place to place. No one town within the region was a self-sufficient economic unit. Each depended on the other. Nor, for that matter, was the region self-contained. It too specialized and drew in needed raw and finished products and in turn shipped out its surplus production to national and world markets.[16]

As a result of the movement of goods from one location to another within the region, the various cities and towns became economically interrelated and intertwined. The emerging concentration of major industrial production in a few urban locations was stimulated by and depended upon the export of these goods and often the import of raw materials either to or from other locations in the region or from outside the region. Such concentrated industrialization interacted with concentrated trade flows to stimulate the commercial and retail sectors of the regional economy which served to match available supplies with pockets of particular demands in the region. To what extent did goods flow through the region? Indications are that a substantial amount of goods moved within the region each year—the pattern was a complex one. The chief reason for the complexity of the regional pattern was in the region's proximity to the coast. There were numerous ports of entry. Goods did not necessarily flow through one port alone to get into or out of the region. Also there were raw materials native to the region which had flow patterns peculiar to their own points of origin. Likewise, particularly due to the product specialization of some areas, the flow pattern of finished goods to ultimate markets was often peculiar to the place of manufacture.

To chart the movement of goods or materials through the region in the early nineteenth century would indeed provide a picture of the general pattern of commodity flows. With such complete data one could easily and, with certitude, delineate the extent to which the flow process depended on a hierarchical network of cities which might emerge to make commodity flows more efficient.

If perfect data were available to measure the movement of goods through the region, a chart could be constructed indicating exactly the exports to and the imports from each town in the region. The ideal chart, as shown in figure III-1, would indicate in detail the inputs and outputs of the economies of each city and town in the region. By looking at any given entry one could determine, for example, how many nails came into town Y during a specific period from towns A, B, and C within the region and how many were imported from towns outside the region. McLane report data for 1833 and the census information

Figure III-1
Hypothetical Input-Output Model for a Regional Economy

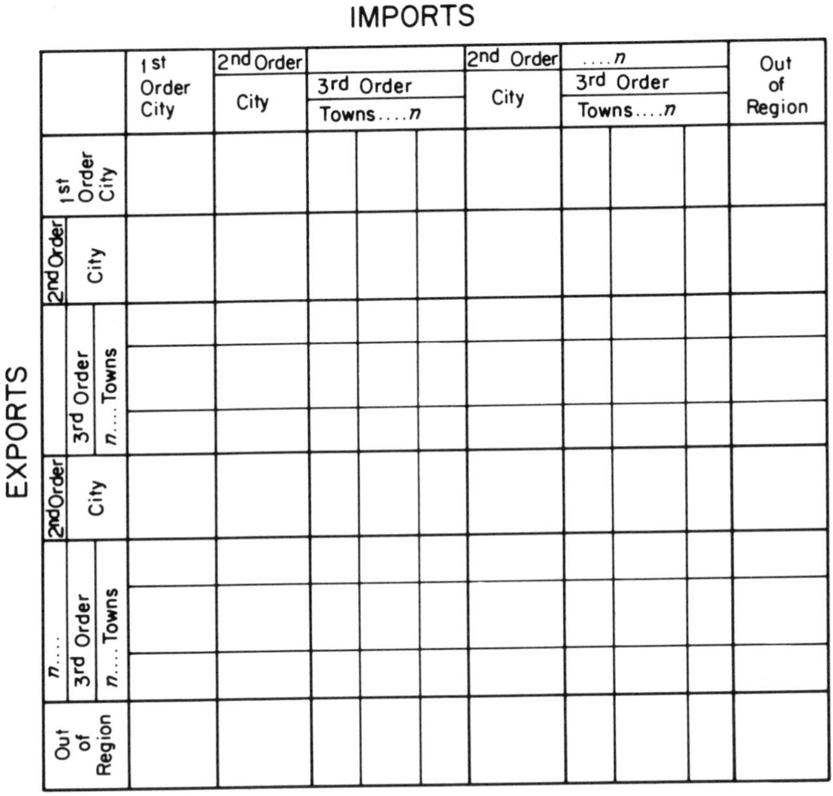

IMPORTS

	1st Order City	2nd Order City	3rd Order Towns....n			2nd Order City	3rd Order Towns....n			Out of Region
1st Order City										
2nd Order — City										
3rd Order — n.... Towns										
2nd Order — City										
n.... 3rd Order — n.... Towns										
Out of Region										

EXPORTS

for 1850 show industrial activity dispersed throughout the region. All towns show some imports and exports. The quantities are not always exactly indicated. However, the quantity of industrial inputs demanded by particular towns would be the aggregate of the quantities demanded by the specific industries of the town.

This pattern challenges any notion that most specialized industries would be found in high order central places with only the least specialized ubiquitous activities located in the smaller hinterland towns. For example, Shirley, a small town with a population in 1830 of 991 and in 1850 of 1,158, was the location of two rather small cotton mills. The town of Groton, with a population of 2,515 in 1850, had in that same year three papermaking firms. The town of Framingham, a middle size place with a population of 4,252 in 1850, had in that year a worsted mill with an annual output of $600,000 worth of goods which indicates a high degree of specialization in the local economy. These facts would be borne out visually if plotted on the hypothetical input-ouput chart (figure 3-1).

Also on the chart, if plotted fully, one might expect to find heavier industries concentrated in the first and second order cities which would have immediate access to efficient transport such as ship and rail as opposed to overland cart. In 1850 machine works were located in thirty-nine towns, five of which accounted for 70 percent of total output: Boston, Lowell, Taunton, Worcester and Lawrence. Boston, Lowell and Worcester were regional transport nodes while Lawrence and Taunton were located on major rail lines. Since heavy metals were important to the machine industry, chart entries for these towns might show large amounts of primary metals imports either from southeastern Massachusetts towns or from abroad. As for the export of the final product, much of the machinery produced in Boston, such as locomotives, would be consumed within the region by the railroads. Similarly in Lowell local mills would purchase locally made textile machinery. Thus the machine exports in these two towns would be a small percentage of total output.

One can distinguish a variety of types of firms in the patterns of materials and products visible in the input-output model. Local market firms might use local raw materials in the manufacture of goods for local markets. Some local market firms are likely to be ubiquitous such as blacksmithing, shoemaking and cabinetmaking. Some firms might be located in a second order city filling subregional demands. Worcester, for example, was an important wire center. Much of this wire was used in the surrounding towns for the manufacture of hats. Local market firms using ubiquitous raw materials such as wood, or labor intensive firms, would likely be dispersed throughout the region. Local market firms depending on imported goods would have to consider access to imports in their location decisions. These firms might then tend to be found on the chart in towns which would assure for the entrepreneur access to these required resources at competitive cost.

In some contrast, the export market firm would most likely use some unique local input whether a raw material, power resource, or special labor. The concentration of these firms would depend not only on the location of these key inputs but would also be sensitive to their need for efficient transport to get goods out of the region to their final markets. The extent to which industry tended to concentrate and cluster in specific areas is tied to the extent to which manufacturing was growing in response to demand generated outside the local town economies and outside the regional economy. In figure 3-1 the largest of these export market firms would probably show up in coastal locations and later in the principal rail centers. Furthermore, as industries expanded rapidly during the period 1830 to 1850, local supplies of some raw materials became inadequate. Thus, over time the import column in figure 3-1 for cities specializing in those industries would become increasingly filled with items which previously were extracted from within the boundaries of the region. As this trend becomes manifest, a trend of location of firms in principal transport centers should also appear.

For development of a detailed approximation to the ideal import/export matrix of figure 3-1, the McLane report is most useful. Its data for Massachusetts, though incomplete, not only indicate annual volume of production, capital, and location, but also the origin of raw materials and the destination of final products. Though it does not always give precise data on origins and destinations, it does offer an unparalleled sense of commodity flows through the region.

The report permits discussion of various patterns in which goods flowed through the region. It indicates a variety of patterns and suggests the extent of the interdependence of the cities and towns of the region. For all of these, Boston was the principal marketplace and the principal source of supply.

Sources of supply and markets depended on the nature of the product made, annual volume produced and the location of the manufacturer. For example, in Worcester County, there was the small town of Milford located just east of the Blackstone basin. With a population of 1,360 Milford sustained activity in fourteen branches of manufacturing, none very extensive. Raw materials came chiefly from Massachusetts but its final products were distributed to a variety of markets. Its woolen yarn production received raw wool from various parts of New England and sent one-fourth of its finished products to Massachusetts, and three-fourths to "east, west and south." The town curriers received hides from New York, Connecticut, and Massachusetts, and distributed the finished leather to Massachusetts markets. The largest industry was in straw goods, probably a cottage type industry since it reputedly employed 500 people! Workers obtained their straw locally but distributed the final goods to "principal cities of the U.S." Coach lace production, a more refined craft industry, found threads locally in Massachusetts, but the finished lace was marketed in

Boston, New York, and Philadelphia. The production of chaises and wagons was a strictly local industry. Materials were taken from all over Massachusetts and all its final product sold in the city of Worcester.[17]

In the Blackstone basin section of Worcester County, the chief industry was cotton textiles. The town of Grafton, for example, (population 1,889) had four small textile factories with a total output of $103,310. The factories obtained their raw cotton from the south and sent the final product to Boston where it was presumably further distributed by the textile agents. The town also engaged in considerable shoe production, using Massachusetts leather and distributing final products to Boston, New York, and Philadelphia. The town's one woolen factory ordered New York wool, and Vermont sperm oil and shipped $100,000 worth of satinets to Boston, New York and Philadelphia—curiously not to Providence.[18]

Fitchburg was a much larger town in the county with a population of 2,169. Its industry was more specialized: hardware, farmtools, paper and textiles. The four companies engaged in production of farm implements drew raw hardwoods, etc. from Massachusetts and distributed the final product locally either to "Massachusetts" or to "Boston." One firm did ship a few to New York. Fitchburg's considerable textile production also utilized southern cotton and shipped final products to Boston. The town had a sizable paper industry, which used local wood and stock, shipped final products to Boston, New York and other parts of Massachusetts.[19]

The towns of Leominster and Lancaster to the north of Worcester both had considerable comb manufacturing—probably with cottage labor. Unlike other industries which used local material, the combmakers imported Spanish horns for their wares. The finished carved combs were then sent to the principal cities of the United States.[20]

Worcester, the economic center of the county, with a population of 4,713 housed nineteen branches of industry, including the county's only machine works of any size. These machine works generally responded to the demands of the local textile industry though according to the McLane report, the six firms sent their final products to all the northern states—principally in New England. Unlike the industries of neighboring smaller towns which generally (except textiles and combs) used local materials, the machinery industry of Worcester imported a variety of materials which included Swedish iron, German steel, English screws and iron. Worcester's textile industry followed patterns similar to other towns. Imported southern cotton was processed into finished yard goods and sent on to the principal east coast cities. Both regional imports typically entered at the port of Boston.[21]

In Middlesex, as in most counties, the shoe industry was important. In Stoneham for example, the large cottage shoe industry employed 370 of the town's residents. The leather used came from local producers as well as from

New York, Pennsylvania and parts of Massachusetts. Linen for the lining came from Rhode Island. The thread used was "foreign material." Three-fourths of the finished shoes were sent to Massachusetts markets with the residue sent to the southern states. The town blacksmith used Virginia coal to fire his foreign steel to meet local demands.[22]

In Lowell, the largest and most advanced producer of textiles in the region, a myriad of materials were brought in not only to provide for the raw cloth but also for printing, bleaching, etc. A list of products used in these various processes would include New Hampshire wood starch, Pennsylvania coal, Massachusetts oil, southern cotton, Maryland flour, Vermont potash, and New England wools. These textiles were listed as being sent to the principal cities of the United States, most notably New York, Philadelphia and Baltimore, as well as throughout the New England area.[23]

In Newton, Massachusetts, among its many industries, were three sizable paper plants. These in accord with current technology generally utilized Massachusetts rags and cotton waste though one did use southern and imported rags. Paper products were sent principally to Massachusetts but also to other locations as well. In addition, Newton had a large soap and candle manufactory, the likes of which were scattered throughout the region. They generally used Massachusetts material in their production; these included tallow, ashes, grease, boxes and wick yarn. Necessary barilla, palm oil and cotton oil were imported by the firm. One-third of the final products were then shipped to locations in Massachusetts, one-third to southern states, and one-third to the West Indies.[24]

East Cambridge had an unusual concentration of glass works which drew in a variety of raw materials including: northern New England ash, Virginia coal, Massachusetts wood, Maine lime, New York firestone, Philadelphia iron, New Jersey sand, Missouri red lead. The glass was distributed nation-wide and one company reported sending one-tenth of its output to Europe.[25]

As industries in the towns of the region became increasingly export oriented and as the expansion of industry increasingly required the importation of raw materials, the local economies of the towns became increasingly interdependent. Gathering the materials necessary in the production of glass, iron, textiles, etc. necessarily required coordinated efforts not only among manufacturers in the region but also among the financial and commercial sectors. These became increasingly important as hinterland and coastal manufacturers had to look further and further for supplies and/or markets.[26]

The McLane report, detailed as it is, does not provide the kind of detailed market information which would permit the study of the extent of subregional isolation. In terms of flows of goods through the region, subregional isolation would mean bypassing the services of the first order city of the region, Boston. Essex County comes to mind immediately as an example of a subregion which might not have been as dependent on Boston as was the interior. Historically,

Essex County was dominated by the port of Salem, and possibly its geographical position would have permitted goods and services to flow through its own port to or from ultimate subregional market locations. Some firms in the county reported specifically that their output was sent to Boston which gives a clue that Essex County was not a completely independent regional subarea. A tobacco firm, one of five in Saugus, sent all its cigars and snuff to Boston. Others sent their products to "Massachusetts" and other parts of the United States. All shoes produced in Saugus were sent to Boston. Furniture and cordage made in Marblehead were sent to Boston. All shoes made in Marblehead and Lynnfield were sent to Boston. Most of Lynn's shoe production went to Boston. Boston also received all flannel produced in Haverhill. Other products were marketed locally or were reported as "sent to Massachusetts." Thus it seems clear that Essex County was indeed economically integrated into the broader region.[27]

Information for Rockingham County, New Hampshire, in the McLane report gives additional clues to the extent of regional flows. Like Essex County, Rockingham also had its own port, Portsmouth, which again could have provided a greater degree of independence from Boston than the interior counties enjoyed. Again, the McLane report indicates otherwise. To be sure, a significant portion of the goods produced in New Hampshire were consumed there, though not necessarily in the town of origin. For example, in Exeter, the most industrial inland town, leather was "sold at home," machinery sold in all northern New England states, brushes in New Hampshire and Massachusetts, hatting in New Hampshire and Massachusetts, bricks at home, candles in New Hampshire and Maine. All morocco went to Boston. Smaller towns such as Rye and Hampton Falls sold their products locally. In a general note about cotton manufactories in the county McLane noted that they were sold principally in Boston, New York, Philadelphia and Baltimore with a portion "exported to S. America and the E. Indies." Even the smaller towns were tied to some extent to other locales higher in the subregional or regional urban hierarchies. Hatters in Hampstead sent their goods to Boston. A note to the returns for the inland town of Raymond states: "sale shoes; the leather is cut in Haverhill, and the shoes when made, return thither."[28] The same was noted for East Kingston. Shoes made in the larger town of Newmarket (population 2,008) were all sold in New Hampshire. Portsmouth, like Exeter, had many more branches of industry (28 listed). Some products were sold only in New Hampshire, such as pottery, brass, blocks, ropes—all generally related to the shipping industry and made by small firms. Some of the larger industries sent products to Massachusetts and other markets. Unlike other large ports, such as Salem and Boston for example, Portsmouth was not a major industrial town.[29]

Boston, the proverbial hub of this regional universe, was the most important trade center of the region. While it is impossible to know from the McLane report data exactly what goods passed through Boston, both theory and fragmentary evidence suggest that a significant percentage of regional imports and exports moved through the port. The city was the main focal point of trade flows. Hence the city was a popular location for merchant and other middleman activities. Boston, however, was not merely the pivotal port of call for many of the region's products. Nor was it simply a service center housing bankers, auctioneers, and merchants. Boston was itself one of the chief manufacturing centers of the region. Its pre-eminence in publishing and in the manufacture of fine instruments has been noted. Boston also housed a variety of other industries including chemicals, combmaking, cordage, machinery, mathematical instruments, distilling, paperhanging, shoe lasts, tobacco processing, shipbuilding, tailoring, etc. Most of the products were sold in Massachusetts. Given the very specialized and craft nature of some products such as surgical and musical instruments, clocks and tailored clothing, the Boston location was the result of the city's access to transportation, communications, specially skilled labor, and of the fact that the city was the principal node of the region. Its publishing, chemical, shipbuilding, gold leaf, iron products, pianos and other goods were sent throughout the United States.[30]

The McLane report indicates considerable movement of raw and finished goods through the region, suggesting in a basic way the interdependence and integration of economic activity among the various cities and towns of the region. The report does not show how products filtered through various intermediary stops on the way to ultimate markets. A Christallerian model would suggest that goods circulated in very set hierarchical patterns. For example, cotton produced in Andover would be shipped to Lowell and then to Boston. Leather produced in Danvers would go to Salem and then to Boston. Similar rigid patterns would exist for goods brought in by the two towns. Such a set pattern would suggest a rigid hierarchical arrangement of cities to which the flow of economic activity would have to conform. The Löschian model on the other hand would be more flexible, suggesting that goods circulated in the most economically efficient way, often conforming to the nodal hierarchy in the urban network, but sometimes following other more efficient channels.

Neither of the classic models are purely applicable to the Boston region in 1833. The early patterns of flows of goods in the region indicate a much more complex relationship among the cities and towns of the region than classic theory would suggest. Some goods did indeed move very nicely through the hierarchy, with basic materials imported from outside the region through Boston, then through an intermediate town and then to the site of the factory. Once the final product was made, it was then shipped from the town, through intermediate locations, through Boston and then exported from the region to its final market. Some manufacturers, however, bypassed the first order city and imported or exported goods through second order ports such as New Bedford or Salem. Other manufacturers dealing with local markets would import through the hierarchy and sell locally. Others using local resources bought locally but exported through the hierarchy. The hierarchy in the region emerged to assist the movement of goods and services. The hierarchy was essentially a commercial and transport based system which manufacturers could utilize as their needs dictated. The textile industry was very dependent on this hierarchical arrangement of cities and towns. The need for water power pulled the industry into the hinterland. The need for large amounts of imported raw cotton and wool required some system through which these raw materials could move from point of entry into the region to the specific mill, not just in the physical sense of moving from point to point but in the broader sense of being purchased, insured, ordered in specific amounts, loaded and unloaded, financed and transported. Likewise cloths manufactured had to be sent to final markets usually outside the region, calling for various intermediaries who both staffed and financed the industry's distribution system at this time.

The aggregate of these decisions indicates the degree of specialization within the particular economies of the cities and towns of the region. These specialized industries were the basic stimulus for the dynamic process of urban and industrial growth within the industrial towns of the region. Needless to say, this scale of growth in all but a few towns was modest indeed but the presence of industry did signal a beginning. To understand the process of urbanization in these towns one must first consider this industrial base. However to establish an industry is one thing, to sustain an industry is quite another. The industries in the towns of the region were sustained by competitive access to resources, including raw materials, and by a relatively steady demand for goods produced. Limited historical sources for the period suggest that this demand was in some cases local within the town, in other cases within the region, and beyond, or a combination of factors, particularly in towns with a diversified manufacturing base.

To the extent that resources necessary to local manufacturing and to the extent that demand for goods produced existed within the boundaries of a particular town, the dynamic process of urban industrial growth as suggested in the Pred model could be said to take place entirely within the context of the particular town. The story of urbanization in the particular town could then be told apart from events or developments in places nearby or far away. However to the extent that capital, raw materials, and new technology on the supply side and markets on the demand side were located in neighboring towns, regions, or nations, the dynamic process of urban industrial growth was dependent upon and affected by the same process in other locations.

In the Boston region, based on the degrees of specialization of activity and based on admittedly limited historical sources regarding marketing patterns, it appears that the process of urbanization was clearly not a phenomenon isolated within the boundaries of a particular city and town, but was rather an interdependent process. New sources of supply and demand came from a variety of places. For example, new pockets of demand in various corners of the region stimulated the process of growth in various manufacturing districts elsewhere. New pockets of demand might well have emerged from new industry in a particular town or expansion of an industry in response to demand outside the region. The point is that due to the spread of industry throughout the region and due to the degree of specialization within various towns, the history of urbanization in the region was a complicated, dynamic and interdependent process which can be fully understood only on a regional scale.

As the towns of the region became increasingly specialized, mechanisms emerged which linked pockets of supply with pockets of demand (producers and buyers) located both within and outside the region. These intermediaries were required to make location decisions as well. They frequently chose major cities in the area which in turn furthered the image of these cities as more important or central among the cities and towns of the region. As argued in chapter II, these cities formed the upper layer of the hierarchy of a system of cities which evolved in the region to facilitate these necessary linkages. The linkages were important on one level to sustain the profitability of regional manufacture and other economic activity. On another level though, these linkages in facilitating the matching of available products with available demand served to sustain the level of urbanization in the region as a whole and the various levels of urbanization achieved by each of the cities and towns which composed the region.

Allan Pred in a later work defines a system of cities as a "set of cities which are interdependent in such a way that any significant change in the economic activities, occupational structure, total income, or population of one member city will directly or indirectly bring about an alteration in the economic activities, occupational structure, total income or population of one or more other set members."[31] What sustains a system of cities? Given the complex economic base of the region even by 1830, the system of cities within the region was sustained by (A) a fairly steady flow of the factors of production both within and outside the region, (B) fairly reliable sources of demand both within and outside the region, and (C) reliable mechanisms to sustain the steady flow of raw and finished goods through the region so that the requirements of the supply sector and the demand sector were satisfactorily met. These mechanisms were of paramount importance in the system. They composed essential elements of the infrastructure of the system of cities. These mechanisms were essentially the linkage which tied the region together and fostered the interdependence of the various cities and towns which compose the region. The three subsequent chapters examine in detail the nature of activities which operated as vital linkages in the region: transportation linkages, credit linkages, and market linkages. A study of these linkages underscores the interdependence of the cities and towns of the region and clearly demonstrates the hierarchical nature of the evolving system of cities in the region.

IV

TRANSPORTATION LINKAGES IN THE REGION, 1810-1850

The process of economic development through a region depends to a large extent on the flow of goods and services through the region. It is this flow which sustains the economic activity of the cities and towns. To facilitate this vital flow, various linkages must be maintained within the region so that goods and services flow efficiently from location to location. The term "flow of goods" here is used as an abstraction to indicate the kinds of movements of goods and services described in the previous two chapters. Linkages on the other hand refer to specific formal or informal institutional means by which goods and services move through the region.

The most necessary and probably the most obvious linkage is transportation. The various means of transportation available in many ways determined the flexibility in location decisions for local entrepreneurs. In addition, the transportation network facilitated movement of goods and services which was essential to the process of regional economic growth: moving goods to markets, raw materials to manufacturers, and moving people who carried out these many transactions.

Efficient transportation generally results when a maximum amount of goods can be shipped at minimal unit cost. In the case of the railroad, for example, transport efficiencies have been achieved through the establishment of a system of main and branch lines. Obvious inefficiencies would result if each city and town attempted to maintain direct lines to all other cities and towns in the region. Therefore choices had to be made regarding transport routes and nodes.

In choosing the location of transport routes access to various resources was important. Transportation involved movement of people as well as goods and services. Thus the more population centers served by a route, the greater the use and return on investment. Freight was also an important consideration; thus access to manufacturing or to agricultural produce centers would be an important consideration as well. To sustain a profitable freight route manufacturers must be in the business of fabricating goods for export from the local town to a regional market or beyond. In the case where routes linked existing population centers or manufacturing centers with other population centers in the region, transport was established to meet a demand for such services.

Once the need for a transport route was perceived, the mode then had to be chosen. By the early nineteenth century, alternatives were available and adoption was usually determined by perceived profitability. In the early part of the nineteenth century transport could be by cart, ship, canal barge, or, later, the railroad. When water resources (i.e., rivers) existed to link inland towns, barges could then be used and if the volume of trade seemed sufficient canals could be dug and rivers deepened to create longer routes. Otherwise overland cart, a most inefficient form of transport, was used in the interior until the level of technology improved to the point where the railroad was an alternative. Involving considerable investments, the railroad routes usually linked major centers providing or anticipating a high volume of traffic. Cost per mile was generally less than similar trips by cart mainly because the railroad could handle far larger volumes of material. Ability to operate in the winter made the railroad more attractive than the cheaper though seasonal canal and water routes. The exception would be coastal shipping which was both economical and competitive except when the harbors froze.

As transport decisions were made in the region, a system of transport linkages gradually evolved. The system of transport linkages was important in the development of the region in two ways. First, when new routes were established, or when existing routes were made more efficient in linking existing manufacturing centers to population centers, reduced costs of transport enabled a manufacturer to become competitive in markets previously closed to his particular product. In the process, the profitability of the individual firm was increased and in turn the level of wealth in the particular town was likewise increased. Through increased exports from the town, the new level of wealth permitted expansion of production leading to expansion in employment and related activities. Thus changes in the transport sector within a region, particularly those which reduced costs, had a direct impact on the growth of individual local economies particularly on the inland towns of the region. Second, when routes were established in anticipation of demand, transport could open up for a particular town competitive access to resources which previously were inaccessible. Thus locations which were unattractive to manufacturers prior to the establishment of the route, became competitive as transportation centers or nodes which facilitated efficient movement of goods within the region.[1] For the railroad this generally meant that important nodes of commercial activity would emerge at strategic intersections of lines or that the railroad would choose to locate a line or route so as to pass through or terminate at an existing node. In the process either a hierarchy of such cities and towns evolved as distribution points based on the transportation pattern or an existing hierarchy was reinforced by the transportation pattern. In either case the process of urban concentration was furthered.

In nineteenth-century Massachusetts, as transportation methods evolved from 1810 to 1850, the flow of goods and services likewise shifted to take advantage of the most efficient means of movement. For analytical purposes, the period 1810 to 1850 has been divided into three subperiods. The first period 1810 to 1825, the pre-railroad era, was a period when cart, stage, and to some extent canals provided the main sources of inland transportation, with rivers and coastal trade important as well. The second period, 1825 to 1840, marked the coming of the railroad and its unsettling consequences for regional flow patterns. The third period, 1840 to 1850 and beyond, marked the emergence of a regional hierarchy based primarily upon the rail network through the region. This would not be challenged until the coming of the automobile.[2]

Before 1825, the common forms of transportation were boat and cart or stage. Boston had always been a busy port and over time shipping traffic had increased among all the seacoast towns of the region as the population increased. Population statistics in chapter II illustrate the predominance of seacoast towns in lists of most populous places in 1810. Newspaper advertisements mention standard packet services to Cape Cod, Salem and other ports.[3] Sources on the extent of the coastal trade are rare, particularly for the local intraregional trade. One can really only infer from the relatively large population size of the coastal towns and from the extent of the packet services that coastal locations provided a distinct advantage during the early period. Also it is clear that overland transportation by wagon was much costlier than water transport. The tendency of various industries to locate along the coast as shown in chapter III suggests that the advantage of a coastal location was perceived by the entrepreneurs of the region.

By 1810, the turnpike routes were very well developed if not well paved. The focus of the overland transport network was Boston with principal turnpikes running north, west and south. Maps drawn in 1830 reveal a complete system of roads linking each town, usually from town center to town center. Charles Hudson, writing in 1868 about the history of Lexington, recalled the roads running west: "Before the railroads diverted the travel, there were three great thoroughfares from Boston into the country running through the entire length of the town." He listed the Concord Tunrpike to the south, the Middlesex through the north and the Old Concord Road which ran through the center of town. He noted that often many stages could be seen on these roads.[4]

Stages did run frequently from many towns. Newspaper advertisements show regular runs to the principal inland towns, Lowell and Worcester, as well as to such coastal ports as Salem, New Bedford and Providence. These were regularly scheduled passenger routes. There was no indication of comparable widespread scheduled freight service.[5] An early historian of Haverhill noted that "Rufus Slocumb began a regular running of a tow horse 'baggage waggon' between Haverhill and Boston for the transportation of freight." His service proved so successful that he was "obliged to increase his freight facilities."[6] His service was used principally by the town's forty-one shoemakers. In 1825 he made 103 trips to Boston, taking with him 2,805 cases of shoes weighing 161 tons and returning with 168 tons of goods (unspecified). It can be assumed that other enterprising owners of horse drawn wagons provided similar services in other towns directed at getting goods to Boston, the principal market.[7]

While such overland transportation was available, there is significant evidence that freight rates were too high and thus hindered significant development of the interior. A petition arguing for a railroad between Salem and Boston claimed that the cost per ton by land over that distance was $3.34 and by coastal transport 85 cents—a significant difference.[8] In 1813, John L. Sullivan published a pamphlet in Boston "Remarks on the Importance of Inland Navigation from Boston." Sullivan noted that Boston had an excellent harbor and through the early years of the new nation enjoyed flourishing commercial development. Of course in 1813 this was threatened and surely the war sparked Sullivan's reassessment of the Massachusetts economy. His line of argument, though, is significant. He argues that to command trade ". . . a good harbour, a city where wealth, intelligence, and commercial skill are found, and an extensive, fertile, well peopled back country are the requisites to permanent and progressive prosperity."[9] In order to achieve this development, he suggested the more efficient use of inland waterways. The two principal potential inland water systems at the time were the Blackstone (not well developed until 1825) and the Middlesex (developed 1798-1804) canals. The Blackstone system provided water transport for southern Worcester County to Providence. The Middlesex canal provided a linkage through Middlesex County and upper Essex County to Boston. Sullivan argued that the coastal population should note the economy of canal transportation and the potential it provided for the economic growth of the region. Sullivan observed that the Middlesex canal sharply reduced the costs of transporting timber to the Boston market. He noted that cattle could be brought to market more efficiently as well—i.e., cheaper and with less chance of damage to the beef.[10] Sullivan, obviously favorable to canal transport, may not have presented a wholly objective analysis, but he did see the advantages of efficient transport for the economic development of the interior towns of the region. Sullivan may have been sensitive to the tendency of large firms to locate on the coast and thus argued the need to have nodes of transport to interior towns which would permit manufacturers to import raw materials and export finished products at prices competitive with firms located near the coast. Indeed the location of important manufacturing industries, particularly textiles, in the two canal basins support the perceived logic of Sullivan's arguments.

The emergence of the two canals marked the first transportation system in the hinterland that was rigid. Canal boats could only travel on certain routes between select points. This required that goods shipped by canal be brought to specific transfer points for loading on barges. This rigid system had an expansionary impact on the service sector of the economy of those towns which became transfer points. In 1822, a group of citizens met in Worcester to explore the possibility of construction of a canal to link the Blackstone basin with Providence, though it was made clear that Boston could benefit as well. Supporters of the canal drew up questions to ask various economic interests in the area. The questions reveal a sensitivity to the role of the hinterland in a strong regional economy. The questions included: "What number of tons of all kinds of goods, merchandise and products is carted from Boston and other seaports annually by the inhabitants of your town?" "Should such a communication reduce the expenses of transportation from Worcester to Boston to Providence two thirds?" and "What articles could you send into the market, which would now yield no profit?"[11] Unfortunately, the answers to the questionnaire have not survived. However, the questions themselves do indicate that the men who explored and ultimately promoted the project were concerned with the potential profit of a strong hinterland, and that the location of new and expanded industries in the hinterland would be attracted by more efficient transportation. The citizens of Worcester "supposed that many Agricultural Products might find a market which are not now transported at all: and that many kinds of manufacturing might be pursued which are now neglected in consequence of the expense of transportation."[12]

In 1825, the canal company met and financed the construction of the canal. By this time a sizable potential market for the services of the waterway existed since the Providence textile entrepreneur Samuel Slater had located a number of mills in the basin, attracted by the waterways more as a source of power than transport. The waterway most likely had an important effect on the town of Worcester in the region since Worcester was the northernmost transfer or distribution point for goods moving via the canal. The actual effect of the canal on the town is difficult to measure precisely.

More important to the region under consideration was the Middlesex Canal linking the upper Merrimack area with Boston. Conceived in 1790, the canal was originally intended to increase Boston's trade with the agricultural areas of the north hinterland and to promote the potential of the northern sections of the region for manufacturing. In operation by 1804, the canal proved particularly useful in facilitating efficient transport of many goods to Charlestown (which lay across Boston Harbor at the terminus of the waterway system). The most important product shipped via the canal was timber. In 1805, 8,905 tons of raw timber and boards were transported along the canal route, which constituted 84 percent of the total business of the canal for that year. This new route for timber transport was primarily responsible for the emergence of Charlestown and inland Medford as shipbuilding centers. In 1810, for example, 400 tons of oak timber were sent to Medford along with ninety-four tons of pine timber and masts and 154,000 B.M. of oak and pine planks.[13]

The canal remained active into the railroad era. In 1817, the canal transported 3,700 tons of timber products plus 807,225 B.M. of lumber and 5,300 cords of wood. With the beginnings of the textile industry in Lowell and elsewhere in the region served by the canal, there was demand for bricks for the construction of the mills and a demand for the freight services of the canal. The canal serviced the principal Lowell mills until the railroad link was established in 1836. Between 1835 and 1836 receipts from Lowell freight on the canal fell from $12,000 to $6,000 per year.[14]

As will be seen, the relationship of the canals to the formation of the urban hierarchy of the region is not as clear as is the relationship between the urban hierarchy and the railroads. Towns did not emerge in response to demands from canal traffic as was the case with the Ohio canals. Perhaps this is because the trip from the extreme ends of the Blackstone Canal and the Middlesex Canal could be made in one day without the need of a service or stopover town. Or, if such stops were required, they could be made in existing towns. Also, the canal system may have been less able to serve efficiently on short runs the local manufacturers who could instead load the products of six months work onto a cart, go to Boston, sell the contents and return home by sundown. The railroad very early began to compete with the Blackstone Canal which really had only ten years without competition. The Middlesex Canal had thirty years without competition on its route but then its upper Essex County customers could just as easily have shipped goods to Salem or Salisbury for transfer to ships for Boston. In any case there is no evidence that canal towns emerged in the region. However, it is at the same time clear that the economic structure of some towns did change in important ways because of access to the canal, most notably Medford, where the shipbuilding industry depended on lumber moved down the canal.[15]

Although the canals were important, they were always in competition with coastal shipping and eventually with the railroad. A more persistent alternative to inland transport was the coastal trade. Ships typically sailed from harbor to harbor, ultimately bringing their goods to Boston. This form of transport dated back to the seventeenth century. It is unfortunately very poorly documented, probably because it was so informal, with small craft hauling small loads for small distances. No records could be found which distinguish ships coming and going from ports in the region from general tonnage statistics. The economic advantage of coastal shipping can only be inferred for the pre-1825 period. A large percentage of the coastal trade involved bringing raw materials from New Hampshire and Maine to the many manufacturers located along the coast. For major buyers, whole shiploads may have been shipped directly from supplier to buyer. Smaller lots likely were distributed at major ports through middlemen. The coastal trade, like the canal system, required transfer points. The large volume of goods to be loaded and unloaded from ships did of course stimulate the service sectors of the principal port cities and towns. It is clear that overland transport was very expensive leading to funding of canals where possible. Further, location trends among major manufacturers for this period would indicate perceptions of distinct advantages in a coastal location which would provide access to cheaper transportation. The commercial facilities and services in Boston were important for larger firms and these facilities were most cheaply accessible via the coast.[16]

The region appears for the most part to have been oriented during the early period toward the coast. No other form of transportation could match coastal shipping as a means of efficiently transporting bulk materials. The construction of the two canals offered an alternative to overland transport but they were not really effective in drawing business away from the coast. Perhaps the canals were too early overshadowed by the railroad in the process of industrialization.

The best evidence relating to the desire of Bostonians and others to get to the hinterland of the region and to the apparent inefficiency of canals and rivers in the region can be seen in the rapidity with which major rail lines were established. By 1835, major routes were established from Boston to Lowell, Providence and Worcester. Shortly thereafter a route to Salem and another to Fitchburg were established. The pattern of railroad development was twofold. The first phase linked existing major urban centers to Boston. While there was some controversy over the exact routes, the ultimate destination of the roads during this phase was not questioned.[17] After the major routes were established, roughly after 1840, various cities and towns then tried to merge into the basic system through branch lines or by establishing independent lines to second order cities not served by Boston transportation.

The process of establishing a rail line involved legislative approval. Petitions to the legislature for routes reveal a good deal about patterns of thought among the economic interests of the region who, for the most part, could expect to gain considerably from the establishment of the suggested lines. The central theme running through all the petitions is that better access of the hinterland to Boston would permit greater development of the hinterland's potential for both agriculture and manufacturing. Boston contained the essential services and shipping facilities necessary for getting goods to wider markets—also Boston itself was a market. The essential link necessary was the dependable, regular, and relatively inexpensive transport provided by the railroad. While canals could service some points in the hinterland as cheaply if not more so, the railroad did not have to depend on the existence of waterways and could thus serve a wider area.[18]

A Boston-Worcester route was the first petitioned for and this was envisioned by some to be the first leg of a Boston-Albany route to cut off New

England's isolation from western produce and markets recently opened up by the Erie Canal. One enclosure to a petition from the citizens of Worcester argued that any railroad "to be useful or profitable to the state . . . must be advantageous to the city of Boston." The author looked forward to the day when all cities and towns would be linked to Boston.[19]

Petitioners for a Boston and Lowell route argued that railroads were a "practicable, cheap and expeditious mode of internal communications."[20] The commitee was interested in getting a line to Lowell as soon as possible. The only controversy among the petitioners was over the engineering of the final route. Towns along the way were either excluded from or chose not to engage in the debate. Their reluctance might have been due to uncertainty over the rate of regional return of this new technology, or to vested interest in stage services. The petitioners emphasized the economic advantage of the road. In 1829 they claimed that sixteen tons of manufactured products per day traveled from Lowell to Boston—7,400 tons per annum. Stages and the canal handled the volume at the time but apparently not to the satisfaction of those petitioning. The canal company fought the establishment of the road but lost out.[21]

When negotiations bogged down on a Boston-Providence line because of objections by the Boston and Providence turnpike interests, a group of citizens of New Bedford, Taunton, Fairhaven and Troy (Fall River) petitioned for a Boston-Taunton line. They too argued that the exchange of goods between their towns and the capital would be greatly facilitated to the mutual advantage of all. They further pointed out that though large quantities of goods are transported by land between Boston and Troy, "the trade for west and east India goods is now chiefly to New York and Providence, there can be no doubt that the trade in these articles will be to and with Boston in preference to all other places, if the facilities of transportation, as they must, be by railroad."[22]

While the petitioners were more than likely ready to deal in New York, Providence and Boston markets, the petition shows that the railroad was expected to open up economic advantages for Boston's commercial and financial interests. The petitioners also envisioned advantages for the Port of New Bedford which might receive goods from ships and transfer them to rail for Boston.[23]

This theme was echoed by petitioners for a Fall River Mill Road Railroad and Ferry Company. They argued that goods could be shipped to Fall River via ship from New Bedford, Nantucket, or Martha's Vineyard and then transported overland via rail to Boston. The scheme was generally thought visionary but its proponents understood the need for cooperation among various elements of the region. Fall River was not interested in becoming a rival of Boston. The town economic interests clearly understood their relationship to other places in the region and were interested in maximizing any advantage. Fall River needed the Boston market and access to its commercial and capital facilities. It also needed food to sustain its factory working population. The railroad would facilitate the necessary movement of goods and services to sustain the city's specialized function—manufacturing.[24]

The most controversial route seemed to be that of the Eastern Railroad which had the strong backing of Thomas H. Perkins, the Boston merchant. The controversy probably arose because the Eastern, unlike the other routes, would pass through the already heavily industrialized corridor of western Suffolk, Middlesex and Essex Counties. The data presented in support of the petition indicates that the stakes were high. Lynn reported that 6,050 tons of merchandise were transported annually between Lynn and Boston, including three million pairs of shoes. (No indication was given as to the breakdown of freight by mode of travel.) Salem reported that about 3,000 tons of merchandise passed between it and Boston by land and 7,600 tons via water (at a cost of 85 cents per ton by water and $3.34 per ton by land—assumed average rates). Beverly reported that in 1835, 1,000 tons of merchandise passed between the town and Boston via land and 3,000 tons by water. Total freight from Ipswich to Boston amounted to 2,000 tons and from Danvers 6,000. These figures are first of all estimates and secondly, compiled by individuals favorable to the improvement of transportation in the area. They do indicate that a large amount of goods were circulating through the region (as suggested in earlier chapters) both by overland and sea transport.[25]

Interestingly, it appears from the papers regarding the Eastern Railroad that the controversy was not due to competition for the railroad but rather to fear of it. At this early date the profit capabilities of this new invention were still unknown. People generally feared that bridges needed for the route might destroy water routes. Rowley, for example, was an important supplier of salt hay, harvesting in the fall hundreds of tons of the material; its citizens feared a proposed railroad bridge would prevent access by salt hay boats to their product. Newburyport did not want the railroad passing through the center of town where it might "endanger the lives and property of our citizens unless their rights be carefully guarded." Beverly also feared a bridge would spoil its "safe, commodios [sic] harbour, [and] easy access from the sea."[26] They argued that the railroad would not open this particular area to economic development as it would more western areas since existing modes of transport were as efficient if not more so. The Eastern Railroad was operating in 1840.

By 1840 the Boston region had an impressive rail network linking the city with major subdistribution and manufacturing areas. The rail network did not fundamentally alter the emerging hierarchical arrangement of cities within the region, but rather confirmed the existing spatial distribution of central places and made the pattern rigid. The rail lines were steel spokes extending to the hinterland which reinforced the existing pre-eminence of interior cities such as Lowell and Worcester as important intermediate points in the pattern of flow of goods through the region. For coastal towns the effect was mixed since the railroad focused hinterland transport on Boston and thus also must have attracted a greater percentage of ocean shipping to Boston. Population figures between 1830 and 1850 underscore this pattern. The population of Lowell increased 415 percent, Worcester increased 308 percent, and Boston increased 122 percent, while Salem increased only 45 percent.

With the basic pattern set and with the potential cost savings of railroads becoming more widely known and experienced, other towns had to determine how best to join the system and assure access to this iron network. From 1829 to 1840 thirty major petitions had been submitted to the legislature for railroads in the region. In the following decade seventy-eight such petitions would be submitted. With some notable exceptions, however, most of the interest in railroads became interest in somehow extending the existing network rather than establishing additional spokes to Boston.

The two important exceptions were the Fitchburg Railroad and the Old Colony. By 1844 when a southeastern route from Boston to the coast near Plymouth was proposed, the economic advantage of the railroad was apparently clear. There was an outpouring of petitions from all towns in the area for a position on the Old Colony line. Braintree argued that it needed such a road because its inhabitants were a "manfacturing People." Grist mills, a chocolate factory, shovels, nails, tacks, paper and shoes were all increasing in business and the "public good seems to require some cheaper and more expeditious means of the conveyance of passengers and merchandise from and through this place to Boston to enable use to compete successfully with similar traders in other places."[27] The economy of Braintree could not realize its full potential unless linked in an efficient way to Boston.

The town of Carver saw a "new impulse to the business and prosperity of the community" from the railroad.[28] Citizens of Pembroke petitioned with "deep interest in the success of this project which will facilitate the intercourse of the inhabitants of this town with both the shiretown of the county and the city of Boston."[29] Dorchester citizens saw advantages in trade and suggested that a railroad would "bring Dorchester so near Boston in point of time as to render it a convenient and desirable place of residence for businessmen . . . very much enhancing the value of its real estate—securing the benefit of a city residence without any of its discord."[30] On Cape Cod the citizens of Sandwich thought the railroad would bring prosperity to their town and argued the importance of having the route pass through.[31]

There was so much interest that a special commission was established to determine the most profitable route for the road. In the process of reporting, the committee gathered the following freight estimates (in tons) for the various towns along the proposed route:

South Braintree	1,875	S. Weymouth	4,875
Randolph	7,856	Abington	6,800
N. Bridgewater	2,703	Hanson	3,050
W. Bridgewater	1,245	Pembroke	200
E. Bridgewater	4,104	Middleborough	2,150
Bridgewater	6,260	Hanover	1,526
Halifax	150		

The ultimately successful petitions for the Old Colony Railroad to locate along the southern coast (see map) provided yet another spoke to Boston. While all the southern coast towns had long established manufactures, the building of the railroad would provide a dependable transport link to the center of the region from the southeastern portion of the hinterland. This in turn would encourage further manufacturing, attract more population and produce more goods. These goods would be shipped to Boston for distribution to wider markets.[32]

Similarly the Fitchburg Railroad was established, first from Fitchburg—the rapidly growing industrial center of the Nashua basin—to Charlestown and then on to Boston by 1850.[33] However, for the most part, citizens and particularly entrepreneurs of the region were interested in better access to central distribution points in the region—not necessarily to Boston. A myriad of petitions arrived at the State House for permission to construct special branch lines to the existing network of rail transport. In 1844, citizens of Salisbury and East Kingston wanted some linkage to the Boston and Maine.[34] Citizens of Georgetown wanted some link to Salem since "the extensive business now carried on in the towns mentioned and the adjoining towns demand this accommodation."[35] The route was to go through Danvers and the petitioners presented a detailed picture of the Danvers economy and noted the need to get skins to local shoe and leather producers. The implication here was that the skins came through Salem from Maine, Vermont and South America to be tanned and curried, and then some were sold locally and the rest exported from the area.[36] The concern for access to Salem of these two smaller towns reflects a classic hierarchical pattern in the system where Salem needed access to Boston and the towns nearby needed access to Salem.

For the region's southern towns this pattern is not so clear. A petition by Randolph, and Bridgewater in 1844 sought access directly to "the Capitol" and cited statistics on the freight and passengers transported between the two towns and Boston.[37] Wareham (tack and nails) noted that though its coasting trade was active (240 arrivals freighting 25,000 tons of iron products, etc. in 1844), they wanted access to Boston by rail.[38] Both petitioners were incorporated into the Old Colony line route.

The various towns in Essex County petitioned for an Essex railroad as "of great advantage to all concerned, by increasing the facilities of exchanging the productions of the sea and those that are seaborne, for those of the country."[39] They were also concerned about comparative cost since wagon freight charges were three times the rail rates.[40] The line was built from Lawrence to Salem. The town of Chelsea just north of Boston found itself in the awkward position of having both the Boston and Maine and the Eastern passing through but with access to neither. Their case for their own rail line to Boston rested on the need to transport five million bricks per year plus substantial amounts of grain and merchandise.[41] That particular road was never built.

Bedford wished connections with Boston to facilitate transportation of its annual output of 3,500 tons of raw, manufactured and agricultural products in addition to the 73,000 cans of milk produced in the town.[42] Stoneham wished a branch rail line to handle its 3,000 tons of agricultural and manufactured goods produced each year.[43] Neither of these lines were built.

In the western part of the state in 1847 a number of towns petitioned to have better access to Worcester and through Worcester to link with the central rail network. The towns of Leicester, Gardner, Rutland and others petitioned for a Barre and Worcester line and quoted the following freight estimates (in tons) for shipment of goods from surrounding towns to Worcester:

Leicester	3,000	Dana	1,237
Paxton/Holden	1,100	Hardwick	1,000
Rutland	1,200	Philipston	1,210
Oakham	1,500	Templeton	4,000
Hubbardston	2,500	Athol	2,000
Barre	4,600	Gardner	1,000
Petersham	1,700	Wichendon	2,000
Royalston	1,000		

Petitioners also suggested the possibility of a Fitchburg, Worcester railroad noting that "Fitchburg is increasing in population, business and wealth almost unprecedented and at no very distant day is destined to be the great town north of Worcester.[44] This road was eventually built and by 1850 Worcester was serviced by four lines.

In 1848, a number of citizens petitioned for a Salem to Lowell railroad. Lynnfield saw such a road as the only way of keeping its marble industry on a profitable basis.[45] With the completion of the Salem to Lowell route, the region was fully interconnected with a network of railroad lines. From Boston rails extended to Salem, Portsmouth, Lawrence, Lowell, Fitchburg, Worcester, Providence, Plymouth and Fall River. Interestingly, New Bedford was on a branch line of the Boston and Providence. A rail line also served to interconnect Providence, Worcester, Lowell, Lawrence and Salem. In addition to these main lines, by 1850 fifteen branch lines had been constructed to serve towns like Quincy, Plymouth, Framingham, Cohasset and Sandwich (see map).

Map IV-1. Map of New England Exhibiting the Railroad and Telegraph Lines
      in Operation, 1850

(Map IV-1)

Such capital as was invested in the network served to get people and the goods they produced in the region to move about as efficiently and as directly as possible. The arguments put forth in support of the network were regional in conception. The hinterland wished better access to the points of distribution of goods and services. When the railroad was perceived as more profitable and reliable than other alternatives, existing major centers were quickly linked together. As a consequence, the hierarchical system became more rigid. The existence of the railroad predetermined for the most part location of distributive services, as well as the location of some retail and manufacturing activity. The railroads reinforced the pre-eminence of the major cities which they linked together. The resulting comparative advantage furthered the agglomerative effect exerted by these cities in the process of location decisions. The rail network was a rigid one. The resulting hierarchical structure would not be challenged until the age of widespread use of the automobile.

Aggregate figures show that the lines were quickly pressed into use. For example, the Boston and Lowell carried 24,869 tons of freight in 1836, and twice that in 1838. It doubled again by 1843 and nearly doubled that again with 222,831 tons in 1846. Some of this growth in volume would reflect the development of various lines which fed into Lowell goods produced further out in the hinterland. But the bulk of the increase probably reflects the growth of the textile industry and the shift of its business from water to rail transport.[46]

Records of business firms of the period also indicate that, once built, the railroads provided the desired means of cheaply and quickly moving goods produced in the region from place of production to points of distribution. As the system evolved, business firms in the region increasingly looked to intermediaries in Boston to take care of moving goods between the port city and the hinterland. Bourne Spooner, agent of the Plymouth Cordage Company, wrote that they had "no convenience for storing in Boston but can send by the railroad when wanted, and the truckage may be direct from railroad to packet. Nearly all our merchandising common with Boston is now transported on railroad."[47] The company did a substantial volume. S. Melcher of the Locks and Canals Company (Lowell) ordered iron from Boston to be shipped by railroad to Lowell.[48] Silas Pierce & Co. of Boston, wholesale grocers, wrote in 1850 to John Gates of Worcester that they had sent "to Worcester RR Depot the goods ordered as pr. bill . . ."[49] The Appleton Company, cotton textile manufacturer in Lowell, made use of the rails. Its agent wrote in 1840 of shipping cotton waste products to both Boston and Worcester by rail.[50] N.F. Cunningham, a Boston agent, wrote of shipping bales of cotton to Fitchburg via rail for use in the textile mills there in 1849.[51] Business correspondence tends to be dry, routine and right to the point. What is available, of which the above is a sample, indicates the obvious—that companies did indeed take advantage of the services of the rail network. As the petitions to the legislature suggested, there was a need for effective transportation linkage between Boston and the various parts of the region. These links were built and used. The availability of cheap and reliable transportation for goods surely was an important factor in the increased development of the interior. The gradual shift of manufacturing from coastal locations to interior areas was largely due to the more advanced transport linkages which emerged toward the end of the period under study. The subsequent history of Lowell, Lawrence, Worcester, Fitchburg and Salem through the age of the railroad, i.e., through to the automobile, would indicate that the railroad had successfully opened up the interior of the region. In some cases this permitted greater options for location decisions—providing access to hinterland resources of raw materials, labor power, as well as to ultimate markets.

Though the railroad was important in this process, other forms of transportation persisted as well. Business records indicate that businessmen of the time apparently continued to find overland wagon-haulers and coastal vessels acceptable, useful and economical for some purposes. Naturally before railroads were constructed, overland routes had to be serviced by wagon teams.[52] Henry Hall, agent of the Tremont and Suffolk Mills in Lowell, mentions teams taking the raw cotton between Lowell and Boston, even in 1833, after the railroad had been built.[53] The railroad petitioners also gave ample evidence that overland travel was a popular way of getting goods to market during the period of building the railroads.

After many of the main railroad routes were established, overland transport continued by wagon as well as by rail. Information is so scarce that it is not possible to determine which kinds of goods went by wagon and which went by rail. It is probably safe to assume that large textile machinery, railroad equipment, and large volume bulk shipments went by rail. Companies producing a large quantity of shoes, wire, etc. probably chose the railroad where there was a cost savings in bulk shipments. An exception would be very heavy items such as nails or raw iron which probably went by ship if possible. Short hauls and hauls connecting to rail distribution points would of course require a wagon. The smaller craft industries which dotted the region may have found it as convenient to ship via cart (personally owned) or by an independent jobber, or by commercial stage.

Wainwright and Tappan, a Boston metal importing firm, wrote in 1842 of receiving a shipment of metal from Salem via the sea and shipping it off to its destination (Ipswich) via wagon.[54] William Richardson, a Stoneham shoemaker and wholesaler, wrote about shipping children's shoes via the Newburyport and Boston stage.[55] Walter Baker, founder of the famous chocolate firm, wrote in 1848 that he had engaged a "teamster owning a wagon" to move his goods and supplies between Boston and Dorchester.[56] Bigelow Kenard & Co., a Boston jeweler wrote in 1840 of sending goods to Worcester and Royalston via team, though rail service between the two towns would have been available.[57] While the railroad was available, all forms of transportation were used to transport goods throughout the region.

Likewise, ships and packets were popular throughout the period for shipping goods, though evidence could only be found for the mid-period. C.W. Morgan, the New Bedford shipping entrepreneur, arranged to ship iron products from Wareham to Boston in 1834.[58] Bourne Spooner of Plymouth Cordage Company frequently sent cordage via ship. Spooner also wrote at length of the economic advantage of having goods sent by water to Plymouth.[59] In 1836, Whittemore and Lovering of Hingham received machinery from the Locks and Canals Company of Lowell which was shipped via the sea.[60] William Richardson, shoemaker from Stoneham, received a letter in 1835 from Portsmouth, New Hampshire ordering shoes: "you will please send them—steam boat *Citizen* from Boston, her days of sailing are Monday and Wednesday and Saturday at 7 a.m. She sails from T wharf and if she should not be there, she may be stored on the warf [sic] under the care of the warfinger."[61] R. Borden of the Fall River Iron Works wrote in 1850 about getting cotton from Boston via boat.[62]

By 1850 the hinterland was very accessible to Boston by rail, sea and road. Boston was the major crossroads of the region where rail lines connected to rail lines, where rail met boat, where cart met rail. Boston was the transportation hub of the region. Lowell, Salem, Fitchburg and Worcester were important subterminals, but Boston clearly overshadowed all towns in the region as a transport center. The major goal in railroad construction and in the movement of goods for non-local consumption was to get to Boston.

As a result there exist in the business records of the period ample indications that goods did pass through Boston from one point to another. This was suggested in the analysis of the McLane Report. Large firms, particularly textile firms located in the hinterland, would send and receive goods via rail that had been processed through Boston. In the transport ledgers of the Lawrence Manufacturing Company one can find an excellent record of this sort of activity. They indicate bulk shipments of cotton fabrics almost daily to and from Boston.[63] In many cases goods were shipped through Boston when direct shipments were not possible. Reed and Barton, silversmiths of Taunton, mentioned such an arrangement in 1843.[64] C. G. & H. M. Plimpton of Walpole, farm implement manufacturers, sent goods on occasion via Boston to hinterland markets.[65] Newmarket Manufacturing Company in New Hampshire, manufacturers of printing cloth, shipped items on occasion through Boston.[66] Wainwright and Tappan, Boston import agents, offered services as an agent for goods shipped to Boston. They would make certain that goods were properly transferred to a wagoner or railroad to reach inland markets.[67] It was generally and logically considered more economical if goods could move directly from place of manufacture to ultimate market. But if the trip had to be broken it was usually broken in Boston and often broken again at an intermediate point such as Worcester or Salem. A composite description of transportation in the region points out that linkages did exist between the various principal nodes in the region. The particular pattern which emerged reflected and reinforced the regional hierarchical arrangement with Boston predominant which had been pretty much determined before the arrival of the railroad. A good, reliable transportation system permitted flexibility in choice of manufacturing location and should be considered a principal factor in the industrialization of the hinterland. Water power made Lowell what it would be. Worcester had traditionally been a market center. The predominance of these two towns was reinforced by the development of the Blackstone and the Middlesex Canals. New Bedford, Salem and Portsmouth had water access. The railroad, when it came, rigidified this structure. The railroad literally linked the existing hierarchy in steel and increased the existing comparative advantage of the subregional transport centers. The advantages of the spread of this more thorough, efficient and relatively cheap new form of transportation seem to have had important implications for the spread of economic activity throughout the region as contemporaries recognized. By 1840 the region, particularly the inland hinterland, had reliable access to the major port. The spread of economic activity into the hinterland as shown in the previous chapter indicates that the new rail network did have an important impact on the spread of growth in the hinterland. The railroad provided new transport alternatives for hinterland manufacturers and provided them with competitive access to markets both in and beyond the region.

Though the process of building rail routes through the region sparked a sense of competition among the various transport modes, the railroads did not displace older forms entirely but rather added a new dimension to the evolving transport system in the region. The existence of the rail network provided new alternatives and in many cases, but not all, cost effective alternatives to the older forms. This total transportation system, powered by rail, steam and horse, linked the cities and towns of the region to each other. But the linkages in many cases were not direct. Routes clustered at specific nodes in the region—Boston primarily but also Worcester, Lowell, Salem, Fitchburg, and New Bedford. The position of these nodes in the system which were emerging in the early period was enhanced and ultimately fixed by the coming of the railroad. The rail system was a fixed system. Thus the position of Lowell, Worcester, and Fitchburg as inland transfer points was enhanced. This in turn contributed to a higher level of urbanization in those areas. Salem and New Bedford had the additional advantage of being a node where a rail system met a water system. Clearly the focus of this entire system was Boston, which served as the focus of a major rail network, the terminus of a river/canal system in addition to being a major port. The broad impact of transfer activities is difficult to measure precisely but clearly they contributed significantly to the level of urbanization in that city as well as to its general preeminence in the hierarchy. An efficient transport system was obviously essential to the flow of goods with the region. The transport linkage was the fundamental but not sole mechanism in the infrastructure of the system of cities in the region. Access to transportation at a reasonable cost was particularly significant for development of the interior towns such as Easton (shovels), Leicester (wood products), Clinton (textiles), and Foxborough (bonnets). These towns relied on the transport linkages to get products to market and likewise relied on the transfer services housed in the principal nodes of the region to handle their goods once they left the factory. This relationship was a mutually dependent one and mutually advantageous one for the manufacturing towns and the principal cities of the system. However transportation was not the sole activity which linked the cities and towns of the region. Finance too was essential to the flow of material and products in the manufacturing process. Local manufacturers during the period were frequently looking for sources of credit. Since little was available locally, they generally had to look elsewhere in the region.

V

CREDIT LINKAGES IN THE REGION, 1810-1850

In the region there were a few institutions, primarily banks, which facilitated the flow of credit to various parts of the region. For the most part, as noted in chapter II, these institutions were clustered in the principal cities of the urban hierarchy. Boston banks had enormous capital resources when compared to other financial centers in the region. Boston banks had 70 percent of the total bank capital in the Massachusetts counties of the region in 1810, 67 percent in 1830 and 61 percent in 1850. The existence of so many institutions, particularly the larger ones, with such resources at their disposal was important to both manufacturers and traders throughout the region[1] (see Appendix II for complete Bank listings).

But formal banking institutions were not the sole means of securing long and short term capital. Though no comparative statistics exist, probably most lending was done on an informal or personal basis through friends or merchants, both on the local level and from town to town or from city to town. Unlike the transport linkages in the region which were based on a transport system easily plotted on a map, credit linkages in the region were much more a matter of influence and connection which varied from firm to firm, entrepreneur to entrepreneur and thus from place to place. Credit linkage can be accurately measured only by assessing the sum total of all credit transactions in the region. Nonetheless, as an element of the infrastructure of the system of cities in the region, these linkages were every bit as important as the more visible and readily identifiable transport linkages.

Finance can be a simple as well as a complicated process. Essentially finance involves paying for goods and services rendered. A simple method of finance would be "self finance" or internal finance. Goods are paid for out of current income or accumulated savings. As a basically cash transaction, this method creates no debt or credit. Self finance by definition is local finance; no dependence is created between a debtor and a creditor.

When self finance is not possible or, if possible, is not the most conducive to profit or growth in the eyes of the entrepreneur, "external finance" becomes necessary. Transactions of this sort create debt and credit. In some cases they require a "chain of credit." The simplest form of external finance is direct external finance which involves the transfer of accumulated savings from the creditor to the debtor for the purpose of purchasing necessary goods and services. A loan of money by a merchant to a shoemaker to pay for new tools would be an example of direct external finance. A less obvious example would be a trade credit which is a transaction in which a manufacturer agrees to receive payment over a period of six or twelve months.

The location of borrowers and lenders in direct external financial transactions is important to the process of regional growth, particularly if borrowers and lenders are in two distinct locations within the region. If a textile machine factory extends trade credit to a cotton mill across the street, allowing six months credit on payment of a specific machine, then accumulated savings of the machine manufacturer are transferred to the mill owner, enabling him to expand his capital and his production. Though this is clearly a case of direct external finance from the point of view of the participating firms, from a community perspective this loan is a case of local finance or "community self finance" in the sense that the transferred savings remain in the same general location. An alternative to local finance would be the case of the mill located in another town. In this case the accumulated savings of a firm in one location are transferred to a firm in another location, thus stimulating the economy of another place. In the process a financial linkage is created not only between the firms but also between the economies of the two towns which depend on those firms. This linkage will often be to the mutual benefit of both locations since the savings will both stimulate the cotton mill and yield a return to the machine manufacturer.

External finance can involve indirect transactions which in turn involve a financial intermediary such as a commercial bank. In the case of "indirect external finance," accumulated savings of the ultimate lender are transferred to the ultimate borrower. The ultimate lender spends less than his current income and relies on an intermediary to invest or directly loan those savings. In the process the intermediary creates paper in effect promising to pay the ultimate lender at a fixed rate for the use of funds. The intermediary also extends credit to the ultimate borrower at a fixed rate for the borrower's use of funds. The locational linkages have a potentially even greater impact on the region in the case of indirect external finance since three parties are involved. If each is located in a different town within the region the transaction will affect the economies of all three locations. Because the ultimate lender does not deal directly with the ultimate borrower, however, the economic impact of these indirect external transactions will depend on the aggregate economic behavior of the intermediary and the behavior of the firms or individuals receiving the loans. To the extent that the financial intermediary draws money from savers outside its own location, the intermediary is creating a linkage with other local economies, using savings accumulated in certain locations for

Table V-1
Capitalization of Boston Banks and of Salem Banks 1810, 1830, and 1850

1810	Boston	$4,600,000	Salem	$ 500,000
1830	Boston	12,350,000	Salem	1,450,000
1850	Boston	20,861,000	Salem	1,750,000

Source: Abstracts of Banks for the Commonwealth of Massachusetts.

investment in others. If the intermediary's investments are sound then the agreed rate of return can be paid to the ultimate lender and generate a profit for the financial intermediary. In the case of the ultimate borrower, the stimulus effect of loans will depend on the performance of the individual or firm. A successful loan (in which the earning exceeds the interest cost) will have a long term stimulative effect on a local economy while a bad loan will have only a short term stimulus.

From a regional perspective, it should be noted that investments can come from outside the region either directly or indirectly. Thus savings from one region will stimulate the economy of another. Also credit can come from outside the region through a "chain." Recall the example of the textile machine manufacturer extending credit to the cotton mill. It may well have been that the machine manufacturer received imported iron on credit himself, and that the foreign iron ore was purchased from Great Britain by a seacoast merchant on credit. Thus through such a series of direct or indirect credit transactions a chain of credit was created which enabled the Boston region to use the savings of Britain or Europe or other American cities, to the benefit of the local economies of each place which participated in the individual transactions. This was provided of course that the terms of the various loans could be met at each point.[2]

Financial arrangements, both direct and indirect, were important structural links within the Boston region. Debt and credit linked producer to financier, buyer to seller, and in the process allowed financier and seller to exert influence in the regional economy. Since the wealthiest financiers were located in Boston and to a much lesser extent in Salem, Worcester, Lowell, New Bedford and Portsmouth, these individuals and the cities in which they lived exerted enormous power within the region. The financial linkages which they provided created a dependent relationship of the small towns upon the larger cities. Manufacturers and traders needed the services available from both the banks and the funds which Boston capitalists controlled. In taking advantage of the available financial services, manufacturing and commercial firms could expand their output and markets and hence maintain or expand the economic base of the city or town in which they were located.

The tangled web of finance in the region is very difficult to document. Since credit arrangements were often direct, records of such transactions were kept informally and often not noted in financial ledgers. However, enough evidence exists to indicate that the spatial diffusion of economic activity upon which the development of inland cities and towns depended, relied very much on financial resources flowing from the principal urban nodes of the region. In finance, Boston played a dominant role. In 1836, an anonymous group of Boston citizens petitioned the legislature in favor of financial reform. They noted that ". . . it is well known that every state, county and town in New England which has any considerable manufacturing or commercial concerns leans in some degree on pecuniary aid obtained from this quarter."[3] There was a general awareness of the financial role of Boston in the development of the region.

In day to day business activity many of the region's larger business firms used the services of chartered banks. Available records indicate that for the most part banks served merely as intermediaries for payment. Buyers would purchase goods with notes which the seller could take to the bank and draw on the buyer's account. If funds were not available, then the buyer, banker and seller would work out a stretched payment arrangement in which the bank wold provide credit to bridge the delay in payment. There are numerous examples revealed in surviving business records. Bourne Spooner, agent of the Plymouth Cordage Company, recorded a simple kind of transaction with a customer: "your favor of yesterday is received advising of the receipt of eight hundred dollars paid by the Union Wharf Co. on account with the Plymouth Cordage Co. which amount is accordingly placed to their credit. I will thank you to deposit the said sum or any other received in like manner at the New England Bank to the credit of Benj. Spooner."[4] Note that the company was located in Plymouth but did its banking in Boston, even though banks did exist in Plymouth. In this case the bank acted strictly as an intermediary to facilitate payments over distances within the region. Ichabod Washburn's Wire Company in Worcester also accepted large payments through banks in Boston and Worcester. His many small transactions were conducted locally through barter and cash.[5] Reed and Barton of Taunton were paid by checks drawn on Providence and Boston.[6] Nathaniel Stevens of Andover paid B. Goodrich of Danvers for wool by depositing a check in the Suffolk Bank in Boston to Goodrich's account.[7]

The payment function of banks had important regional implications since they provided institutional means for buyer to pay seller without having to be physically present. Such arrangements provided greater flexibility in location throughout the region for firms with substantial cash flow. Chapter 6 will note other institutions which arose to enable buyer and seller to exchange goods without being physically present. Many large firms such as Tremont and Suffolk Mills, Jacob Peabody, Wainwright and Tappan, and N.F. Cunningham took advantage of this service.[8] Banks as central institutions in these transactions required a central location. Boston was such a location with easy transportation access to all corners of the region; hence the largest financial sector of the region developed in the highest order city of the regional hierarchy.

In the Pred model for urban growth, the emergence of this financial activity in Boston would be one of the root bases for the growth of the city economy. Since the financial services in Boston depended on payments from industry within the city and industries outside the city, the financial institutions earned income which provided jobs which in turn pumped cash into the local economy and accounted for further multiplied growth in the financial, retail, construction and other sectors of the urban economy. During the early nineteenth century this financial sector remained small in its share of total Boston employment.

Often, particularly in times of scarce money, payments or notes could not be met and special credit arrangements had to be negotiated. Plymouth Cordage repeatedly used the facilities of the Plymouth Bank for credit extensions. When those resources were exhausted, they looked to Boston. Bourne Spooner wrote often to his agent in Boston of the need to raise money in Boston to meet notes falling due.[9] The Plymouth Bank, particularly in periods of tight money, would become extremely cautious. However, in each of his letters, Spooner indicates that in more prosperous times the Plymouth Bank was a willing lender.

In some cases sellers presented buyers' checks to banks only to discover that the buyer's account was empty. Usually in such cases it became the seller's responsibility to secure the funds. The bank's services would cease. Letters appear from Wainwright and Tappan, and Bigelow, Kennard Co., as holders of unpaid notes, to firms asking what schedule of payment might be anticipated. In some cases the seller might extend credit to the buyer to be paid through the bank. Banks were seldom more than a payment intermediary in such arrangements.[10]

Because of their conservative and cautious policies, banks appear not to have been the most popular source of credit among the businessmen of the region. Plimpton Iron Works of Walpole, Massachusetts avoided dealing with banks if at all possible, particularly in their later years (1840's and 50's).[11] Charles Phelps of Phelps and Rand, a Boston merchant firm, wrote in 1820 that "since I left business in 1808, I have had nothing to do with the banks: and I have no disposition to get myself enthralled with them again."[12] Charles W. Morgan, the New Bedford merchant, was the most explicit in his correspondence. Writing in New Bedford in 1842, he lamented "my position is dreadful having received all the aid it is possible I can receive here. I have to depend on Boston banks where there is no sympathy for me and where they only give me money when their own people do not want it so I never feel safe for a moment."[13]

Morgan was frustrated less with banks than with his position in the hierarchy. If Morgan's observations are true then the conservative policies of banks limited their usefulness to small town businessmen and may have worked to the advantage of Boston interests. It could also be argued that conservative policies worked to the advantage of neither in the long run, because the severe restrictions of credit added to economic instability and perhaps limited economic growth. "I cannot give my note for anything" Morgan wrote. "I can pass nothing in Boston without one of my brother's names."[14] This crisis in Morgan's finances was probably a function of tight money during the depression as he is more positive about affairs in Boston in later letters. But it does illustrate the hierarchical structure and his perceptions of such arrangements.[15] Judging from activities of Nathan Appleton, the Boston textile merchant, Charles Morgan may have been correct. Boston banks may indeed have catered to Boston interests. But this would not preclude their making regional investments. Appleton was a prime mover in the development of the Lowell textile mills and depended on banks and other credit sources in Boston for loans. Living in Boston, he had the advantage of being closer to the financial center of the region and had better access to interests which might have the means and appreciation for his ideas. Though the number and amount of loans extended to Appleton are not entirely clear from company records or from personal papers, as part of the "Boston Associates" he virtually built organized financial institutions largely to serve the ambitions of the Associates to industrialize the hinterland.

From Appleton's intense interest in maintaining stability in the banking structure of New England, one could conclude along with his biographers that he had a good deal to gain from banks and the other emerging financial institutions in the region. His large scale investments and those of others in the region needed assurance of sound currency and a reliable and steady source of institutional credit in the region for their own investments to succeed. Thus they moved to coordinate more strictly the flow of credit through the region, and the locus of this control was Boston.

In a pamphlet written in 1831, Appleton praised the centralized structure of banking in the region. In 1814, the New England banks had adopted the measure of receiving bills of all the banks in New England at a discount varying according to distance but not exceeding one percent. In 1824, the system was revised and, as described by Appleton:

certain banks in Boston have contributed a sum agreed on, to a common fund; and in consideration of the use of that fund, one of them, the Suffolk, undertakes to receive all New England bills from the associated banks as cash, and collects them from the country banks. The mode of doing it is as follows: the country banks are invited to keep a fund in deposit at the Suffolk Bank, for the redemption of their bills, and by doing so, it becomes a very simple operation to both parties. If they decline, the bills are sent home for payment, in which case nothing is received but specie. The trouble and inconvenience attending this mode of payment soon induce the country bank to yield to its true interest and keep up the deposit; since thereby, it can keep in circulation a larger amount of its bills than it would otherwise be safe to attempt.[16]

Appleton took pride in the fact that Boston currency remained strong throughout the first decade of the system at least. He remarked that "all New England bank notes are virtually redeemable in specie, at par at the counters of the associated banks in Boston and this equally, whether the banks issuing the notes agree to it or not."[17] Apparently the "country" banks were not particularly excited with the arrangement, which suggests that Boston interests were behind the scheme. Appleton noted, "It was in fact the subject of great complaint with many country banks, that their bills should thus be raised in value to an equality with specie against their own consent, but the public being benefitted, by the change, they have been obliged to submit in silence."[18]

It is not clear what public Appleton had in mind, particularly since bartering was quite common in the hinterland. He did mention that virtually everyone would benefit "whether the specie has been advanced by friend or foe, by broker or banker, at par or at discount, it was the fact that, or the belief that, money could be had for it at Boston which alone has given it general currency."[19]

While the idea behind the Suffolk system was generally attractive to Appleton, he did note certain problems. Chief among these was the inability of the system to guard against bank failures—he noticed ten in the period 1810 to 1830. He felt that such failures occurred because the banks rested on too small a capital base which made them vulnerable to the speculations of the directors. Appleton proposed a solution based on the principle "large capital and small circulation." He urged that "no bank should be allowed to issue notes for circulation, having less than a million of dollars, or at the very lowest, certainly half a million. The right to issue notes should be restricted to one third the amount of capital." The effect of this proposition of course would be "that no bank of circulation would be established, except in the large commercial towns, in Massachusetts, perhaps only in Boston."[20] The advantage of that location for such institutions would be that they would be "under a surveillance" which would be the best possible assurance to the public "for correctness of their management."[21]

The pamphlet represents one idea of one man, so it is difficult to assess the universality of these beliefs among the higher strata of financial interests in Boston. But from the writings of Charles Morgan it does appear that the Boston interests were a tight knit group. A.A. Lawrence, in a letter to his son in 1830, lamented the number of bank failures in the region and hoped for a more structured system. He was concerned that the Suffolk bank system might not be performing as well as its authors had intended.[22] The movement to coordinate banking and currency at the center of the region came from Boston interests and was largely to benefit those interests in their attempts to industrialize the region. For this study the importance of Appleton's argument is its underlying attitude that Boston should be the financial center of the region and that lower order towns had neither the large fluid capital resources nor the expertise to engage in such activity.

The New England bank, to which Appleton referred, was not the only bank which kept country bank reserves. Bray Hammond has discussed in detail the activities of the Suffolk Bank, referred to by Appleton. Hammond has seen the bank as exerting a stabilizing force in the region's currency fluctuations from 1824 to 1850.[23] Other banks in Boston also accumulated reserves of "distant banks." In 1835, the Merchant's Bank of Boston reported over $3,000 due the Dedham Bank; $20,000 due the Fitchburg Bank; $3,000 due Plymouth Bank; and $300 due to the Wareham Bank.[24] A report on New Hampshire banks in 1837 indicates a sizable "amount of specie in the vault and deposits in Boston banks for redemption of bills."[25] These include the Portsmouth, Rockingham, Piscataqua, Exeter and Commercial Banks, all in Rockingham County.

Chartered banking in the region thus appears to conform very much to the hierarchical structure of the region—indeed such a financial structure reinforced the hierarchy, particularly as institutional banking would become an increasingly important source of credit. Except for the writings of Charles Morgan and a few others, it is difficult to determine the extent to which the banks extended credit outside the cities in which they were located and thus assisted more broadly in the economic development of the region. Appleton's intense interest in the need for stable banking may indicate that his regional interest gained by regional economic stability as did the interests of many others. To that extent surely the banking structure located principally in Boston, but also in other large towns, and did indeed facilitate economic development.

Research has been done by Gerald White on the Massachusetts Hospital Life Insurance Company which had substantial assets, though it was not precisely a bank. By the end of 1830, the company was "administering 1,123 deposits in trust amounting to $4,865,254." In 1837, the fund had grown to over $6.2 million, mostly in trust accounts and "was little affected by the panic of 1837."[26] The company's own capital amounted to half a million dollars. All this money, of course, had to be invested. Generally the funds were invested conservatively in land mortgages. The company had elaborate procedures for making such investments, wishing to deal with "none but punctual men who will by the day interest comes due, see that it is paid in Boston (in Boston money) . . ."[27]

In 1823, nearly all their mortgages were in and around Boston. However, in 1824 the company, in financing the land purchases of western farmers, began to grant mortgages in hinterland areas. During 1824, the company placed 323 new mortgages of which 166 were located in Franklin, fifty in Hampshire, ten in Hampden, three in Berkshire (all outside the region) and seventeen in Worcester, fifteen in Middlesex, four in Essex, four in Norfolk and fifty-four in Suffolk counties in the region. Though located in Boston, the company was cognizant of the economic promise of the region and of the state as a whole. This pattern continued through 1838 when the greatest number of mortgages were in the hinterland of the region and in the western part of the state but the greatest amount of money was invested in Boston. Mortgages in the Boston area averaged $3,650 in contrast to $650 for mortgages elsewhere.[28]

In addition to lending on mortgages, Massachusetts Hospital Life served the business and financial interests of the region with loans primarily to banks, financial houses, and manufacturing firms. The company was intertwined with the upper financial circles of Boston. It made frequent deposits in all the banks in the city, which substantially increased their resources. In the period 1835-1850, the company became very closely associated with the entrepreneurs most responsible for the development of the textile industry in the region. Nathan Appleton for example served as director of the company from 1823 to 1848 and president from 1849 to 1861. It was Appleton and P.T. Jackson who received the first textile loan from the company for their mill in Waltham. By 1850 the company had records of direct loans to virtually all the major textile mills in the region.[29]

Institutional banking did play an important role in the development and structure of the region. Funds filtered down the urban hierarchy under the direction and supervision of the Boston financial community. Institutional arrangements favored economic interests in cities in the upper level of the hierarchy or which had direct access to those institutions. Over time it appears that institutional financiers became increasingly aware of the economic potential of the region's hinterland, particulaly as a location for large scale manufacturing of textiles (discussed further in Chapter VI). Boston remained the center for institutional finance throughout the period. Though other cities on the intermediate level in the hierarchy had a few banks, none compared in amounts with the institutional capital located in Boston. From the perspective of urbanization in the region, the concentration of this economic activity in the city of Boston permitted a very high level of urbanization since the returns on financial investments brought in substantial amounts of money which could then be filtered through salaries and earnings to sustain and expand the retail and other economic sectors of the city. At the same time, of course, loans extended from the Boston area to the hinterland did permit economic expansion in comparatively savings-poor areas of the region. Those locations, in order to achieve a higher rate of expansion, had to depend on local returns generated by the economic activity into which these external bank funds were channeled. Transactions of this kind over separate geographical locations linked the economic development of one city with the economic development of another.

Though banks were certainly important, particularly in linking major urban centers of the region together through credit flow and currency control, the bulk of credit throughout the period seems to have been on a direct personal basis rather than through chartered or incorporated institutions. Small town firms generally did not have the access to institutional credit that provided larger firms with substantial sums. Nor did larger firms outside Boston have desired access to credit, particularly in times of tight money, as was illustrated by the Charles Morgan case. All this, of course, did not mean that credit was unavailable in these quarters. Throughout the region there was a large network of friendships and business relationships through which credit could be obtained. Various merchant or manufacturing firms would permit credit to customers over time on an informal basis. These credit arrangements were vital to the economic health of the region. Largely through these direct credit arrangements, the bulk of the economic firms in the region survived.

A multitude of such informal direct credit arrangements existed in the region. Within small towns, credit was carried on through bookkeeping and bartering arrangements where residents would exchange their goods and services daily and then settle accounts every four or six months, at the same intervals as storekeepers and other importers of goods and materials from outside the town settled their accounts. This barter-credit system minimized cash flow and provided for active exchange of goods on an informal credit basis to the benefit of the local economy.

From records of larger firms which operated in the region the importance of reliance on informal credit arrangements can be seen more clearly. Credit was often discussed in many routine transactions. Most common was the delivery of goods on a credit basis—short term, usually various terms within one year. The large metals marketing firm of Wainwright and Tappan of Boston frequently sold goods on short term credit to clients in Salem, Templeton, Newton, Worcester, Newburyport, Holden, Haverhill, Lynn, and others. Normally Wainwright and Tappan would submit a bill and ask for "payment at earliest convenience."[30] To less well known firms, they would ask "In case you do not send the money with the order, have the goodness to give us a name here [meaning Boston] for reference."[31] One of the company's important customers was J. & C. Washburn of Worcester, wire makers. Obviously metal supplies received from Wainwright and Tappan were vital to the manufacturing of wire there and to the whole Worcester wire industry.[32] Wainwright and Tappan normally extended credit for six to nine months. Presumably the buyer could fabricate the metal, sell it and then pay for the raw material and interest. Such was the nature of informal cash and credit flow linkages through the region. One can assume that if Wainwright and Tappan needed credit, the firm could secure loans in Boston or from the European metals suppliers.[33]

The flow of credit generally was from Boston outward through the hierarchy. Plymouth Cordage Company, with financial offices in Boston, frequently extended credit to purchasers of their product. This worked to the advantage of the coastal fishing industries who were able to secure needed cordage on six to twelve month credit terms.[34] Likewise the Fall River Iron Company extended credit to those whom they felt were good risks. They generally insisted that their borrowers have sufficient capital as collateral for such loans.[35] Records of Bigelow Brothers, a jewelry retailer in Boston, show that they had notes due from nearly every town in the region.[36]

This sort of direct mercantile credit was extremely important in providing raw materials, capital goods and wholesale goods to the hinterland. As long as everyone could pay their bills, the system would work to the mutual benefit of each firm and consequently each city and town in the region. But, because the fortunes of one or another firm were always in flux—in addition to fluctuations in the business cycle—the delicate structure of credit in the region was occasionally thrown out of balance. While these problems do illustrate certain inadequacies of the system, the very existence of these kinds of problems and the extent to which they are manifest in the surviving records of business firms documents the dependence of the cities and towns of the region on this kind of credit flow for sustained growth.

Often problems were solved simply by a further extension of credit. Josiah Quincy, President of the Western Railroad Company, wrote to the Boston textile entrepreneur P.T. Jackson in 1841: "I will gladly accept your offer of permitting the note for $11,117.75 that comes due tomorrow remain on demand at a week's notice."[37] Bigelow Brothers of Boston, who extended credit quite often, had an account in arrears. In 1842, the firm of George H. Brown of South Bridgewater could not pay but asked for an extension or for permission to pay in hardware goods. Bigelow Brothers, in need of funds at the time, accepted the hardware to make it "easy" on Mr. Brown.[38] With the Dunbar and Story Company of Worcester, Bigelow Brothers had to request a modest extension on a loan. But then three months later the roles were reversed as Bigelow Brothers wrote in September of 1840: "We understand that your Mr. Story has gone to Connecticut. Perhaps he may make some arrangement to take up one or both of his notes. Should he not do so and you are not able to pay us something, would it be unreasonable to ask you to accept a Draft or two in the manner that you have done several times before that we may be put in funds by means of a discount."[39]

In other cases when extensions were requested, creditors were not so receptive. Reed and Barton, silversmiths in Taunton, denied all requests for long credit extensions. Perhaps because of the substantial investment required in the production of their goods, the firm tried if possible to get a 25 percent advance on all orders. Agents throughout the region were often encouraged to secure cash for goods.[40] Benjamin Loring of Plymouth Cordage Company had extended credit for twelve months to a Samuel Vease who still could not pay. A disgusted Mr. Loring wrote: "One would think that 12 month credit would be sufficient to secure punctuality from any gentleman who had the ability to pay. I can only add that it is best to suspend business that will not command payments."[41]

Silas Pierce & Company, Boston Food Wholesalers, inadvertently noted the hierarchical structure of informal credit within the region in writing to O.M. Donahoe of Lowell in 1848 refusing to extend credit further. Pierce & Company wrote that ordinarily credit could be extended when the Pierce firm could "hire" money "but just now the case is very different and we cannot by [sic] money less than 15% per ann." Pierce & Company needed the money to meet their own payments and suggested that Donahoe could "buy the money probably cheaper in Lowell than we can here."[42] Records also indicate that major agents such as N.B. Gordon, J. Fairfield and John Hancock had established informal credit lines as well.

The experiences of the straw bonnet industry suggest that in some cases entire industries depended on these informal lines of credit. In an "essay on the Manufacture of Straw Bonnets," written by an anonymous author in 1825, the dependence of that hinterland industry (concentrated in Worcester County according to the McLane report) was noted and argued as a condition unfavorable to the hinterland manufacturers. The treatise noted that "the long credit" which they were often obliged to give in order to dispose of their bonnets created problems. "Goods purchased in Boston or elsewhere on sixty or ninety days credit could usually be disposed of for bonnets in that time."[43] But the bonnets apparently "could seldom be disposed of for cash in twice that time." Thus they had to carry their business on credit "at a distance."[44] Bonnets were usually sold in Boston for export out of the region "to the principal cities of the Union."[45] During this period, according to the essay, times were difficult for the straw bonnet industry. But the McLane report indicated that many firms were still operating nearly a decade later. It thus appears that though credit arrangements were not satisfactory in all quarters of the industry, production continued through a continual infusion of credit. The straw bonnet industry is an example of a hinterland industry relying on informal sources for credit in order to survive. The manufacturers apparently obtained their credit through agents such as N.B. Gordon or wholesalers such as Silas Pierce who were generally located in principal cities, particularly Boston. These merchants acted as intermediaries transmitting urban credit to needy hinterland borrowers.[46]

Finding the precise sources for direct lines of credit is difficult. Boston appears to have been the principal place one went to find credit. It was the center for both direct and indirect sources of credit, particularly when money was tight. Many large entrepreneurs in the region mention their correspondents' finding funds in Boston—not in banks, but rather through friends and connections. Smaller high risk operations probably would be unable to find credit sources in Boston and would have to rely on local connections. The evidence on the smaller firms, aside from that relating to merchandise credit, is scarce. From existing business records it appears that such transactions were seldom successfully conducted by letter. Men like C.W. Morgan and others speak continually of the need to travel to Boston in order to secure funds personally. James Whiton, a Boston dry goods merchant, wrote in his 1829 diary of becoming an independent agent. He "managed through my friends in Boston to procure money and credit to the amount of $5,000."[47] He used these funds to invest in his initial inventory and to travel to England to make connections there. An 1837 entry indicated that Whiton was on the verge of bankruptcy and noted the interest rates in Boston to be in the 30 to 40 percent range.[48] Such informal Boston credit, which was local credit for Mr. Whiton, was crucial to the survival of his firm, and he apparently watched the credit market with great concern. Similarly the firm of I. Howland & Company paid a bill to the Plymouth Cordage Company by a draft, not on a bank but on Josiah Bradlee & Company, a Boston merchant.[49]

Charles Morgan, the New Bedford merchant so articulate on financial matters, apparently had fairly good Boston financial connections. His account books contain references to outstanding loans with such prominent Boston merchants as Coolidge & Haskel, John Patrick, Samuel Frothingham, and Josiah Bradlee & Company. His letters of the 1840's contain frequent references to his plans for traveling to Boston to check connections for cash loans. In March of 1842, he mentions going to "Boston tomorrow to raise some money—but I have no active paper to raise it on." This is followed three weeks later by a request to Josiah Bradlee for a loan.[50] By July he requested a renewal of a $10,000 loan from the Fall River Savings Bank and an additional loan of $20,000.[51] His requests to Fall River indicate a reliance on closer sources of credit. However, his records indicate that despite the availability of credit in nearby towns, access to Boston sources was crucial to the operation of this business. In 1846, he confided to his close associate W.L. Fisher that "the money market has been so tight that my whole time has been taken up in contriving ways and means and in travelling to Boston to see banks and brokers."[52]

Not only was credit a problem for Morgan and presumably for other individual entrepreneurs in the region, but also the inability to secure funds precisely when needed and any resulting squeeze on a firm's liquidity would send rumors flying throughout the informal credit network. In 1842, Morgan mentions "making horrible sacrifices of money and credit to obtain what is needful [for his brother and for the family iron works in Pennsylvania] and am sure it is injuring me. My paper is in the Boston markets and inquiries have been sent here to know my responsibilities. This is dreadful to me."[53]

Another perspective on finance in the region can be gained from the papers of the lenders. Regional financial giants like Nathan Appleton, Thomas Lamb and A.A. Lawrence all allude to their role as sources of financial aid to regional businessmen. Each of these men was listed among the stockholders in the major New England textile firms and Boston banks. These kinds of men and the institutions which they represented were important sources and were exclusive sources of large sums of cash when required by businesses in the region.

Appleton, for example, was both a financier and a borrower. He was able to raise vast amounts of money. One of his companies had over 140 stockholders.[54] While many businessmen in the region were failing in the 1837 period of tight money, Appleton's companies paid dividends. His partner J.W. Paige wrote him in 1836 that "money has been more scarce here than I ever knew it since my first coming to this place in 1816. I do not see how we went through with it yet it has been done with few or no failures and much less aid required by the jobbers—we have paid as high as 1½% per month for money in some instances yet the price of goods has kept up so that all of our concerns could make dividends . . . money is easy."[55] This financial crisis underscored C.W. Morgan's frustrations and his perception that Boston interests had clear advantages in money markets. Paige's statement also underscores the relative advantage held by the textile industry in attracting investment from the pool of available capital resources. Though certainly an exceptional figure in regional financial circles, Appleton was very much entwined with high Boston financial circles, holding stock in the Massachusetts Hospital Life Insurance Company, Tremont Bank, Fire and Marine Insurance Company and the Suffolk Bank.

Thomas Lamb, another prominent Boston merchant, invested heavily in Boston wharfage facilities and had a considerable fortune. Like Appleton, he was very involved in upper financial circles in Boston. In the late 1840's he was president of the Washington Insurance Company and the New England Bank. He had stock investments not only in the large textile concerns and in Boston firms, but also in hinterland firms such as the Sandwich Glass Company and the Taunton Copper Company.[56] He was also a recognized source of loans. In 1837, he received a letter from T. Dawes of New Bedford requesting funds ("to go back to [the subject of] money, W. Warren tells me it is plenty in Boston").[57] The letter also notes that Charles W. Morgan, Thomas Pope and others had obtained funds.

Abbott A. Lawrence was another financier who invested in the regional economy. A list of his stock holdings in 1847 indicates that he held stock in the State, Suffolk and Merchant Banks—all in Boston—five insurance companies, thirteen textile mills and bleacheries plus wharfs, stores and power companies. In all the list indicates a total investment in various stock enterprises throughout the region of $784,000, most of it in Boston finance and regional textile mills. Through his stock purchases and through whatever informal loans Lawrence saw fit to give, he too was an important source of credit in the region.[58]

Lance Davis has systematically studied the sources of loans to the New England Textile Industry from 1840 to 1860. The structure of the textile firms were much more capital intensive, and they were the only manufacturers organized as corporations and selling stocks publicly. However, their rather complete financial records provide good data on sources of investment capital. Davis's summary findings are reproduced in Table V-2. Davis noted that most "textile credit was obtained from sources in Boston. When it became difficult to obtain funds in that city, the mill owners did not hesitate to turn to other areas." By "other areas" Davis means institutional sources from outside the region and noninstitutional sources within the region. The choice of source of credit depended on availability of money and comparative interest rates. Institutional loans tended to be less expensive as commercial banks were governed by Massachusetts usury laws during the period limiting the cost of loans to 6 percent.[59]

He has also studied sources of stock investment in the industry and isolated three specific groups: merchants, including individual nontextile merchants and nontextile mercantile firms; financial institutions including commercial banks, savings banks, insurance companies and brokerage houses; and financiers including officers of commercial banks, trusts, and insurance companies. Very few of these institutions and individuals represented non-Massachusetts capital. They did in fact represent considerable sums drawn from the aggregate accumulated savings of the mercantile and financial communities of the region.[60]

The relationship of the major financiers and investors in Boston to the entire question of regional credit flows is difficult to establish precisely. The most measurable flow of credit and investment from Boston to the hinterland was through the textile industry. Planned and managed in Boston, the industry, in order to capitalize on the power resources of the rivers of the region, invested considerable sums of money during the period for textile mills located outside Boston in lower order cities. The impact of this investment on the patterns of growth of towns like Lowell, Lawrence, Andover, Exeter, Newmarket, and others, is legend. The extent of investment in the textile industry from sources outside the region is difficult to determine. Though Davis finds little direct investment, his findings do not preclude indirect investment through institutional intermediaries.

The emphasis on Boston in this chapter may short-change direct sources of credit available in the region at other locations. Existing records of small firms generally do not show loans in daybooks. This absence of formal accounts suggests that such activity occurred on a personal basis, through the exchange of notes—which were seldom entered in the records. The existence of banks in the hinterland does suggest subregional flows of credit from those institutions. Also wealthier citizens in smaller towns could perform credit services as well. Henry B. Hough's history of the Wamsutta Mills of New Bedford suggests that the textile firm was financed through local resources which were "reluctant to divert funds from highly profitable commercial shipping."[61]

The pattern of finance in the region suggests a strong primate city arrangement with Boston at the top exerting strong financial influence. The credit linkage comes closest of the three linkage arrangements studied to a simple city-hinterland model. The hinterland was clearly dependent on Boston credit but Boston was not necessarily dependent on the hinterland as a place for investment. This is in contrast to the transport linkage and the market linkage which served to link activities in the region clearly dependent on each other. Credit linkages in the region flowed from Boston outward for the most part. Many firms relied on direct sources of credit in the Boston area. Boston financial institutions were influential not only as sources of investment but also as clearers of notes of smaller hinterland banks. From available evidence it seems certain that Boston was the financial center and financial pulse of the region. However, evidence regarding self-finance and local finance is difficult to find. The savings of the men and institutions in Boston did certainly filter out to the hinterland at a significant if not overwhelming rate, but the precise rate is impossible to determine.

Nevertheless, the tendency for Boston credit to flow out into the region had an important stimulative effect on the development of the hinterland and in the process created direct linkages between the economic development of the hinterland towns and that of Boston itself. The general availability, particularly of informal direct credit, permitted more efficient movement of goods in the region. It permitted distance between buyer and supplier by financing the inventories, by financing the time delays in processing and by financing and insuring the movement of goods in the region and beyond. Also, of course, the wide availability of informal direct credit was more influential in the growth of firms in the hinterland, especially ventures considered too high a risk by the large financial institutions.

However, the credit from Boston and elsewhere which did flow into the various economic activities in the cities and towns of the region helped sustain and in some cases expand these activities. This in turn sustained or contributed to a rise in the level of urbanization in the cities and towns. Likewise, the returns on investments made in the region—and elsewhere too—sustained the financial sector, which was such a crucial component of the economic base of the city of Boston. Like the transport network, though in a somewhat different way, the credit flows too underscored the interdependence of the local economies of the region. Even Boston, the powerful hub of this transport network and the center of finance, depended heavily on and thrived because of the success of economic activity well beyond its political boundaries.

Table V-2

**Twenty Years Summary of Relative Contributions of Eight Lender Groups
to New Formal Loans by Length of Loan
(Renewals and Trade Credit not Treated)**

[in per cent]

Lender	Demand and up to 30 Days	30 Days to Six Months	Six Months to One Year	One Year And Over	Total Of 2,385 Loans
Commercial Banks	22.7	86.9	63.0	3.5	58.1
Savings Banks	2.0	1.4	4.3	39.7	10.1
Trust Companies	5.5	0.6	6.0	29.1	8.2
Insurance Companies	1.2	0.3	1.7	1.5	0.9
Individuals	19.5	2.5	10.8	22.0	9.9
Mercantile Houses	20.5	4.1	13.2	2.8	7.3
Manufacturing Firms	26.2	3.9	1.0	0.6	4.9
Misc. Institutions	2.4	0.3	0.0	0.8	0.6

Source: Lance E. Davis, "The New England Textile Mills and the Capital Markets: A Study of Industrial Borrowing 1840-1860," *Journal of Economic History*, vol. 20, no. 1 (March 1960), p. 6 (reproduced).

MARKETING LINKAGES IN THE REGION, 1810-1850

The existence of an active, available and efficient transportation network was critical for the movement of goods through the region. Goods could easily move physically from one location to another. However, the regional economy did not depend simply on the movement of goods from one place to another. Goods had to be sold and sold profitably in both local and distant markets in order to realize the necessary rates of return for a local economic activity to remain in business. Smaller businesses could not afford the luxury of their own agents strategically placed at various important nodes, particularly Boston. Rather they relied on a myriad of individual agents and institutions to send their products to market at a competitive price. The existence of these agents and institutions permitted the location of manufacturing throughout the region, since middlemen could provide the link between the location of manufacturing and the location of principal markets, whether within or outside the region. Based on available evidence in local business records, this chapter suggests ways in which these links served the manufacturing interests, enhanced economic development of the total region, and most importantly, provided a mechanism which worked to increase the level of urbanization in the region.

In general the institutional components of these market linkages were either external or internal to individual business operations. The institutions external to the firms included individuals such as jobbers, peddlers and small merchants who performed a variety of services as independent intermediaries. By 1850 when such services were provided on a large scale, the intermediary was frequently a more structured firm such as a merchant house, wholesale house or auction house, which provided more specialized services. Toward 1850, however, with the emergence of the large stock-owned corporations in the region, many functions formerly conducted by independent individuals or firms were performed by the corporation itself. Individuals were employed by the corporation to perform duties that smaller firms might have contracted out to an independent intermediary. These internal links were part of the structure of the large firms.

The independent intermediaries generally were located in the principal population centers of the region. The form of linkages among the cities and towns varied depending on the services required by each specific firm. During the early period the most ubiquitous and common services which linked the hinterland with the central places of commerce or distribution were the jobbers and agents. These individuals functioned as risk takers, transporters and sellers. Their role was to see that supply was linked with demand within the region and beyond. Their behavior is an important factor both in the integration of regional economic activity and in the urbanization process. Jobbers were typically individuals, self-employed, who performed the important tasks of buying whole-sale goods in large quantities, breaking them up in small lots and selling them to retailers. Their services were not cheap, but because dry goods were produced in such quantity in specialized locations, a jobber was required to perform a distributive service. Often in the process, he informally extended credit to small country retailers.

Information on specific jobbers is difficult to find, despite their importance to the operation of the economy of the early nineteenth century.[1] A.S. Lawrence, the wool wholesaler, noted in 1850 that jobbers could pay comparatively high prices for finished products and were often in competition with large wholesaling firms marketing goods for export. Jobber transactions were generally with small retail stores and jobbers usually located in Boston.[2] Waterson, Pray and Company were a large dry goods jobber operation which sold small lots of textile goods and other dry goods to dry goods stores both in Boston and out of town in quantities rarely valued over $500.00. An analysis of one and one half weeks of their business indicated fifty-three transactions with stores subsequently found listed in the Boston city directory and seventy-seven transactions with firms presumably located out of town. It is likely, though not certain, that many customers were located within the region.[3] Hatch and Fearing of Boston was a smaller jobber operation which sold clothing, blankets, drugs, etc., all in small quantities.[4] The records of the Boston Sugar Refinery Company indicate that jobbers periodically picked up bulk sugar supplies and sold them in the hinterland.[5] From buyers' records, their dependence on jobbers is evident. The records of Burr and Pritchard, a Concord, Massachusetts, general store, show transactions between the store and individual jobbers through which sugar, dry goods, spirits, etc. were purchased.[6]

These independent suppliers were particularly important as linkages in the urbanization process for the region. Located in Boston at the pinnacle of the hierarchy, they in fact survived because of production of goods and demands for goods generated in the hinterland. Their good fortune depended on the productivity of the larger region which as it grew created more and more demand for intermediary services in Boston. Hence urbanization in Boston was sustained through the expansion of the service sector in Boston—which responded to growth not only within the city, but in the region as well.

This Boston service sector was not limited wholly to the activities of jobbers. Larger transactions were generated in the large merchant houses and by the agents which were involved in the importing of goods from abroad and the exporting of goods such as straw hats, shoes, and textiles from the region. Where jobbers were the common link between buyers and sellers within the region, agents and merchants generally linked regional producers with the world beyond the regional boundaries.

The achievement of greater urban growth and larger city size by the cities and towns depended on the expansion of the agricultural and manufacturing sectors of the local economy, and these industries could expand only to the level of demand. The jobbers within the region would distribute goods primarily in small lots in response to local or regional demands. However, as previously noted, the region also depended both on the importation of goods and the exportation of goods from outside the region as well. The expansion of exports to places within the region, and outside the region as well, encouraged expansion of the manufacturing sector and thus of the base for larger city size.

Monitoring the extra-regional export sector were the merchants and agents who served as intermediaries between hinterland manufacturers or retailers and the markets or suppliers primarily beyond the regional boundaries. The business of these merchants and agents was generally transacted in Boston, which thus created further dependent relationships or linkages between the hub and the hinterland. The scale of services required in the port city depended on the scale of manufacturing and other demands generated in the hinterland and in the manufacturing sector of Boston itself. Some agents and merchants were also located in Salem, New Bedford and Worcester, the second level exporting and importing cities.[7] The presence of these merchants in the second level cities both reflected and augmented the increased manufacturing activity in the region. Through their world-wide connections they channeled much of the raw material to inland manufacturers, and provided the markets to sustain or increase the level of urbanization particularly in the emerging manufacturing towns.

The relationship of merchants to the manufacturing based economy of the early nineteenth century was quite different from what it had been to the commercial economy of the period before 1812. Their services became more specialized and oriented to the growth in the production of goods manufactured in the region. Porter and Livesay in their study of this relationship have noted that "merchants were the agents of transfer, a role which resulted naturally from their position at the nexus of American commerce." They argue that the growth of American markets for manufactured goods in the period, "presented an incentive and a compulsion for mercantile participation in mercantile finance." As agents of transfer in the period, merchants became involved in transportation, insurance, packing in bulk or dividing bulk into small lots, credit, wholesaling, and the locating and purchasing of raw materials.[8]

Patterns of specialization among merchants varied. The Boston firm of Lawrence and Sons Co. specialized in all aspects of the textile industry, including locating raw cotton and marketing the finished products of fifteen mills located primarily in Lowell. In the 1840's, the firm of N.F. Cunningham of Boston specialized primarily in cotton though it dealt also in flour, corn, hides, rosewood and pianos as a wholesale merchant. Other firms such as that of Daniel and Charles Jackson of Plymouth, Massachusetts, specialized in marketing goods brought to Plymouth by its own ships. The Jacksons were a small firm dealing in many goods. The much larger Boston firm of Thomas Wigglesworth, active from 1806 to 1847, also dealt in a wide range of services, including importing, exporting, handling bills of exchange, insurance and general commission business.

While merchants did specialize, firm categories are difficult to determine. The early nineteenth century was a period of change as the economy of the region moved from being primarily commercial based to primarily manufacturing based. Some merchants clung to the traditional role of merchant underwriting the transfer of world commodities. Others were primarily involved with the newer trade flows resulting from the growth of domestic manufacture in the region. Some were involved a bit in both. It is clear that during the period merchant services were important to manufacturers who depended on them for the location and shipment of raw materials and for the marketing of final products. Between 1810 and 1850 as the economy expanded and the volume of domestic manufacturing increased, merchants, agents, and jobbers increasingly specialized in particular products or services. Firms such as Lawrence and Sons specialized in the marketing and distribution of specific products. Despite the trend toward specialization among these intermediaries, Boston remained the primary center of this sort of activity though the expanding manufacturing base which encouraged greater specialization of merchant, agent and jobber activity took place in the smaller cities and towns of the region.

With this growth in the scale of manufacturing in the region, merchants could by 1850 focus on fewer commodities and/or functions, whether it be distribution of textiles or iron, underwriting or foreign exchange. The growth of manufacturing, which permitted greater city size in the lower order towns of the hierarchy, contributed to the expansion and diversification of commercial activity which tended to cluster in the principal nodes of the region. At the same time the growth, specialization and diversification of the commercial sector facilitated in a dynamic way the expansion of manufacturing and of the demand for manufactured goods in the hinterland. This was the marketing linkage operating in the region.

In the early part of the nineteenth century, mercantile activity was recovering from the devastation of the European wars. Papers which do exist for the period 1810 to 1820 illustrate the various services the merchant and agent performed, which not only served to assist regional manufacturers and to make money for merchants themselves, but also to help fully integrate all resources of the region.

Merchants kept up to date on current prices. They knew the larger market accurately. For shoemakers like William F. Richardson out in Stoneham, this information was essential for deciding when to send goods into town.[9] In negotiating sales, agents would at times extend credit to the purchasers, as in the case of a sale of Richardson's goods in 1817.[10] Through this and other agent transactions, goods produced in Stoneham and other parts of the hinterland, found their way to pockets of demand in cities throughout the nation. In the process the merchant/agent sector of the Boston economy experienced considerable growth.[11]

The most important transactions in the early years of the century were to be found in the ledgers and logbooks of the very large merchant houses such as that of Hancock or of Phelps and Rand. They imported and exported goods needed to keep the economy of the region active. In the correspondence of the House of Hancock for instance, one can see the merchant role in building the infant industries of the region. In 1810, Hancock served as an exporter of candles for A. Hunting, Candlemaker, of Watertown, and exporter of iron products for Lazelle Perkins of Bridgewater and a supplier of powder to D. & L. Laws of Salem.[12]

At the earliest stages of manufacturing, merchants and agents played an important role, and saw opportunities for growth in the manufacturing sector. By 1820, manufacturing was firmly implanted in many parts of the region and merchants and agents responded more routinely to the demands of manufacturers for a variety of services. Still located primarily in Boston, merchants and agents increased their involvement with manufacturers and a wholesaling sector emerged in Boston primarily to sell goods of hinterland manufacture. Of course, the emergence of this sector furthered the growth of the region's principal city.

Agents could also locate high quality raw materials and other inputs as demanded by manufacturers. Mr. L. Alger helped P.T. Jackson obtain iron "of particularly high quality and suitable for machinery" from Clyde, Calder and Dundee, an iron producer (no location given, probably England). Jackson was a principal investor and overseer of the emerging textile machinery industry, particularly of factories located in Lowell.[13] Merchants were shipping intermediaries for goods flowing into and out of the region, handling both the actual transportation and the underwriting risks involved in such transport. C.W. Morgan, a New Bedford merchant, was very much involved in the shipment of goods from New Bedford to Boston (particularly before the rail network), taking care that goods were delivered "in the like good order and well conditioned." Risks of many of his shipments were underwritten by the Boston merchant J.P. Bradlee and Sons. These transport and underwriting services located in higher order cities depended on a productive region for business as much as the region depended on them for services rendered.[14] Thomas Lamb of Boston provided similar services: informing customers of current prices, arranging shipment and underwriting risk and in some cases speculating on commodities in shipment.[15] Mason and Lawrence Company of Boston served as agents for the Pepperell textile mill "receiving for their services the usual compensation."[16] This flow of "compensation" to Boston from the hinterland stimulated still greater growth which led to a higher level of urbanization in the city.

Dodd and Son of Boston would take orders for goods from the hinterland businessmen, locate the goods and see that they arrived where needed.[17] Many merchants engaged in wholesaling goods, some exclusively. Smith and Hopkins of Boston wholesaled goods while relying on other wholesale merchants and agents to distribute the goods to the retailers in their regions.[18] Reed & Barton of Taunton sold their britannia ware exclusively to select wholesalers in cities throughout the United States, including Boston. In reply to one inquiry, they noted "we have not sought to sell direct to the retailers choosing to have our customers supply them."[19] One of the larger wholesale firms in Boston was that of Silas Pierce & Co. which dealt in food products. Their account books reveal dealings with retail outlets in nearly every town in the region. Silas Pierce also served as wholesalers for food producers such as the large Boston Sugar Refinery, distributing the company's sugar products throughout the region.[20] Bigelow Brothers were a wholesale jewelry organization and, like Silas Pierce, had accounts in virtually every town in the region. They dealt with second order cities such as Fitchburg (S.H. Goodnow) and Worcester (D. Goddard & Company) as well as with smaller towns such as Leominster, Sandwich and Holliston. Besides attempting to provide small retailers with appropriate and desired goods, Bigelow Brothers were very generous in extending credit for purchases. Their correspondence is full of such gentle reminders as rendered to Dunbar and Story of Worcester in 1840:

> We write to you at this time to say that a note signed by your Mr. Story 10th '38 at 18 months became due yesterday. We understood you to say that these notes would be paid at maturity. Supposing from the great length of time it had to run that it may have been forgotten, we conclude to drop you a line respecting it, hoping we shall receive the desired reply as early as the 20th, inst. when we have got a large acceptance to pay . . .[21]

In an analysis of one company letter book of fifty-five letters pertaining to accounts in the region, thirty pertained to credit arrangements. This case further illustrates Boston as a locus for credit and shows that Bigelow Brothers themselves relied on credit from elsehwhere, presumably through the Boston community.[22]

The large merchant firms continued to be important during the 1820's, 1830's and 1840's, particularly as links between the region and national and international markets. One such firm which has left a fair amount of records was the large Boston merchant house, Wainwright and Tappan. The transactions described in their letters show the extent to which large firms were such a window to the outside world and how they facilitated intraregional transfer of goods. Wainwright and Tappan dealt in large quantities and in a variety of goods important to manufacturing in the region. The firm brought in iron rails through Liverpool and Boston, which were used in building the Eastern, and the Boston and Lowell Railroads. Iron chain and anchors were also imported for the shippers of Newburyport. Russian hemp by the ton was imported for a Portsmouth rope factory. They exported goods as well, including much of the wax produced by William G. Appleton of Quincy, which was sent to buyers as nearby as Salem and as far as Philadelphia and Rio. In many cases, Wainwright and Tappan stood ready to extend credit, usually at six months, on goods sold through them.[23]

In the early stages of the industrial growth of the region the economic activity of towns depended a great deal on the services of the agents and middle men. These intermediaries, handsomely paid, not only moved goods through the region, but also worked to insure that quality raw and finished material passed in and out of the region. Thus there was a semblance of quality control as well. Wainwright and Tappan informed William Appleton in 1843 that clear and well bleached wax was preferred by customers to that which was "very dark."[24] They also referred to a shipment of bad cotton "not suitable for making any numbers of yarn."[25]

Manufacturers welcomed and utilized the services of intermediaries to take care of functions thought either irrelevant to their business or too far away from their location to care for. High as merchant rates and commissions were for services, it was still cheaper to leave such functions to individuals with connections and located in Boston, rather than coming in day after day or lodging in Boston over weeks, waiting out the often unpredictable price fluctuations, shipping schedules, etc. Walter Baker depended on major agents to secure the right grade of cocoa for his chocolate produced in Dorchester and to export it from the region. He also depended on lesser agents to wander around the region to publicize and secure orders for his chocolate in local general stores. Baker generally extended credit himself for from four to six months.[26]

The Plymouth Cordage Company employed the services of many agents located in the principal ports of the region and elsewhere to sell their cordage.

The company in some cases would extend credit through the agents, in others would regulate the terms of credit offered by the agent.[27] The Nathaniel Stevens papers (Andover textile manufacturer) show extensive use of Boston agents. Stevens regularly purchased oil through Edward Lamb of Boston, sold flannels through Clapp and Steele of Boston and, typical of the hierarchical arrangement of the region, arranged a purchase of lumber from P.J. Farnum of Salem by meeting Farnum's agent in Boston.[28]

It was essentially through this interaction between manufacturer and merchant/agent that the process of urban industrial growth in the region began to proceed in a dynamic way, given an increasingly thorough and efficient transport system and the availability of credit. The manufacturer needed the expertise of the agent and the agent needed the goods manufactured. In the process of the interaction of these two groups the pace of urbanization in the region was increased.

Naturally, in the manufacturing areas urban size increased because the manufactories were able to employ significant numbers of people, generally living in close proximity to the place of work. For example, in Andover there were, in 1830, five flannel factories employing 201 individuals and two cordage factories employing 110. By 1850, there were seven textile factories in Andover, employing 906 individuals and six cordage factories in Plymouth employing 142.[29] While these figures do not indicate metropolitan size growth, they are significant for many reasons. They illustrate a growth in the manufacturing export sector of the local economy, the success of which led to the growth of tertiary activities within the town due to expanded demand. The growth of infant manufacturers in the hinterland generated increased demand and rates of return on economic activity located primarily in higher order central places, thus not only furthering urbanization in the larger cities, but establishing a new and essentially industrial base for that urbanization, though the industries were located primarily, though not at all exclusively, in the hinterland of the region. Funds generated by the merchants and agents of Boston (that city's chief export sector) gave rise to tertiary industries as well, leading to a spiral of urban growth which was given an industrial dimension both from the rise of Boston manufacturers and the rise of hinterland manufacturers.

Business activity in some of the smaller towns was sustained by regional demands as well. William Richardson of Stoneham employed a considerable number of home workers in Stoneham and surrounding towns making shoes. Many of these shoes were intended for export out of the region, but his letters also indicate that he actively sought sales within the region as well.[30]

But the records of nearly all firms consulted show some dependence on the services of Boston. The India Rubber Hat Company of Lexington bought rubber scraps in Boston. The accounts of John Goodwin (1810-1834), a small Reading shoemaker, reveal that he delivered most of his products to Boston and purchased his supplies there as well. The large Plymouth Cordage Company imported its Russian hemp through Boston. The Boston and Lynn India Rubber Manufacturing Company exported its goods via Boston, sending its rubberized cloth to the hub via coastal vessel. Much of its cloth was bought by local Lynn shoemakers as well. Washburn and Goddard purchased iron through Boston commission houses. All this activity, of course, stimulated the Boston urban economy.[31]

Patterns of demand within the hinterland area also acted as a stimulus to growth in individual towns at the lower levels of the hierarchy. As various towns began to specialize in one or another industry, each to some degree had need of the industrial products of the other. In East Middleborough, William Eddy & Company manufactured shovels and other tools from 1827 to 1873. His accounts for the 1840's show purchases of iron from Lazelle Perkins Company of South Bridgewater. Miscellaneous Eddy receipts for the 1840's show that he made purchases at Plymouth, Middleborough, Taunton and Boston. In Boston he picked up other goods. Bulk imports from distant places usually came through Boston, such as the many handles he would order from Augusta, Maine.[32] Through the successful operation of his shovel manufactory, Eddy influenced perhaps in a small way the level of urbanization in Augusta, North Bridgewater, Boston and Taunton, as well as his own East Middleborough, upon which the existence of his company would have the most profound effect. A similar effect can be deduced from the purchasing patterns of Washburn and Goddard. The Worcester wire firm bought iron from Fall River Iron Works and distributed the finished wire about the area to local hat makers.[33] Lazelle Perkins of South Bridgewater supplied the Lowell Machine Shop with locomotive crank axles, connecting rods, etc., for the Boston and Lowell Railroad.[34]

The links to Boston were strong indeed. The city was the focal point for the movement of goods so essential to the growth of the region. Boston not only was the center for individuals with expertise but also was the place most central to the transportation, credit and other networks in the region. It was the center for the institutions through which goods were bought and sold, particularly in smaller quantities.

Probably the most important of these institutions was the auction house, which aided in moving in small lots the goods of the many small producers in the region. Located in Boston, Salem and possibly other cities, these houses facilitated the sale of the goods of hinterland manufacturers to regional and even to world markets through agents or jobbers who would buy the lots of goods. Thus the hinterland producer could think in terms of a market wider than his own small town and in the process create a demand for additional services in Boston and other central places. A few catalogs of these auctions survive, hinting at the process which probably occurred daily since Boston and

Salem had established auction houses. In 1828, Whitwell and Bond and Company of Boston held an auction in Faneuil Hall of 305 lots (10-220 pairs of shoes per lot). In 1835, Coolidge and Haskell, Auctioneers, held an auction in Quincy Hall of foreign and domestic wool. In 1850 at Oak Hall, an auction house, G.W. Simmons of Boston held a sale of his firm's ready made clothing. Terms of sale differed in each case. The Whitwell Bond catalog mentioned "term of credit will be named at the sale." Coolidge and Haskell accepted "satisfactory endorsed paper at six months" (the buyer had to transport at his own risk). G.W. Simmons mentioned nothing about credit but did promise that "package of goods purchased at Oak Hall will be delivered at any depot in season for any train according to the direction of the purchasers" which indicates that at least many of the goods manufactured in Boston were destined for markets within the region. The G.W. Simmons firm produced over $475,000 worth of ready made clothing in 1850, employed 250 tailors and was only one of 136 tailoring firms located in the city of Boston in 1850.[35]

J.L. Cunningham was a Boston auctioneer whose business legacy amounts to two letters. In these he indicates he had his own auction house or room. In th mid-nineteenth century he sold boots, shoes, wrapping paper and other goods, taking care that his auctions be centered around one or two commodities. This work often involved soliciting hinterland manufactures for available lots.[36] The firm of Jacob Peabody in Salem and Boston, whose records survive, auctioned a wide variety of goods manufactured in the region: flannels for Nathaniel Stevens of Andover in 1825, patterns and muslins for Nathan P. Smith in 1825, quills for Samuel Haskell of Beverly in 1822, sleigh bells for N. Bradley in 1822, shoes for William Bandlett of Portsmouth, New Hampshire in 1823, hides for C. and J. Smith in 1822.[37]

In the process of auctioning these goods, the auctioneer provided a variety of services for his hinterland buyers and sellers. He established and published current prices and kept customers informed of fluctuations. To Nathan Smith, Peabody in Boston wrote, "we have rec'd your favor of this date and should like to have you send us your gown patterns and muslins and feel confident we can get you more for them here than they will bring in Salem."[38] To Nathaniel Stevens that August 26, 1825, he wrote "being a warm day and not much spirit for woolens, we thought best to keep the residue for our next sale."[39]

When goods were selling briskly the auctioneers encouraged manufacturers to send further supplies, as was the case with the quills made by Samuel Haskell (of Beverly):

> We have one case of your quills on hand which we have just shown to a purchaser and offered them to him at 185 cash, he wants about 100 in and we can furnish them we think he will take them.The object of writing to you now is to know if you have two cases more of the same quality and if we cannot get 185 whether you prefer to take a little less rather than keep them on hand.[40]

In December of 1822, Peabody had trouble moving N. Bradley's sleigh bells because "our market is quite overstocked with that article. The season is so far advanced that they would not sell till next fall—They are sold mostly to country dealers [jobbers] and they buy their stock early in the season."[41] Thus the auctioneer in larger cities gave a certain rhythm to the circulation of goods in the region, anticipating demand, and meeting fluctuations in the larger market. All these services were very valuable if not essential to hinterland producers.

To pay for these services auctioneers took most goods on consignment. J.L. Cunningham sold goods on "consignment" or "commission" and also once noted, "If you require any advance, I shall be willing to furnish the money to a reasonable amount, in which case the usual guarantee will be [met], and the balance paid as soon as the accounts are settled." Auctioneers were also in the business of extending credit, though consignment arrangements would suggest that the manufacturer was also providing some credit, by covering the inventory costs for the time between date of manufacture and date of sale.[42]

Consignment was a popular arrangement for goods to be sold within the region. Agents often received goods on consignment from manufacturers. Walter Baker often sent amounts of chocolate to agents on consignment urging them to secure the best price.[43] Isaac Howland and Company took consignments from the Plymouth Cordage Company.[44] N.B. Gordon, a Boston agent, often took goods on consignment, usually in large quantities.[45] Reed & Barton manufacturers felt that their product was of high quality and in sufficient demand; they sold their goods to merchants and were concerned if those merchants would then consign. The firm feared that goods on consignment sold more slowly.[46]

The jobber, merchant, agent, and auctioneer shared common functions. Together, these businessmen were the key to the dynamic growth of the region as a whole and facilitated through their services the beginnings of urban and industrial growth on a regional scale. The manufacturing was primarily located in the hinterland and the service (mercantile) sector, primarily located in the larger central places of the region. It was through the interdependence of these two sectors over space and time that the capacity for urbanization in the region expanded and the level of urbanization in the region thus increased.

The larger cities in the hierarchy, especially Boston, in part existed on commissions on the distribution of hinterland goods and investment into hinterland development. Boston was the chief port of entry for goods passing through the region and as goods filtered through the service sector of Boston to satisfy demand within the hinterland the independent service sector took its percentage. Likewise goods passing through to their ultimate markets outside the region were handled by this independent service sector. Thus the circulation of goods as outlined through the information in the McLane report at the end of chapter III became the basis for the increased urbanization throughout the region. As goods moved from place to place in a region where economic activity was spatially diffused, the very movement of goods implied a demand for services in the central places of the region, thus giving rise to an army of independent intermediaries populating the central places. Some merchants, auctioneers, and jobbers were at the top of the list. These individuals were in a position to make fortunes in the business. But others gained livelihood from this process as well. The wharfinger, the hackney, the bank clerk, all supported and gained livelihood from the service sector of the central places.

The relationship of Boston to the hinterland as one of service center to producer came in the early nineteenth century to be injected into the structure of economic activity, particularly as firms began to "vertically integrate" various economic functions within the corporate structure. Under such arrangements, firms which were in name Boston firms were able through the dispersed locations of their production facilities to influence the course of urbanization in a number of places other than Boston. Such arrangements were new forms of structural linkages between the hinterland and the higher order central places. The functions of hinterland activities were similar to smaller independent hinterland firms. Likewise, much of what was done in the higher order cities was similar to those services performed by independent merchants. The difference was in the form since both functions were under the same corporate structure— since the firms which adopted this form of organization were among the largest in the region. Their influence in the process of urbanization far outweighs their numbers. Vertical integration of economic activity within the structure of the firm was seen in a number of industries. Most notable was the textile industry, but it also emerged in shoemaking and cordage.

The shoe industry, particularly during the prefactory days (pre-1855), assumed a variety of organizationl structures. It was for the most part ubiquitous throughout the region. In 1850 there were 154 towns listing shoemakers. However, those towns varied in total output from $600.00 in Gardner to $4.05 million in Lynn; the scale of production varied enormously through the region. Blanche Hazard, in her important study of the organization of the boot and shoe industry in Massachusetts, has suggested that a number of structural changes occurred in the industry during the period, particularly 1810 to 1855, while the industry was characterized by the putting out system.

By 1820 the industry reached a level of specialization in which hides were cut in a central shop and then distributed to individuals not located at the shop to be put together.[47] This required a certain level of capital accumulation on the part of entrepreneurs and a certain organizational structure. Hazard cites one such advanced organization, the Littlefield Brothers of East Stoughton (Avon) Massachusetts. These were four brothers who divided responsibilities among themselves. One, Darius Littlefield used to drive to Boston Monday and stay until Wednesday and again on Thursday and stay until Saturday, keeping watch on the Boston affairs, probably, accounts, shipments, loans, etc. James Littlefield was a traveling salesman, exploring markets in the south and eastern seacoast cities. In Stoughton, for a while under the eye of Nathaniel Littlefield, a central shop existed for the preparation of shoe parts which were then distributed to mostly unskilled workers from Stoughton as well as the surrounding towns of Abington, Mansfield and Middleborough for finishing. In the 1820's, Darius Littlefield also diversified into a general store business so that he could buy goods wholesale and give them at retail value to his workers in lieu of cash payment. He was also postmaster, a position which carried a franking privilege, thus cutting costs in his New Orleans correspondence.[48]

The company had an average annual output of $100,000.00 from 1828 until their failure brought on by the depression of 1837. What is relevant to this study is the way the organizational framework of the partnership reflected and affected the urbanization process in the region. No one locale received the full benefit of the $100,000.00 annual output. Part was pumped back into the Boston operation (out of a hotel room), part pumped back into the Stoughton central shop and part pumped back through the workers in other towns.[49] Thus the levels of urbanization of both Boston and the smaller towns in the hinterland were increased by the variety of locations of economic activity chosen by this one firm. Considering that by 1850 the total output of shoes in the region amounted to $24,302,509 (12% of which came from Boston shops), this industry generated a large number of manufacturing jobs and dollars for the region.[50] Not all shoe companies were organized as were the Littlefields, but the structure reveals a peculiar need for entrepreneurs to capitalize on the resources of the hinterland, in this case unskilled part-time labor. Despite the pull of this hinterland locational advantage, the link to Boston had to be retained—the dependence is clear and as with so many other firms, a portion of the earnings of Littlefield and Company of Stoughton were channeled into a Boston office—into the local Boston economy, thus raising the level of urbanization in Boston, based on manufacturing performed elsewhere. The population of Stoughton rose from 1,591 in 1830 to 3,494 in 1850, raising it from the ninth to the fifth largest town in Norfolk County (excluding Roxbury and Dorchester, which were neighboring towns to Boston).[51]

The impact of the structure of the shoe industry on the course of urbanization in the hinterland and in Boston in the early nineteenth century did not go unnoticed by contemporaries. Writing in 1858, W.H. Richardson noted that the shoe and leather trade emerged as a "prominent branch of commerce" around 1830 "caused principally by the change made in conducting the business." He defined the change as manufacturers selling shoes directly on their own accounts instead of consigning them to dealers. As a result, he noted, Boston was made headquarters for nearly all the manufactories of New England

and "although the city of Lynn and the towns of Haverhill, Danvers, etc., sell a large portion of their goods at home, a large number of the manufactories have offices in Boston for the sale of their goods." Richardson then links this structural change to the process of urbanization, noting that "if the domestic trade of Boston had been conducted on the home principle, the expansion of the city would have greatly exceeded its present limits."[52] Richardson is essentially discussing the relationship of industrial development to the level of urbanization, suggesting that had the entire shoe industry been established within Boston, a far greater population would be required to provide the labor. As a result of the structural division of firms over space, the industrialization contributed to the increased level of urbanization of a number of cities and towns though the activity appeared to be centered in Boston. It should be noted that the effect of this change in shoe company organization was due largely to increased scale where it paid to have a permanent employee (rather high-paid and high-spending) located in Boston. This individual would take over functions performed by intermediaries. Thus these "corporate agents" gradually increased their share of the commercial sector at the expense of independent agents and jobbers.[53]

Of all industries in the early nineteenth century, the textile industry was the most important in the process of urbanization. Its scale of production gave it enormous economic power and from very early it was organized much differently than the smaller industries previously discussed.

Textile production in the nineteenth century required a considerable capital outlay, resulting in some of the first stock corporations in America. Most of the important mills in the region were linked together financially as indicated by the same names appearing on stock lists, such as Appleton, Jackson, and Lawrence. Though technically independent companies, the Boston Manufactory Company, the Waltham Mills, the Merrimack, and Tremont and Suffolk, all shared stockholders.

These large companies were essentially Boston companies dominated by Boston men; their factories, however, were scattered throughout the region and thus had a profound impact on urbanization in many areas, most notably Waltham and Lowell. The need particularly for adequate power resources forced entrepreneurs such as the Lowells and the Lawrences to locate their considerable capital investments in generally unpopulated areas.

In the early nineteenth century, the larger New England textile industries invested in machine shops as well as looms, dye works and bleacheries. They also in some cases marketed their own products and ordered their own supplies. The structural integration of various activities relating to the production and distribution of textiles produced in the region meant that important corporate structural linkages were formed connecting the various corporate economic units of economic activity located at different points in the region. This process occurred gradually over the period 1810 to 1850 as the industry became increasingly integrated.

George S. Gibb in his study of the Saco-Lowell shops pays particular attention to the integrated structure of the textile industry. He notes that the Boston Manufacturing Company had mills in Waltham and Lowell, also a machine shop in Lowell. The directors of the firm also held a major interest in the Locks and Canal Company of Lowell which controlled the power resources of the town. The treasurer of the firm was located in Boston. The economic activity of this particular firm therefore generated income for Waltham, Lowell and Boston and formed an important structural linkage between Boston and the two hinterland towns.

Gibb explores the nature of this linkage in some detail in his discussion of the Saco (Maine) Manufacturing Company. He notes that the "traditional location of the treasurers office in Boston arose from the necessity, in this era of slow communications, for close physical proximity to the financial district. This location was dictated by the fact that most of the stockholders and all the directors were Boston men."[54] Gibb describes the functions of the treasurer as a financial officer responsible for corporate finance. He also notes that the treasurer assumed functions traditionally left to independent agents in less integrated operations such as purchase of supplies.

The relationship between the Boston office and the hinterland factory were not always smooth. Instructions from the directors and treasurer "were frequently slow in arriving and often were ambiguous and inadequate to meet the local conditions."[55] Treasurers often complained that superintendents' accounts arrived late and not in time for directors' meetings. Even with improved railroad transportation there was a "psychological cleavage" between the two places. Gibb suggests that "distance tended to lend awe, if not enchantment to the Boston office and the well groomed men associated with it."[56]

Despite any mutual suspicions of Boston financiers and hinterland superintendents of manufacturing operations, diverse locations of various activities within one firm was common practice in the large textile companies. Superior power resources in the hinterland and superior financial resources in Boston formed the basis for these location decisions. The Lawrence Manufacturing Company kept its treasurer in Boston where the official books of the company were kept though duplicate information was kept in Lowell at the mills.[57] The Boston Manufacturing Company and the Merrimack Manufacturing Company also kept their treasurers or "agents" in Boston. The Newmarket (New Hampshire) Manufacturing Company was an investment of men from Salem, Massachusetts, and thus its treasurer was located in Salem.

Though these structural linkages existed between branches of relatively few firms in the region, their importance lies less in their numbers than in the quantity of output of the individual firms. The textile firms comprised the

the leading manufacturing activity of the region from 1830 to 1850. In 1830, for example, the Merrimack Manufacturing Company had an annual output valued at $660,600, the Appleton Company $427,584.[58] By 1850, these same firms produced cotton cloth valued annually at $1,468,478 and $550,000 respectively. The value of cotton cloth produced by twelve mills in Lowell in 1850 amounted to $9,518,000.[59] These firms though few in number infused large amounts of money into the towns in which their factories were located in the form of wages. The cotton textile industry employed over 11,000 individuals in Lowell alone in 1850.[60] In addition, through profits and return of investments, which were substantial, large sums were channeled to Boston which in some cases were, in turn, reinvested in the hinterland. The structural charateristics of the large integrated firms of the region most represented in the shoe and textile industries had an important impact on the course of urbanization in the hinterland by providing a strong and expanding economic base for a number of factory towns dependent on corporate organizations headquartered for the most part in Boston.

In general the entire service sector, both independent and structured, was the export sector of the central places, particularly Boston. Services rendered brought in payments from throughout the region, which, injected into the local economy, gave rise to demand for goods which led to Boston becoming a market for goods as well as an entrepôt. Shrewd C.W. Morgan of New Bedford wrote that good boiler iron would always sell in Boston and good nails would sell regularly.[61] This could refer to sale for export or for local demand. In any case, the volume of merchants and service activity in Boston did generate considerable demand for goods leading to the further development of the tertiary sector (principally retail and light manufacturing) to serve the needs and demands of a considerable urban population and one of considerable wealth and disposable income (see chapter II for number of shops).

Though Boston was certainly the service center of the region, it is important to note that the Boston economy was very diversified and had a considerable manufacturing sector. The McLane report lists ten blank book manufacturers, twelve printing and publishing houses, two chemical factories, and 100 tailors. The 1850 census lists twenty-five musical instrument makers, eight breweries, two chemical factories, nine jewelers, five gilders, etc., all highly specialized industries. In Boston, for example, there were located the only blank book manufacturers in the region; these existed surely because of a great local demand from the service sector, but also supplied the hinterland demand as well. Nearly all the records of firms consulted for this study were kept on Boston-made blank books.[62]

As certain cities, including Boston, Salem, Lowell, Fitchburg, became increasingly centers of finance and transport in the region, these cities exerted a comparative agglomerative effect through competitive advantage as service centers with access to all forms of transport. The cities became the center for discussion of business and for large transactions. In Boston, for example, men like C.W. Morgan and Nathaniel Stevens frequently remarked that their trips to Boston were for discussions and transactions of a more serious nature. Such trips generated further demand for tertiary services, such as hotels and other meeting places, again bringing income into the Boston economy.[63]

Ultimately, though, dollars would not have flowed into the urban economies of these early nineteenth century service centers had income not first been generated by value added in the manufacturing sector (or agricultural sector) of the hinterland or of the manufacturing sector in the principal cities themselves. The service sector by definition needed activity to serve and a great percentage of that activity was located in the various cities and towns of the hinterland. Hinterland incomes were gathered through value added in the manufacturing process or agricultural production. It was on the dollars generated by those sectors that the growth and development of the region ultimately rested. The manufacturers were manufacturing and the farmers were growing those items which constituted the export sector of the towns in which the manufacturing and farming was located. In the process of manufacturing goods for local, regional demand and for export from the region, raw materials were brought in, creating the patterns of flow of goods into, out of and within the region and, in the process, through an urban hierarchy dominated by service nodes.

The service sector was really subservient to or dependent on the manufacturing sector only in the sense that their commissions or salaries for services rendered depended on the existence of a productive sector. As much as the merchants responded to demand for such services, they also were able to generate demand for goods produced through their connections and their advantage in being centrally located. The independent agents and corporate officers of the early nineteenth century were an important linkage between the central city and the towns of the hinterland. They coordinated, speculated, transported, all within the fluctuations and risks of a free market economy. The growth of the region and especially the urban dimension of that growth illustrated the success of this service sector in the aggregate. Thus the pattern which emerges within the region in the early nineteenth century was one of growing interdependence of the city and town economies. Even though Boston, Salem, Lowell and New Bedford dominated in terms of population growth, the relationship and interdependence of these cities with the 205 other towns of the region was intricate, dynamic and very real.

The services which constituted the marketing linkages in the region, whether informal or structural, were particularly important to the process of urbanization in the hinterland. These intermediaries served to link producer to appropriate markets and thus were essential institutional elements in the infrastructure of the system of cities in the region. Since many location decisions were based on the need for access to resources, whether natural, power, or labor, used in the manufacturing of goods, entrepreneurs of the region depended on various intermediaries to service the transfer of goods from place of production to place of final sale. The existence of these linkages permitted viable investments in relatively obscure locations in the region and ultimately provided the channels for the movement of goods which could sustain growing populations in remote areas. In turn, the general growth of manufacturing output in the hinterland provided the economic base for an expansion of the service sector located in Boston, which was an important factor in increasing the level of urbanization in the core city of the region.

CONCLUSION

The pattern of urban industrial growth in the Boston region 1810 to 1850 was an interdependent one involving each of the 219 cities and towns which comprised the region. The process of urbanization in the various cities and towns depended on an expansion of specialized economic activity in each locale. New technology, regional and extraregional demand, and a capacity to produce goods at competitive costs encouraged new industry which led to the expansion of the manufacturing sector. The specific location in the region of each activity was based on decisions that reflected the need for access at competitive cost to specific resources. The total of these decisions resulted in a spread of specialized economic activity throughout the region. The dynamics of urban and industrial growth in each town as Pred suggests depended on the expansion of the specific specialized activities within each individual town. This expansion did not, however, occur in isolation but rather was dependent on and interrelated with the expansion of specialized activities (manufacturing, agriculture or services) in other cities or towns. As activity became increasingly specialized, there was an increasing need to exchange goods and to facilitate this exchange of goods. The patterns of this exchange over space indicated the degree and direction of interdependence of the specific cities and towns, thus providing a sense of the economic region.

The spread of economic activity in the region and the resulting interdependence of particular specialized activities through the region required specific linkage which would assure the efficient movement or flow of needed supplies through the region and facilitate the sale of final products in competitive markets. The transport, credit and market linkages as discussed in the previous chapters were the principal mechanisms through which these necessary flows occurred. These mechanisms together evolved into a necessary infrastructure within the region which permitted the spread of specialized economic activity over space as well as time. The patterns which emerged in the transport, credit and market linkages not only underscored the interdependence of variables in the process of economic growth and development in the local economies of the region but also defined certain nodes as places particularly central and thus particularly service oriented which monitored and facilitated regional flows. These linkages thus formed the basic elements of an infrastructure of an evolving system of cities hierarchially arranged within the region.

Clearly within this system Boston as the principal service center was the focal point of the region. As the primary transport node, the primary financial center and the primary marketing center, its services were vital to the economic health of all the towns of the region. However, by 1850 Worcester, Fitchburg, Salem, New Bedford and Lowell had emerged as essentially intermediate service centers or nodes in the system. As intermediate transfer centers in the transport network, these lower level central places were particularly important. As their own manufacturing base increased as well as the manufacturing base of those towns nearby, these intermediate nodes became increasingly financial and service centers as well. But throughout the period the system was based on the existence of many small specialized productive towns in the region.

The dynamics of growth of the manufacturing and/or service sectors in each of the cities and towns of the region depended on and fed each other creating an interdependent and dynamic spiral of urban and industrial growth through the region. Of course, the cities and towns of the region shared and contributed to the process in varying amounts. As the manufacturing activities increased in volume, services multiplied and specialized, resulting in the development of these intermediate service areas to facilitate the transport of goods, the financing of new activities, and the marketing of manufactured goods.

Fundamental to understanding the process of urbanization in the Boston region is an understanding of the development of the economic base of the various cities and towns and the interdependent process by which this base was able to expand. An expanding economic base permitted increased levels of population. When this expansion was in the specialized manufacturing or service sector which required small amounts of space relative to agriculture, conditions emerged in many of the cities and towns of the region which permitted a considerable population to occupy a small amount of space—a precondition for an urban environment. Essential of course to the economy of these compact and specialized urban areas were the links to other urban areas which generated demand for specialized products. These links were the basis of the infrastructure which tied together a regional system of cities and channelled sources of supply and goods to markets within and beyond the region.

The theoretical concepts and historical process outlined in my study attempt to address fundamental questions which look to the root causes of urbanization. These questions look at a given space and examine the process through which populated differentiated space in the Boston region moved from one of a few scattered densely populated settlements to a space of a considerably larger number of larger such settlements during the early nineteenth century. The process through which these urbanized populations are sustained is clearly an economic one and one which can be understood only on a regional scale.

As a space so urbanizes, other significant questions arise which can be directed both to the region as a whole and the individual location. What is the response of the population to this economic change and the differentiation of regional space? What is the rate of participation in decisions affecting the regional economy? What are the dislocations caused by the process? How does this affect the labor force, family structure, or general demographic changes? How does this ultimately lead to changing values as space moves from primarily rural to primarily urban or in a later period from urban to suburban? What is the degree of awareness of this interdependent process? To what extent, if at all, is this increased interdependence reflected in changing federal, state, and local policy? These are questions which single studies of urban places have not answered altogether adequately, and can really only be understood by looking beyond a single urban place.

This story of urbanization in the Boston region 1810 to 1850 has emphasized the evolution of an interrelated and interdependent economic process among a significant number of cities and towns which comprised a working and cohesive economic region. To understand the process of urbanization in one particular city it is essential to understand the relationship of that city to others nearby. This is more complex than a city-hinterland perspective. It suggests that cities are not isolated self-contained economic units but rather are directly dependent on economic activities in other cities and towns. The direction and nature of these relationships constitute a systematic array of urban and not so urban places. The case of Boston in the early nineteenth century suggests a complex system of cities, hierarchically arranged to facilitate the interaction of the economic activities of the over two hundred cities and towns of the region and its sizable and increasingly urbanized population.

Appendix I

Population of Towns in the Region Over 2,000 Ranked in Order of Population Size for 1810, 1830, and 1850

Source: Census (U.S.) for 1810, 1830, 1850

Rank	1810 Town	Pop.	1830 Town	Pop.	1850 Town	Pop.
1	Boston	33,250	Boston	61,392	Boston	136,881
2	Salem	12,613	Salem	13,895	Lowell	33,383
3	Newburyport	7,634	Charlestown	8,783	Salem	20,264
4	Portsmouth	6,934	Portsmouth	8,025	Roxbury	18,364
5	Gloucester	5,943	New Bedford	7,592	Charlestown	17,216
6	Marblehead	5,900	Gloucester	7,510	Worcester	17,043
7	New Bedford	5,651	Lowell	6,474	New Bedford	16,443
8	Newbury	5,176	Newburyport	6,375	Cambridge	15,215
9	Bridgewater	5,157	Lynn	6,138	Lynn	14,257
10	Charlestown	4,959	Cambridge	6,072	Fall River	11,524
11	Rehoboth	4,866	Taunton	6,042	Taunton	10,441
12	Beverly	4,608	Roxbury	5,247	Portsmouth	9,738
13	Middleborough	4,400	Marblehead	5,149	Newburyport	9,572
14	Plymouth	4,228	Middleborough	5,008	Lawrence	8,282
15	Lynn	4,087	Plymouth	4,758	Danvers	8,109
16	Taunton	3,907	Andover	4,530	Dorchester	7,969
17	Roxbury	3,669	Danvers	4,228	Gloucester	7,786
18	Barnstable	3,646	Worcester	4,173	Andover	6,945
19	Ipswich	3,569	Fall River	4,158	Chelsea	6,701
20	Dartmouth	3,219	Dorchester	4,094	Marblehead	6,167
21	Andover	3,164	Beverly	4,073	Plymouth	6,024
22	Danvers	3,127	Barnstable	3,974	Haverhill	5,877

Appendix I (continued)

Rank	1810 Town	Pop.	1830 Town	Pop.	1850 Town	Pop.
23	Scituate	2,969	Haverhill	3,896	Beverly	5,376
24	Rochester	2,954	Dartmouth	3,816	Weymouth	5,369
25	Dorchester	2,930	Newbury	3,603	Middleborough	5,336
26	Londonderry	2,766	Rochester	3,556	Abington	5,269
27	Attleboro	2,716	Scituate	3,468	Newton	5,258
28	Haverhill	2,682	Hingham	3,387	Fitchburg	5,120
29	Sutton	2,660	Sandwich	3,361	Quincy	5,017
30	Westport	2,585	Attleboro	3,215	Barnstable	4,901
31	Worcester	2,577	Dedham	3,177	Milford	4,819
32	Wrentham	2,478	Mendon	3,152	Randolph	4,741
33	Hingham	2,382	Fairhaven	3,034	Waltham	4,464
34	Sandwich	2,382	Ipswich	2,949	Dedham	4,447
35	Cambridge	2,323	Weymouth	2,837	Newbury	4,426
36	Falmouth	2,237	Westport	2,779	Blackstone	4,391
37	Reading	2,228	Exeter	2,753	Sandwich	4,368
38	Duxbury	2,201	Duxbury	2,716	Fairhaven	4,304
39	Charlton	2,180	Wrentham	2,698	Framingham	4,252
40	Dedham	2,172	Falmouth	2,548	Attleboro	4,200
41	Yarmouth	2,134	Salisbury	2,519	Hingham	3,980
42	Pembroke	2,051	Rehoboth	2,459	Woburn	3,956
43	Salisbury	2,047	Harwich	2,453	N. Bridgewater	3,939
44	Chester	2,030	Amesbury	2,445	Grafton	3,904
45			Abington	2,423	Dartmouth	3,868
46			Newton	2,376	Rochester	3,808
47			Dennis	2,317	Medford	3,749
48			Framingham	2,313	Somerville	3,540
49			Yarmouth	2,251	Malden	3,520

Appendix I (continued)

Rank	Town	Pop.	Town	Pop.	Town	Pop.
		1810		1830		1850
50			Quincy	2,201	Dracut	3,503
51			Randolph	2,200	Stoughton	3,494
52			Sutton	2,186	Ipswich	3,349
53			Derry	2,176	Exeter	3,329
54			Charlton	2,173	Rockport	3,274
55			Fitchburg	2,169	Harwich	3,258
56			Dudley	2,155	Dennis	3,257
57			Seekonk	2,133	Wareham	3,186
58			Chatham	2,130	Provincetown	3,157
59			Deerfield	2,090	Amesbury	3,143
60			Uxbridge	2,086	Leominster	3,121
61			Marlborough	2,077	Clinton	3,113
62			Wellfleet	2,046	Reading	3,108
63			Oxford	2,034	Salisbury	3,100
64			Chester	2,028	Millbury	3,081
65			Lancaster	2,014	Wrentham	3,037
66			Malden	2,010	Braintree	2,969
67			New Market	2,008	Marlborough	2,941
68			Methuen	2,006	Watertown	2,837
69					Hopkington	2,801
70					Westport	2,795
71					Bridgewater	2,790
72					Medway	2,778
73					Natick	2,744
74					Duxbury	2,679
75					Falmouth	2,621

Appendix I (continued)

Rank	1810 Town	Pop.	1830 Town	Pop.	1850 Town	Pop.
76					Canton	2,598
77					Sutton	2,595
78					Yarmouth	2,595
79					E. Bridgewater	2,545
80					Methuen	2,538
81					Brookline	2,516
82					Groton	2,515
83					Uxbridge	2,457
84					Chatham	2,439
85					Holliston	2,428
86					Wellfleet	2,411
87					Wakefield	2,407
88					Oxford	2,380
89					Westborough	2,371
90					Brighton	2,356
91					Easton	2,337
92					Leicester	2,269
93					Concord	2,249
94					Spencer	2,244
95					Seekonk	2,243
96					Milton	2,241
97					Northbridge	2,230
98					Arlington	2,202
99					Scituate	2,149
100					Rehoboth	2,104
101					Chelmsford	2,097

Appendix I (continued)

Rank	1810		1830		1850	
	Town	Pop.	Town	Pop.	Town	Pop.
102					Stoneham	2,085
103					Georgetown	2,052
104					Truro	2,051
105					Upton	2,023
106					Deerfield	2,022
107					Charlton	2,015

Appendix II
Capital of Banks in the Region Ranked by Town for 1810, 1830, and 1850

Source: Abstract of Banks for the Commonwealth of Massachusetts for each of the years 1810, 1830, 1850
Note: (all figures in 000)

Rank	1810 Town	No. of Banks	Tot. Cap.	1830 Town	No. of Banks	Tot. Cap.	1850 Town	No. of Banks	Tot. Cap.
1	Boston	3	$4,600	Boston	17	$11,450	Boston	29	$20,861
2	Salem	2	500	Salem	6	1,450	Salem	7	1,750
3	Newburyport	1	550	New Bedford	2	500	Worcester	5	750
4	Beverly	1	160	Newburyport	2	410	New Bedford	4	1,300
5	New Bedford	1	150	Worcester	2	300	Lowell	4	1,022
6	Worcester	1	150	Roxbury	1	200	Newburyport	3	510
7	Plymouth	1	100	Fall River	1	200	Taunton	3	500
8	Marblehead	1	100	Taunton	1	175	Haverhill	3	430
9	Gloucester	1	100	Haverhill	1	150	Danvers	3	390
10				Cambridge	1	150	Fall River	2	400
11				Lowell	1	150	Fitchburg	2	300
12				Charlestown	1	150	Lynn	2	250
13				Danvers	1	120	Marblehead	2	220
14				Gloucester	1	120	Cambridge	2	200
15				Marblehead	1	120	Dorchester	2	200
16				Andover	1	100	Plymouth	2	200
17				Beverly	1	100	Lawrence	1	300
18				Lynn	1	100	Andover	1	250
19				Leicester	1	100	Gloucester	1	200
20				Mendon	1	100	Charlestown	1	200
21				Millbury	1	100	Framingham	1	200

Appendix II (continued)

Rank	1810 Town	No. of Banks	Tot. Cap.	1830 Town	No. of Banks	Tot. Cap.	1850 Town	No. of Banks	Tot. Cap.
22				Oxford	1	100	Dedham	1	200
23				Uxbridge	1	100	Fairhaven	1	200
24				Dedham	1	100	Yarmouth	1	200
25				Pawtucket	1	100	Newton	1	150
26				Plymouth	1	100	Randolph	1	150
27				Falmouth	1	100	Roxbury	1	150
28				Barnstable	1	100	Wrentham	1	150
29							Beverly	1	125
30							Lancaster	1	125
31							Hingham	1	105
32							Georgetown	1	100
33							Salisbury	1	100
34							Concord	1	100
35							Waltham	1	100
36							Blackstone	1	100
37							Leicester	1	100
38							Milford	1	100
39							Millbury	1	100
40							Oxford	1	100
41							Southbridge	1	100
42							Uxbridge	1	100
43							Canton	1	100
44							Quincy	1	100
45							Weymouth	1	100
46							Attleborough	1	100
47							Wareham	1	100
48							Falmouth	1	100
49							Chelsea	1	61

Appendix III
Classification of Towns in the Region by Number of Firms with an Annual Output Valued Greater than $100,000 for 1833 and 1850

Source for 1833 data: the McLane Report
Source for 1850 data: the Manuscript Returns for the Census (U.S.) of Manufactures for Massachusetts, 1850

A. Classification for 1833

No. of Large Firms	Town	Assigned Category	Items of Materials Produced by the Large Firms
-*	Boston	I	not listed
-*	Salem	I	not listed
6	Lowell	II	Textiles
3	Taunton	II	Iron, Copper, Lead, Calico
3	Mendon	II	Cotton, Satinet
2	Newton	III	Cotton, Paper
2	Dudley	III	Wool
2	Wareham	III	Nails
2	Roxbury	III	Iron, Yarn
1	Salisbury	IV	Wool
1	Cambridge	IV	Soap
1	Charlestown	IV	Distillery
1	Methuen	IV	Cotton
1	Framingham	IV	Wool
1	Medford	IV	Shipbuilding

Appendix III (continued)

1833

No. of Large Firms	Town	Assigned Category	Items of Materials Produced by the Large Firms
1	Watertown	IV	Cotton
1	Waltham	IV	Cotton
1	Exeter	IV	Cotton
1	Newmarket	IV	Cotton
1	Uxbridge	IV	Cotton
1	Grafton	IV	Wool
1	Millbury	IV	Wool
1	Plymouth	IV	Nails
1	Dedham	IV	Wool

B. Classification for 1850

No. of Large Firms	Town	Assigned Category	Items of Materials Produced by the Large Firms
65	Boston	I	Lead, Copper, Piano, Machines, Distillery, Clothing, Sugar, Oil, Lard, Silver, Glass, Gas, Pickle, Flour, Stove, Farm tools.
21	New Bedford	II	Whale fishing, Oil, Cotton, Cordage.
15	Lowell	II	Textiles, Machinery, Lumber.
10	Roxbury	II	Rope, Lead, Leather, Carpet, Ribbons, Wool.
9	Worcester	II	Castings, Wire, Machinery, Shoe, Cars (rail).
7	Fall River	II	Cotton textile, Machinery, Copper, Iron.

Appendix III (continued)

1850

No. of Large Firms	Town	Assigned Category	Items of Materials Produced by the Large Firms
6	Andover	II	Textiles
6	Lynn	II	Shoes, Leather
5	Medford	II	Shipbuilding
5	Salem	II	Guns, Cotton, Machinery, Oil, Leather
4	Cambridge	III	Soap, Bacon, Lead, Tin, Cars (rail)
4	Haverhill	III	Shoes
4	Newburyport	III	Textiles
4	Portsmouth	III	Shipbuilding, Hosiery, Cotton
4	Taunton	III	Tacks, Machinery, Wool
4	Wareham	III	Nails
3	Abington	III	Shoes
3	Blackstone	III	Wool
3	Canton	III	Machine, Cotton, Copper
3	Clinton	III	Textiles
3	Lawrence	III	Textiles, Machinery
3	Newton	III	Paper, Machine, Nails
3	Plymouth	III	Cordage, Wood/Cotton
3	Waltham	III	Textiles, Chemical
2	Charlestown	IV	Furniture, Leadpipe
2	Danvers	IV	Shoes
2	Dracut	IV	Cotton/Wool textiles
2	E. Bridgewater	IV	Nails, Shoes
2	Fitchburg	IV	Rail Car, Cotton
2	Foxborough	IV	Bonnets

Appendix III (continued)

1850

No. of Large Firms	Town	Assigned Category	Items of Materials Produced by the Large Firms
2	Hopkington	IV	Shoes
2	Leicester	IV	Wood products
2	Marblehead	IV	Cordage, Shoes
2	Millford	IV	Shoes
2	Northbridge	IV	Cotton, Machinery
2	Raynham	IV	Shoes, Shovel & Nail
2	Stoughton	IV	Shoes
2	Weymouth	IV	Shoes, Nails
1	Amesbury	IV	Flannel
1	Dorchester	IV	Cotton
1	Billerica	IV	Wood, Chemical
1	Bridgewater	IV	Iron
1	Chelmsford	IV	Cotton
1	Concord	IV	Rails
1	Douglas	IV	Axes & tools
1	Easton	IV	Shovels
1	Exeter	IV	Cotton
1	Framingham	IV	Wool
1	Grafton	IV	Shoes
1	Medway	IV	Cotton
1	Mendon	IV	Shoes
1	Methuen	IV	Bedboards
1	Milton	IV	Wool

Appendix III (continued)

1850

No. of Large Firms	Town	Assigned Category	Items of Materials Produced by the Large Firms
1	Natick	IV	Shoes
1	Newmarket	IV	Cotton
1	Norton	IV	Copper
1	Pawtucket	IV	Textile
1	Rockport	IV	Cotton
1	Salisbury	IV	Wool
1	Sandwich	IV	Glass
1	Saugus	IV	Flannel
1	Somerset	IV	Shipbuilding
1	Sommerville	IV	Spike-Nail
1	Southborough	IV	Cotton
1	Stow	IV	Wool
1	Sudbury	IV	Carpet
1	Upton	IV	Bonnets
1	Wakefield	IV	Shoes
1	Webster	IV	Wool
1	West Cambridge	IV	Spice
1	Winchester	IV	Tanner

* The McLane Report only notes considerable industry for Boston and Salem. No individual firms are listed for the two major ports. No major firms are listed for New Bedford, Newburyport, Marblehead, or Portsmouth.

Appendix IV
Annual Volume of Textile Production in the Region Ranked by Town for 1833 and 1850

Source for 1833: The McLane Report
Source for 1850: The Manuscript Returns for the Census (U.S.) of Manufactures for Massachusetts, 1850

Total Textile Production in the Region for 1833: $11,437,316.
Total Textile Production in the Region for 1850: $32,101,132.

Rank	1833			1850		
	% of Total	Town	Value of Production	% of Total	Town	Value of Production
1	18.6	Lowell	$2,132,589	31.0	Lowell	$9,952,045
2	7.9	Fall River	904,880	8.2	Fall River	2,656,095
3	5.7	Mendon	661,180	6.4	Clinton	2,056,092
4	4.2	Dedham	483,800	5.4	Pawtucket	1,729,224
5	3.2	Millbury	374,825	4.7	Lawrence	1,494,210
6	3.1	Uxbridge	353,940	4.1	Blackstone	1,329,680
7	2.4	Leicester	280,000	3.4	Andover	1,075,450
8	2.4	Taunton	278,550	2.6	Newburyport	835,083
9	2.3	Andover	267,940	1.9	Framingham	600,000
10	2.3	Dudley	259,687	1.7	Salisbury	550,000
11	2.2	Newmarket	255,496	1.4	Waltham	440,575
12	2.2	Pawtucket	252,991	1.3	Salem	425,000
13	1.9	Waltham	218,500	1.2	Taunton	392,378
14	1.9	Webster	216,557	1.1	Worcester	370,632
15	1.9	Grafton	216,360	1.1	Newmarket	352,000
16	1.8	Attleborough	212,011	1.0	Webster	336,440
17	1.7	Watertown	203,400	1.0	Portsmouth	335,000
18	1.7	Oxford	190,200	.9	Roxbury	318,000
19	1.4	Fitchburg	162,200	.9	Medway	295,725

Appendix IV (continued)

Rank	1833			1850		
	% of Total	Town	Value of Production	Town	% of Total	Value of Production
20	1.4	Walpole	$161,600	New Bedford	.9	$288,057
21	1.4	Methuen	160,600	Amesbury	.8	260,000
22	1.4	Medway	158,000	Dracut	.8	250,000
23	1.3	Salisbury	150,000	Danvers	.8	248,750
24	1.3	Northbridge	144,000	Grafton	.8	241,730
25	1.2	Worcester	137,565	Northbridge	.7	225,000
26		Sutton	136,900	Rockport		216,980
27		Shirley	136,500	Oxford		215,285
28		Exeter	135,000	Saugus		207,500
29		W. Boylston	126,836	Chelmsford		206,750
30		Dorchester	120,000	Uxbridge		189,000
31		Haverhill	113,800	Attleborough		186,017
32		Newton	100,000	Canton		182,800
33		Holden	95,875	Plymouth		180,000
34		Spencer	90,500	Sudbury		171,090
35		Upton	84,500	Millbury		165,700
36		Franklin	73,868	Dorchester		150,000
37		Seekonk	73,766	Stow		150,000
38		Raynam & Mansfield	67,960			
39		Douglas	65,000	West Boylston		131,060
40		Dighton	63,652	Dudley		123,900
41		Framingham	63,100	Fitchburg		122,210
42		Wrentham	61,412	Southborough		120,000
43		Saugus	60,000	Milton		118,250
44		Canton	60,000	Sutton		116,700
45		Milford	59,000	Exeter		115,000
				Holden		101,200

Appendix IV (continued)

Rank	1833		1850	
	Town	Value of Production	Town	Value of Production
46	Hopkington	$58,880	Wrentham	$95,140
47	Bellingham	55,650	Leicester	91,800
48	Plymouth	51,250	Newton	85,000
49	Marlborough	50,000	Norton	74,810
50	Middleborough	42,710	Douglas	74,000
51	Danvers	42,000	Fairhaven	73,500
52	Norton	41,160	Auburn	70,000
53	Ipswich	40,000	Hamilton	70,000
54	Rehoboth	36,300	Dedham	69,139
55	Holliston	36,009	Watertown	67,600
56	Halifax	36,000	Ipswich	67,400
57	Needham	35,800	Seekonk	64,684
58	Plympton	35,480	Billerica	63,000
59	Stow	35,000	Spencer	58,300
60	Easton	34,125	Dighton	56,000
61	Stoughton	34,000	Ashburnham	50,308
62	Lancaster	29,200	Haverhill	50,000
63	Sharon	27,414	Rehoboth	49,250
64	Fairhaven	26,640	W. Cambridge	42,500
65	Billerica	26,000	Boylston	40,000
66	Braintree	21,600	Braintree	39,000
67	Newburyport	21,500	Franklin	36,350
68	Northborough	20,400	Stoughton	33,500
69	Foxborough	18,050	Shirley	32,500
70	Concord	17,910	Mansfield	31,497
71	Westminster	16,000	Walpole	30,025
72	Hanson	16,000	Lancaster	30,000

Appendix IV (continued)

Rank	1833 Town	Value of Production	1850 Town	Value of Production
73	Duxbury	$15,000	Holliston	$27,720
74	Rutland	15,000	Sharon	26,200
75	Kingston	15,000	Falmouth	22,900
76	Marshfield	14,985	Ashland	22,500
77	Pembroke	14,120	Bellingham	21,250
78	E. Bridgewater	11,200	Milford	20,300
79	Princeton	10,000	Lynfield	20,240
80	Falmouth	8,500	Middleborough	18,900
81	Harvard	7,350	Bridgewater	18,500
82	Sandwich	4,000	Epping	18,200
83	Northwood	3,743	Rutland	15,000
84	Londonderry	3,500	Easton	13,680
85	Poplin	600	Kingston	12,000
86	Brentwood	550	Foxborough	11,500
87	Sandown	340	Duxbury	11,340
88			Plympton	10,647
89			Hampton Falls	9,500
90			Brookline	9,100
91			Charlestown	7,200
92			Chelsea	7,200
93			Woburn	3,744
94			Greenland	1,600

Appendix V

Annual Volume of Machinery Production in the Region Ranked by Town for 1833 and 1850

Source for 1833: The McLane Report
Source for 1850: The Manuscript Returns for the Census (U.S.) of Manufactures for Massachusetts, 1850

Total Machinery Production in the Region for 1833: $1,567,924.
Total Machinery Production in the Region for 1850: $4,441,130.

		1833			1850	
Rank	% of Total	Town	Value of Production	Town	Value of Production	% of Total
1	12.4	Boston	$195,000	Boston	$1,416,500	31.8
2	12.2	Worcester	192,155	Lowell	569,000	12.8
3	7.0	Leicester	111,282	Taunton	460,000	10.3
4	4.2	Taunton	66,000	Worcester	427,500	9.6
5	3.8	Andover	60,000	Lawrence	250,000	5.6
6	3.6	Pawtucket	57,540	Canton	201,700	4.5
7	2.9	Fall River	46,000	Northbridge	200,000	4.5
8	2.8	Exeter	45,000	Salem	140,000	3.1
9	2.3	Millbury	36,180	Fall River	120,759	2.7
10	1.5	Foxborough	24,600	Newton	103,472	2.3
11		W. Boylston	23,310	Leicester	70,000	1.5
12		Walpole	20,000	Walpole	65,350	1.4
13		Bridgewater	16,000	E. Bridgewater	59,000	1.3
14		Attleborough	12,250	Fitchburg	55,400	1.2
15		Dedham	12,000	Chelmsford	45,000	1.0
16		Holden	12,000	Charlestown	35,000	
17		Methuen	8,000	Newburyport	33,900	

Appendix V (continued)

Rank	1833			1850	
	Town	Value of Production		Town	Value of Production
18	Wrentham	$8,000		Mansfield	$30,000
19	Bellingham	7,958		Dedham	21,600
20	Oxford	6,600		S. Newmarket	20,000
21	Canton	6,000		Waltham	20,000
22	Sharon	5,000		Billerica	19,520
23	Leominster	4,500		Newmarket	15,000
24	Northborough	4,000		Weston	12,000
25	Lancaster	2,500		Winchester	10,000
26	Harvard	1,500		Andover	8,560
27	Spencer	1,372		Lancaster	6,500
28	Fitchburg	1,000		Pawtucket	4,100
29	Deerfield	500		N. Bedford	3,800
30				Grafton	3,500
31				Bridgewater	3,219
32				Framingham	2,800
33				Brentwood	2,000
34				Medway	1,600
35				Georgetown	1,300
36				W. Newbury	1,100
37				Leominster	1,000
38				Townsend	950

Appendix VI
Annual Volume of Boot and Shoe Production in the Region Ranked by Town for 1833 and 1850

Source for 1833: The McLane Report
Source for 1850: The Manuscript Returns for the Census (U.S.) of Manufactures for Massachusetts, 1850

Total Boot and Shoe Production in the Region for 1833: $6,701,749.
Total Boot and Shoe Production in the Region for 1850: $24,302,509.

Rank	1833			1850		
	% of Total	Town	Value of Production	% of Total	Town	Value of Production
1	12.1	Lynn	$811,799	16.6	Lynn	$4,050,500
2	5.6	Haverhill	372,986	6.7	Haverhill	1,651,075
3	5.2	Danvers	351,050	6.7	Abington	1,638,423
4	4.6	Randolph	308,000	4.6	Randolph	1,119,529
5	3.6	Abington	243,750	4.0	Weymouth	977,350
6	3.4	So. Reading	225,000	4.0	Worcester	976,250
7	3.1	Malden	210,000	3.5	Danvers	846,875
8	3.1	Salem	210,000	3.5	Natick	838,590
9	3.0	Bradford	203,250	3.3	Stoughton	805,700
10	3.0	Boston	200,000	3.3	Marblehead	753,800
11	2.9	Woburn	195,894	3.1	Millford	600,000
12	2.8	Stoughton	190,000	2.4	Hopkington	547,200
13	2.4	Weymouth	162,900	2.3	Grafton	415,178
14	2.4	Holliston	162,000	1.7	Stoneham	402,451
15	2.1	Grafton	141,666	1.7	Braintree	387,830
16	2.1	E. Bridgewater	140,000	1.6	N. Bridgewater	333,435
17	2.0	Stoneham	135,000	1.4	Georgetown	326,878
18	1.9	Reading	124,400	1.3	Boston	294,700
				1.2		

Appendix VI (continued)

Rank	1833 % of Total	Town	Value of Production	1850 % of Total	Town	Value of Production
19	1.8	N. Bridgewater	$118,000	1.1	E. Bridgewater	$278,140
20	1.7	Methuen	113,400	1.0	South Reading	252,900
21	1.4	Quincy	92,653	1.0	Oxford	249,647
22	1.3	Rowley	89,675	.9	Quincy	226,647
23	1.2	Milford	85,000	.9	Reading	224,420
24	1.1	Upton	78,300	.9	Woburn	212,800
25	1.1	Braintree	75,000	.8	Spencer	200,000
26		Exeter	70,600		Plymouth	172,500
27		Shrewsbury	67,000		Medway	171,950
28		Westborough	65,000		Middleborough	170,925
29		Newburyport	60,000		Holliston	170,175
30		Wrentham	60,000		Ashland	168,475
31		Weston	58,613		Mendon	165,650
32		Southborough	57,450		Groveland	163,824
33		Hopkington	55,750		Raynam	151,750
34		Marblehead	53,400		Methuen	135,680
35		Saugus	49,496		Lowell	133,300
36		Newbury	40,000		Salem	125,550
37		Hingham	38,151		Marlborough	124,730
38		W. Newbury	37,500		Saugus	123,000
39		Sharon	36,000		Uxbridge	115,504
40		Millbury	34,400		Northwood	112,591
41		Leicester	33,584		Shewsbury	111,220
42		Bedford	33,300		W. Newbury	106,200
43		Charlestown	32,000		Chelsea	102,725
44		Andover	30,400		Millbury	98,200

Appendix VI (continued)

Rank	1833		1850	
	Town	Value of Production	Town	Value of Production
45	Northborough	$26,500	Rowley	$92,950
46	Hampstead	25,416	Hingham	92,365
47	Easton	25,200	Melrose	89,980
48	W. Cambridge	25,000	Beverly	86,800
49	Spencer	23,650	Topsfield	81,800
50	Paxton	22,611	Upton	80,100
51	Kingston	22,325	Newburyport	78,109
52	Northbridge	21,800	Bellingham	76,300
53	Scituate	20,000	Webster	75,000
54	Ipswich	19,575	Sutton	71,200
55	Fall River	18,590	Dudley	71,000
56	Portsmouth	18,400	New Castle	61,400
57	Newtown	18,000	Wrentham	58,714
58	Salem (N.H.)	16,000	Candia	58,000
59	Taunton	15,800	Wayland	57,600
60	Cambridge	15,650	Salem (N.H.)	57,052
61	Oxford	15,000	Middleton	49,788
62	Newmarket	14,618	Hanover	48,600
63	Plaistow	14,500	Ipswich	48,375
64	Lynnfield	13,810	Gloucester	48,000
65	Waltham	13,100	Sharon	47,500
66	Uxbridge	13,000	Lynnfield	44,500
67	E. Cambridge	12,400	Wenham	43,906
68	Lexington	11,450	Exeter	42,000
69	Burlington	10,900	Derry	39,908
70	Framingham	10,000	Kingston	39,360

Appendix VI (continued)

Rank	1833 Town	1833 Value of Production	1850 Town	1850 Value of Production
71	Topsfield	$9,050	Londonderry	$38,640
72	Auburn	9,000	Berlin	35,620
73	Brentwood	9,000	Epping	33,335
74	Needham	9,000	N. Bedford	32,920
75	Sandwich	9,000	Charlton	31,000
76	Wenham	9,000	W. Bridgewater	30,875
77	Stratham	8,850	Needham	30,000
78	Bolton	8,800	Raymond	29,369
79	Lunnenburg	8,000	Framingham	29,250
80	Harvard	7,850	Acton	29,000
81	Lincoln	7,300	Deerfield	28,146
82	Holden	7,300	Northbridge	28,000
83	Medford	7,050	Pepperell	26,000
84	Worcester	7,000	Bradford	24,625
85	Hubbardston	5,500	Sherberne	24,500
86	Hanson	5,250	Portsmouth	23,900
87	Derry	5,120	Sandown	23,440
88	Billerica	5,100	Easton	23,000
89	Atkinson	5,000	Amesbury	22,937
90	Fitchburg	5,000	Walpole	22,548
91	Leominster	5,000	Bedford	22,000
92	Kensington	4,700	Canton	20,000
93	Sudbury	4,637	Roxbury	19,900
94	Falmouth	4,600	Fitchburg	19,057
95	Barnstable	4,500	Hanson	18,000
96	Deerfield	4,500	Groton	17,500

Appendix VI (continued)

| | 1833 | | 1850 | |
Rank	Town	Value of Production	Town	Value of Production
97	Provincetown	$4,500	Atkinson	$17,140
98	Brewster	4,000	W. Cambridge	17,000
99	Princeton	4,000	Danville	15,370
100	Salisbury	4,000	Brentwood	13,387
101	E. Kingston	3,937	Lawrence	13,362
102	Sterling	3,900	Kensington	13,200
103	Harwick	3,800	Boxford	11,375
104	Poplin	3,673	Weston	11,300
105	Natick	3,600	Concord	10,900
106	Berlin	3,500	Newton (N.H.)	10,720
107	Bellingham	3,500	Hamilton	10,712
108	Lancaster	3,500	Fall River	9,900
109	Yarmouth	3,450	Poplin	9,790
110	Londonderry	3,200	Duxbury	9,300
111	Amesbury	3,000	Nottingham	9,200
112	Charlton	3,000	Burlington	8,800
113	Hampton	3,000	Eastham	7,905
114	Orleans	2,900	Newmarket	7,900
115	Seabrook	2,880	Douglas	7,780
116	Dennis	2,760	So. Hampton	7,700
117	Rye	2,700	Swanzey	7,656
118	Epping	2,550	Andover	7,469
119	Hampton Falls	2,500	Marshfield	7,400
120	Newton	2,415	Leominster	6,875
121	Gardner	2,400	Charlestown	6,650
122	Chatham	2,150	Winchester	6,588
123	W. Boylston	2,000	Brewster	6,500

Appendix VI (continued)

Rank	1833 Town	Value of Production	1850 Town	Value of Production
124	E. Sudbury	$1,945	Harvard	$6,500
125	Boxford	1,800	Provincetown	6,100
126	Pawtucket	1,800	Dedham	5,757
127	Candia	1,700	Mansfield	5,500
128	Eastham	1,650	Newbury	5,500
129	N. Hampton	1,500	W. Boylston	5,000
130	Wellfleet	1,460	Rockport	4,100
131	Windham	1,350	Bellerica	3,650
132	Chester	1,200	Sudbury	3,500
133	Truro	1,150	Fairhaven	3,000
134	Hawke	1,120	Orleans	2,750
135	Greenland	1,100	Leicester	2,500
136	Somerset	1,000	Wellfleet	2,500
137	Sandown	860	Westminster	2,040
138	Freetown	800	Littleton	2,000
139	Newington	640	Watertown	1,630
140	Brookline	600	Brookline	1,500
141	New Castle	600	Clinton	1,500
142			Hampton Falls	1,500
143			Westford	1,500
144			Blackstone	1,350
145			Ashburnham	1,200
146			So. Newmarket	1,200
147			Plaistow	1,125
148			Harwich	1,000
149			Lancaster	1,000
150			N. Chelsea	875
151			Carlisle	800
152			Wilmington	682
153			Sommerset	662
154			Gardner	600

Appendix VII

Annual Volume of Tanned Leather Production in the Region Ranked by Town for 1833 and 1850

Source for 1833: The McLane Report
Source for 1850: The Manuscript Returns for the Census (U.S.) of Manufactures for Massachusetts, 1850.

Total Tanned Leather Production in the Region for 1833: $2,203,499.
Total Tanned Leather Production in the Region for 1850: $6,082,071.

Rank	1833			1850		
	% of Total	Town	Value of Production	% of Total	Town	Value of Production
1	16.5	Danvers	$365,600	26.9	Salem	$1,636,950
2	10.5	Roxbury	232,000	15.9	Danvers	967,133
3	8.4	Charlestown	186,000	9.7	Lynn	587,500
4	4.9	Haverhill	108,850	9.1	Roxbury	554,500
5	4.8	Dorchester	105,000	6.7	Boston	405,400
6	4.7	Lynn	103,188	4.7	Woburn	284,700
7	3.6	Salem	80,000	3.1	Chelsea	191,912
8	3.2	Grafton	70,000	2.9	Winchester	177,000
9	2.7	Woburn	59,750	2.7	Milton	166,400
10	2.5	Watertown	56,000	2.5	Charlestown	152,000
11	2.2	Dedham	48,414	2.3	Haverhill	138,000
12	1.8	Salisbury	40,000	1.6	Quincy	96,000
13	1.6	Weymouth	36,000	1.2	Stoneham	73,258
14	1.6	Portsmouth	35,960	1.1	Dorchester	68,600
15	1.6	Rowley	34,950	.9	Dedham	54,750
16	1.4	Shrewsbury	30,000	.6	Salisbury	39,500
17	1.3	Milford	29,200	.5	Grafton	31,887
18	1.3	Milton	28,757	.5	Leicester	30,750
19	1.3	Ipswich	27,900	.5	Tewkesbury	30,000

Appendix VII (continued)

Rank		1833		1850		
	% of Total	Town	Value of Production	Town	Value of Production	% of Total
20	1.1	Northborough	$24,625	Worcester	$28,440	.5
21	1.0	Stoneham	22,035	Ipswich	27,500	.4
22	.9	Cambridge	19,000	Shrewsbury	26,652	.4
23	.8	Brighton	18,000	Georgetown	26,348	.4
24	.7	Weston	16,150	Manchester	20,000	.3
25	.6	Tewkesbury	14,000	Weymouth	17,200	.3
26		Worcester	14,000	Amesbury	16,200	
27		So. Reading	13,890	Hingham	14,850	
28		Medford	12,600	Brookline	12,500	
29		Harvard	12,400	Attleborough	10,500	
30		Saugus	12,000	Ashburnham	10,412	
31		Foxborough	12,000	Cambridge	10,000	
32		Paxton	11,840	Rowley	8,800	
33		Hingham	11,800	Auburn	8,400	
34		Exeter	11,540	Groveland	8,100	
35		Leominster	11,500	Portsmouth	8,100	
36		Princeton	10,850	Fall River	8,000	
37		Bradford	10,800	Stoughton	8,000	
38		Uxbridge	9,925	Brentwood	7,600	
39		Lincoln	9,800	Townsend	7,583	
40		Scituate	8,500	Exeter	7,200	
41		Bellingham	8,000	Uxbridge	7,200	
42		Derry	8,000	Essex	6,800	
43		Lunnenburg	8,000	Medfield	6,300	
44		Millbury	7,125	Brewster	6,000	
45		Gardner	7,000	Natick	6,000	
46		Fairhaven	6,560	Dudley	5,000	

Appendix VII (continued)

Rank	1833 Town	Value of Production	1850 Town	Value of Production
47	Andover	$6,000	Weston	$5,000
48	Brewster	6,000	New Bedford	4,900
49	Fall River	6,000	Newbury	4,780
50	Fitchburg	6,000	Shirley	4,700
51	Westminster	6,000	Candia	4,375
52	Auburn	5,725	Holden	4,300
53	Dartmouth	5,600	Auburn	3,700
54	Charlton	5,500	Epping	3,500
55	Holliston	5,500	Raymond	3,200
56	Marlborough	5,300	Newmarket	3,000
57	Brentwood	5,120	Ashby	2,770
58	W. Boylston	5,100	Bradford	2,363
59	Deerfield	5,000	Westminster	2,240
60	Middleborough	4,000	Dartmouth	2,200
61	Attleborough	4,000	Swanzey	2,100
62	Billerica	3,750	W. Boylston	2,000
63	Barnstable	3,740	Hanover	1,900
64	E. Kingston	3,700	Nottingham	1,300
65	Falmouth	3,510	Sandown	1,200
66	Dudley	3,500	Hanson	1,060
67	Framingham	3,400	E. Kingston	1,025
68	Waltham	3,300	Seekonk	1,025
69	Methuen	3,225	Westford	859
70	Holden	3,000	Duxbury	780
71	Brookline	3,000	Groton	669
72	Southborough	2,900	Derry	600
73	W. Cambridge	2,825	Shirley	600

Appendix VII (continued)

Rank	1833 Town	Value of Production
74	Bolton	$2,800
75	Sterling	2,700
76	Epping	2,675
77	Seabrook	2,650
78	Rye	2,575
79	Hampstead	2,500
80	Reading	2,475
81	Raynham	2,450
82	Lancaster	2,300
83	Newburyport	2,240
84	Hopkington	2,200
85	Oxford	2,200
86	Salem	2,000
87	W. Newbury	2,000
88	Yarmouth	1,900
89	Windham	1,781
90	Sandwich	1,700
91	Westborough	1,650
92	Plaistow	1,600
93	Northwood	1,550
94	Newmarket	1,425
95	Stratham	1,300
96	N. Hampton	1,235
97	Candia	1,230
98	Kensington	1,100
99	Hampton Falls	1,075

Appendix VII (continued)

Rank	1833 Town	Value of Production
100	Chatham	$1,050
101	Hampton	1,025
102	Mansfield	1,000
103	Franklin	900
104	Raymond	900
105	New Bedford	792
106	Taunton	700
107	Burlington	600
108	Orleans	600
109	Harwich	524
110	Dennis	350
111	Medfield	300
112	Sandown	300
113	Eastham	288
114	Poplin	95

Appendix VIII
Annual Volume of Printing and Publishing in the Region Ranked by Town for 1833 and 1850

Source for 1833: The McLane Report
Source for 1850: The Manuscript Returns for the Census (U.S.) of Manufactures for Massachusetts, 1850

Total Printing and Publishing Production in the Region for 1833: $1,289,900.
Total Printing and Publishing Production in the Region for 1850: $2,171,403.

Rank	1833				1850		
	% of Total	Town	Value of Production		Town	% of Total	Value of Production
1	91.3	Boston	$1,178,000		Boston	89.3	$1,940,825
2	3.8	Lancaster*	50,000		Andover	2.5	56,232
3	2.3	Roxbury	30,000		Cambridge	2.3	51,200
4	2.3	Salem	30,000		Lowell	1.9	41,300
5	.9	Lunnenburg	12,000		Salem	1.4	30,000
6		Hingham	5,400		Leominster		18,776
7		Exeter	4,500		Fall River		7,200
8		Watertown	3,000		Fitchburg		6,600
9		Barnstable	2,500		Methuen		4,000
10		Portsmouth	2,300		Framingham		3,500
11		Framingham	1,300		Watertown		3,120
12		Newburyport	900		Charlestown		3,000
13					Randolph		2,500
14					New Bedford		2,400
15					Waltham		750

* Lancaster firm also engaged in other activity—not all printing related.

Appendix IX

Annual Volume of Musical Instruments Made in the Region Ranked by Town for 1833 and 1850

Source for 1833: The McLane Report
Source for 1850: The Manuscript Returns for the Census (U.S.) of Manufactures for Massachusetts, 1850

Total Musical Instruments Made in the Region for 1833: $166,200
Total Musical Instruments Made in the Region for 1850: $832,006

Rank	1833			1850		
	% of Total	Town	Value of Production	% of Total	Town	Value of Production
1	99.2	Boston	$165,000	91.6	Boston	$762,500
2	.8	Deerfield (N.H.)	1,200	3.8	Lawrence	32,000
3				1.7	Fitchburg	14,406
4				.8	Canton	6,900
5				.4	Haverhill	4,000
6				.4	Medway	3,600
7				.4	Dorchester	3,500
8				.3	Portsmouth	2,700
9				.3	Boxborough	2,400

Appendix X
Annual Volume of Tack and Nail Production in the Region Ranked by Town for 1833 and 1850

Source for 1833: The McLane Report
Source for 1850: The Manuscript Returns for the Census (U.S.) of Manufactures for Massachusetts, 1850

Total Tack and Nail Production in the Region for 1833: $1,525,395
Total Tack and Nail Production in the Region for 1850: $2,601,253

Rank	1833			1850		
	% of Total	Town	Value of Production	Town	% of Total	Value of Production
1	35.2	Wareham	$537,500	Wareham	39.9	$1,039,000
2	11.5	Plymouth	174,850	Raynham	15.1	394,000
3	9.7	Taunton	152,050	E. Bridgewater	9.9	256,500
4	6.5	E. Bridgewater	100,000	Somerville	5.8	152,000
5	6.2	Fall River	95,000	Taunton	4.8	124,000
6	6.1	Plympton	93,000	Newton	4.6	120,000
7	5.2	Danvers	80,000	Plymouth	3.6	95,000
8	4.6	Malden	70,000	Malden	3.3	86,000
9	3.6	Newton	55,000	Medford	2.7	70,000
10	3.1	Abington	47,425	Abington	2.3	59,904
11		Bridgewater	36,000	Braintree		43,000
12		Mansfield	33,020	Hanover		36,000
13		Hanson	19,000	Worcester		30,500
14		Scituate	11,500	Hanson		27,340
15		Raynham	9,000	Lancaster		15,000
16		Hanover	7,500	Middleborough		11,700

Appendix X (continued)

Rank	1833			1850		
	% of Total	Town	Value of Production	% of Total	Town	Value of Production
17		W. Bridgewater	$4,000		Dighton	$10,500
18		Leominster	550		Freetown	10,000
19					Duxbury	9,200
20					Scituate	3,550
21					Plympton	3,500
22					Sandwich	2,400
23					Southborough	2,145

NOTES

CHAPTER I

1. Stephen Thernstrom, *Poverty and Progress: Social Mobility in a Nineteenth Century City* (Cambridge, Mass., 1964); Stephen Thernstrom & Richard Sennett (eds.), *Nineteenth Century Cities: Essays in the New Urban History* (New Haven, 1969); Stephen Thernstrom, "Reflections on the New Urban History" in *Daedalus*, vol. 100 (1971), p. 359.

2. Peter Knights, *The Plain People of Boston* (New York, 1971); Richard Sennett, *Families Against the City* (New York, 1974); Joan Scott, *The Glassworkers of Carmeaux* (Cambridge, Mass., 1974).

3. Sam B. Warner, *The Private City: Philadelphia* (Philadelphia, 1968); *Streetcar Suburbs: The Process of Growth in Boston* (Cambridge, Mass., 1962); *The Urban Wilderness* (New York, 1972); "If all the World were Philadelphia: Scaffolding for Urban History" in *American Historical Review*, vol. 74 (1968), p. 26.

4. Allan R. Pred, *The Spatial Dynamics of Urban Industrial Growth* (Cambridge, Mass., 1966); *Urban Growth and the Circulation of Information, 1790-1840* (Cambridge, Mass., 1973); Eric Lampard, "Evolving Systems of Cities in the United States" in Harvey Perloff and Lowdon Wingo, *Issues in Urban Economics* (Baltimore, 1968), pp. 81-139; "The History of Cities in Economically Advanced Areas" in *Economic Development and Cultural Change*, vol. 3, pp. 81-136.

5. Wilbur R. Thompson, *A Preface to Urban Economics* (Baltimore, 1968).

6. Thompson, *Preface*, p. 16. For a critique of Thompson, see Lampard's "Evolving Systems," pp. 93-94.

7. Pred, *Spatial Dynamics*, p. 178.

8. Ibid., pp. 25-32.

9. Ibid., pp. 33-37.

10. Ibid., pp. 41-46.

11. Ibid., pp. 33-37.

12. Harvey Perloff et al., *Regions, Resources, and Economic Growth* (Lincoln, 1960), p. 75.

13. August Lösch, "The Nature of Economic Regions" in *Southern Economic Journal*, vol. 5 (1938), p. 73.

14. Ibid., p. 74.

15. Thompson, *Preface,* chap. 1.

16. Lampard, "Evolving Systems," p. 88.

17. Walter Christaller, *The Central Places of Southern Germany* (Englewood, 1966), especially chapter B. The original German edition of this work appeared in 1934.

18. Lampard, "Evolving Systems," pp. 86-87.

19. Brian J.L. Berry, *Geography of Market Centers and Retail Distribution* (Englewood, 1967), p. vii.

20. Berry, *Market Centers,* chaps. 1 & 2.

21. Ibid., p. 12.

22. Walter Isard, *Location and Space Economy* (Cambridge, Mass., 1956), chap. 1.

23. Ibid.

24. Ibid., p. 78.

25. Isard, *Space Economy,* p. 81.

26. Ibid., p. 87.

27. Ibid., pp. 93-94.

28. Ibid., p. 183.

29. Martin Beckmann, *Location Theory* (New York, 1968), pp. 75-83. See also Fred Lukermann, "Empirical Expressions of Nodality and Hierarchy in a Circulation Manifold" in *East Lakes Geographer,* vol. 2 (1960), pp. 17-44. Lukermann's model sets limits on the tendency toward nodality and hierarchy in the process of regional development.

30. Perloff, Dunn et al., *Regions, Resources,* p. 63.

31. Ibid., chap. 5.

32. Ibid., chap. 6.

33. Perloff, Dunn et al., *Regions, Resources,* p. 53.

34. Lampard, "Evolving Systems," pp. 97, 103. This theme is further developed in Lampard's "History of Cities," pp. 81-136. Also see Nathan Rosenberg's case study of the dynamics of specialization: "Technological Change in the Machine Tool Industry" in *Journal of Economic History,* vol. 23 (1963), pp. 414-434.

35. Lampard, "Evolving Systems," p. 137.

36. Otis D. Duncan, et al., *Metropolis and Region* (Baltimore, 1960), as quoted in Lampard, "Evolving Systems," pp. 105-125.

37. Lampard, "Evolving Systems," p. 138.

38. Stuart Blumin, *The Urban Threshold* (Chicago, 1976).

39. Diane Lindstrom, *Urban Growth in the Philadelphia Region 1810-1850* (New York, 1977).

40. Roberta B. Miller, *City and Hinterland* (Westport, 1979).

41. The studies of the Boston region in the early nineteenth century by Jeffrey Williamson and John Swanson, and by John B. Sharpless illustrate the nature and limits of systematic quantitative data available for the period. See Jeffrey Williamson and John Swanson, "Growth of Cities in the American Northeast" in *Explorations in Entrepreneurial History*, 2nd Ser., 1965, Vol. 4 supplement; and John B. Sharpless, *City Growth in the United States, England and Wales, 1820-1861: The Effects of Location, Size and Economic Structure on Inter-Urban Variations in Demographic Growth* (New York, 1976).

42. Berloff et al., *Regions, Resources*, p. 4.

43. Barry Supple and Arthur Johnson, *Boston Capitalists and Western Railroads* (Cambridge, Mass., 1967), pp. 16-17. See also Edward C. Kirkland, *Men, Cities, and Transportation*, 2 vols. (Cambridge, Mass., 1948). Kirkland looks at the growth of cities through a detailed investigation of the transportation sector. His study is limited by the absence of any theoretical framework by which to integrate the process of growth of this one sector with the largest process of urban development. See Lance E. Davis, "The New England Textile Mills and the Capital Markets: A Study of Industrial Borrowing 1840-1860" in *Journal of Economic History*, vol. 20 (1960), pp. 1-30. See also Lance Davis, "Stock Ownership in the Early New England Textile Industry" in *Business History Review*, vol. 32 (1958), pp. 204-222. Stephen Salsbury, *The State, Investor and the Railroad* (Cambridge, Mass., 1967).

44. Pred, *Spatial Dynamics*, p. 33.

CHAPTER II

1. See Josiah Cox Russell, *Medieval Cities and Their Regions* (London, 1972); Jean Gottman, *Megalopolis* (New York, 1961). On the problem of precise regional boundaries, see H. Green, "Hinterland Boundaries of New York City and Boston in Southern New England" in Harold M. Mayer and Clyde B. Kohn (eds.), *Readings in Urban Geography* (Chicago, 1959), pp. 185-201. See also Allan Pred, *Urban Growth and the Circulation of Information* (Cambridge, Mass., 1973). John Borchert, "American Metropolitan Evolution" in *Geographical Review*, vol. 57 (1967), pp. 301-322.

2. Douglass C. North, *The Economic Growth of the United States 1790-1860* (New York, 1961); Samuel Eliot Morison, *The Maritime History of Massachusetts* (Boston, 1961);

Paul David, "The Growth of Real Product in the United States Before 1840; New Evidence, Controlled Conjectures" in *The Journal of Economic History,* vol. 27 (1967), pp. 151-197.

3. An example of a large regional study would be Jean Gottman, *Megalopolis;* and an example of the study of a smaller region would be John G. Clark, *Towns and Minerals in Southwestern Kansas* (Lawrence, 1970). See also Robert G. Albion, *The Rise of the Port of New York* (New York, 1939).

4. Oliver N. Bacon, *History of Natick* (Boston, 1856), p. 156.

5. The number 219 is an approximation since towns were added during the 40 year period. See Kevin White, *Historical Data on Massachusetts Cities and Towns* (Boston, 1966). On the change from towns to city government in Massachusetts, see Francis X. Blouin Jr.'s "Boston 1822, The Change From Town to City Government," unpublished M.A. thesis, University of Minnesota, 1969.

6. See Walter M. Whitehill, *Boston, A Topographical History* (Cambridge, Mass., 1966); Morison, *Maritime History,* chap. 15. Average annual arrivals from foreign ports at Boston by decades:

1790-1800	569
1800-1810	789
1810-1820	610
1820-1830	787
1830-1840	1,199
1840-1850	1,473

(Source: Morison, *Maritime History,* p. 225)
Annual arrivals of coasting vessels:

1830	2,938
1840	4,406
1844	5,312
1849	6,199
1851	6,334

(Source: *Hazards U.S. Register and Boston Shipping List*)

7. Peter J. Coleman, *The Transformation of Rhode Island* (Providence, 1963), chaps. 1 & 2.

8. See Michael Frisch, *Town into City, A History of Springfield Mass.* (Cambridge, Mass., 1972), chap. 1; Albion, *Port of New York;* Stephen Salsbury, *The State, The Investor, and the Railroad* (Cambridge, Mass., 1967), chap. 1, and p. 182.

9. 1850 Census of Population (U.S.).

10. Figures derived from comparative census data.
Population of Manchester:

1830	877
1840	3,235
1850	13,932

11. Louis McLane, *Documents Relative to the Manufactures in the United States Collected and Transmitted to the House of Representatives by the Secretary of the Treasury,* 2 vols. (Washington, 1833), Serial Sect. 222, 223; hereafter cited as the McLane Report.

12. McLane Report, pp. 304-305.

13. McLane Report, pp. 18-51. Maine was part of Massachusetts until 1820.

14. Kirkland, *Men, Cities,* vol. 1, pp. 208-209.

15. Ibid., pp. 81-84, 245-250; Historical Committee of the Town of Millbury, *Centennial History of the Town of Millbury* (Millbury, 1915), pp. 110-118; the original papers of chapter 56 of the general laws of the Commonwealth of Massachusetts, 1831, June 22, 1831; Coleman, *Transformation,* pp. 170-176.

16. McLane Report, pp. 164-173; Coleman, *Transformation,* p. 123.

17. McLane Report, pp. 162-163; George Sweet Gibb, *The Whitesmiths of Taunton, A History of Reed and Barton* (New York, 1969; reprint of 1943 edition), p. 10.

18. McLane Report, pp. 182-185, 250-251, 602-603; Morison, *Maritime History,* chap. 14.

19. Richard C. Wade, *The Urban Frontier* (Chicago, 1964), pp. 43-49.

20. Marshall Smelser, *The Democratic Republic* (New York, 1968), pp. 172-173; North, *Economic Growth,* chaps. 3, 4, and 5.

21. Note that the map used here is a modern map of Massachusetts. Town boundaries continued to change throughout the period 1810-1850. In 1810 the town of Bridgewater included not only present day Bridgewater but also present day East and West Bridgewater, Brockton and part of Halifax, giving it a considerably large land area. Middleborough included Lakeville and parts of Carver. Rehoboth included Seekonk. See White, *Historical Data,* pp. 17, 45, 56. The Census of 1820 lists nonagricultural employment as follows: Rehoboth 14.3, Middleborough 12.4, and Bridgewater as 31.9 percent.

22. Clarence S. Brigham, *History and Bibliography of Early American Newspapers* (Worcester, 1947). It should be noted that unlike other parts of the nation, in New England the tradition of town government was a strong one and the tradition of county government quite weak. Though Worcester was the county seat, that fact alone would not necessarily account for the dominance of the town. On town government, see John Sly, *Town Government in Massachusetts* (Cambridge, Mass., 1930).

23. "Abstract of Banks 1810 in the Commonwealth of Massachusetts" broadside in the Massachusetts State Library.

24. Census of Manufactures, 1820, p. 34.

25. Ibid., pp. 4-12.

26. Blanche E. Hazard, *Organization of the Boot and Shoe Industry* (Cambridge, Mass., 1921); Oscar Handlin, *Boston's Immigrants* (Cambridge, Mass., 1959).

27. North, *Economic Growth,* pp. 66-74. The McLane Report gives a good indication of the extent to which mills were scattered throughout the region.

28. Computed from the McLane Report and from the population figures from the 1830 census of population.

29. Postal Receipts listed in the American State Papers.

30. "Abstract of Bank Returns, 1830, the Commonwealth of Massachusetts" broadside in the Massachusetts State Library.

31. 1830 Aggregate Valuation, manuscript compilation in the Massachusetts State Library.

32. McLane Report, *passim.*

33. McLane Report, *passim.*

34. Benjamin Labaree, *Patriots and Partisans* (Cambridge, Mass., 1963); Stephen Thernstrom, *Poverty and Progress* (Cambridge, Mass., 1964).

35. Philip Greven, *Four Generations, Population, Land, and Family in Colonial Andover, Massachusetts* (Ithaca, 1970).

36. This ranking is based generally on the tables in the appendix. However, it has been supplemented by reading in the many town histories available for nearly all towns in the region. These volumes are listed in the bibliography.

37. See North, *Economic Growth,* and Morison, *Maritime History.* Population statistics taken from the census of 1850.

38. Census of population.

39. *Abstracts of Banks 1850* issued by the Commonwealth of Massachusetts, 1850.

40. Valuation of the Commonwealth of Massachusetts, 1850 (Manuscript compilation in the Massachusetts State Library).

41. Ibid.

42. Vertical integration of business firms is described well by Alfred D. Chandler in "The Beginnings of Big Business in America" in *Business History Review,* vol. 33 (1959), pp. 1-27. A proper definition for manufacturing, particularly in the early nineteenth century, is difficult to pin down. Much of the early industry was extractive, i.e., fishing, lumber and leather, etc. Also, much was carried on in small shops by what should rightly be called craftsmen. Distinctions should be made between craft and larger scale manufacturing as in textiles and cordage, which could be classified as manufactories. Since this study is basically a study of the growth of urban places rather than of industry per se, a broad definition of manufacturing will be used to reflect the range of occupations which sustained the urban population. See Margaret Walsh, "The Census as an Accurate Source of Information: The Value of Mid-Century Manufacturing

Returns, The Printed Census and the Manuscript Census Compilations Compared," in *Historical Methods Newsletter,* No. 4 (March 1971), pp. 43-51.

43. Manuscript returns of the 1850 census for Massachusetts in the Massachusetts State Library (for New Hampshire in the New Hampshire State Library). On the circulation of information and its impact on the national urban network, see Pred, *Circulation.*

44. Manuscript returns of the 1850 census of manufactures.

45. See papers of James Waldock, tailor, and Endicott E. Oliver, tailor, BA211, BA212.

46. Census of Manufactures for 1850 (manuscript returns).

47. Population census for each census year 1800-1850.

48. See articles in Brian J.L. Berry and Frank E. Horton (eds.), *Geographic Perspectives on the Urban Systems* (Englewood Cliffs, 1970).

CHAPTER III

1. On textiles in Massachusetts and New Hampshire, see Caroline Ware, *The Early New England Cotton Manufacture* (New York, 1931); Paul McGouldrick, *New England Textiles in the Nineteenth Century* (Cambridge, Mass., 1968).

2. Compiled from Census of Manufactures for 1810.

3. Compiled from the McLane Report.

4. Compiled from the manuscript returns for the census of manufactures for 1850.

5. 1810 figures are drawn from the census of manufactures, 1833 figures are from the McLane Report, and 1850 figures are from the manuscript returns for the 1850 census of manufactures.

6. Unfortunately the McLane Report does not give any clue as to exactly what was called a machine. Toward 1850 it becomes obvious that textile and railroad machinery form the bulk of production but that is not so clear for the earlier period. Sources on machinery statistics: the 1810 census of manufactures, the McLane Report and the manuscript returns for the census of manufactures 1850. In 1810 machinery is not listed since machinery was made by the textile firms themselves. See Nathan Rosenberg, "Technological Change in the Machine Tool Industry, 1840-1910," in the *Journal of Economic History,* vol. 23 (1963), pp. 414-434.

7. 1810 census of manufacturing, McLane Report, and manuscript returns for the census of manufactures for 1850. See Blanche Hazard, *The Organization of the Boot and Shoe Industry in Massachusetts before 1875* (Cambridge, Mass., 1921).

8. Robert LeBlanc, *The Location of Manufacturing in New England in the Nineteenth Century* (Hanover, 1969), p. 64; Hazard, *Boot and Shoe,* pp. 95-96.

9. 1810 census of manufactures, McLane Report, and manuscript returns for the census of manufactures for 1850.

10. LeBlanc, *Location of Manufacturing,* p. 67.

11. The papers of the Tremont Nail Company of Wareham, Mass. have been deposited in the Baker Library of Harvard University but contain little information for the early years of the company which coincide with the period of this study.

12. The census of manufactures for 1850 (mss. returns and printed) gives little information on the manufacture of hats in the region. The McLane Report does provide more information for 1833. On mobility in the region, see Peter Knights, *The Plain People of Boston* (New York, 1972).

13. Compiled from the McLane Report and the manuscript returns of the census of manufactures for 1850.

14. Ibid. Printing and publishing included newspapers and magazines of course. See chap. 2 for the relative numbers of newspapers in each city.

15. It is likely that many inland towns had craftsmen who made musical instruments part time or for home use and did not report such activities. The bulk of those who did report from the hinterland made organs and pianofortes.

16. The notion of regional specialization is discussed in Douglass North, *The Economic Growth of the United States* (New York, 1961). North only distinguished specialization at the broadest regional level, i.e., Northeast in manufactures, West in agricultural produce, and the South in cotton. This categorization has come under some recent criticism. The analysis of specialization in this study is intended to show the extent of product specialization within a subregion of the North's "northeast."

17. McLane Report, Milford entry, pp. 512-513.

18. McLane Report, Grafton entry, pp. 490-491.

19. McLane Report, Fitchburg entry, pp, 488-489.

20. McLane Report, Lancaster and Leominster entries, pp. 498-501, 504-505.

21. There was a machine shop in Holden, a near neighbor to Worcester. McLane Report, Worcester entry, pp. 568-575.

22. McLane Report, Stoneham entry, pp. 352-353. Note the McLane Report contains a separate column for goods imported from abroad. The country or city of origin of these goods is not always listed.

23. McLane Report, Lowell entry, pp. 340-344.

24. McLane Report, Newton entry, pp. 348-349.

25. McLane Report, East Cambridge entry, pp. 324-325.

26. Wilbur R. Thompson, *A Preface to Urban Economics* (Baltimore, 1968). For the North this meant significant importation of foodstuffs.

27. McLane Report, Essex County entries, pp. 230-231, 236-241, 256-257.

28. McLane Report, Raymond entry, p. 626.

29. The entries for Rockingham County in the McLane Report tend to be less detailed than those for Massachusetts.

30. McLane Report, Boston entry, pp. 432-469.

31. Allan R. Pred, *Urban Growth and the Circulation of Information* (Cambridge, Mass., 1973).

CHAPTER IV

1. See Paul H. Cootner, "The Role of Railroads in United States Economic Growth" in *Journal of Economic History,* vol. 23 (1963), pp. 477-521; and Albert Fishlow, *American Railroads and the Transformation of the Antebellum Economy* (Cambridge, Mass., 1965).

2. See John Borchert, "American Metropolitan Evolution" in *Geographical Review,* vol. 57 (1967), pp. 301-332. For a less systematic but interesting treatment of the role of transportation in urban growth, see David Ward, *Cities and Immigrants* (New York, 1971) and the works of Sam Bass Warner, particularly *The Urban Wilderness* (New York, 1972), and *Streetcar Suburbs: The Process of Growth in Boston 1870-1900* (Cambridge, Mass., 1962).

3. Isaac Howland to Bourne Spooner, 3 Nov. 1832 (BA 207).

4. Charles Hudson, *History of the Town of Lexington* (Boston, 1868), p. 441.

5. See advertisements in such newspapers as the *Boston Daily Advertiser, Boston Commercial Gazette,* and the *Boston Independent Chronicle.* See also Charles Nutt, *History of Worcester and its People,* 4 vols. (New York, 1919), p. 979.

6. George Wingate Chase, *The History of Haverhill Mass.* (Haverhill, 1861), p. 535.

7. Ibid., p. 536.

8. Original papers of Chapter 232 of the General Laws of the Commonwealth of Massachusetts of 1836.

9. John L. Sullivan, *Remarks on the Importance of Inland Navigation from Boston* (Boston, 1813), p. 7.

10. Ibid., pp. 10-14.

11. Millbury Historical Committee, *Centennial History of the Town of Millbury* (Millbury, 1915), pp. 111-113.

12. Ibid.

13. Christopher Roberts, *The Middlesex Canal 1793-1860* (Cambridge, Mass., 1937), pp. 160-164. See also the McLane Report, Medford entry, pp. 346-347.

14. Ibid., p. 171.

15. See Richard Wade, *The Urban Frontier* (Cambridge, Mass., 1959); and Harry Scheiber, *The Ohio Canal Era* (Athens, 1969).

16. The services of towns in the region are laid out in detail in chapter 6. See also letter of Moses Appleton to Nathan Appleton, 30 Sept. 1825, MHS Appleton papers in which he briefly discusses the importance of the coastal trade in a wider regional context.

17. There is an extensive literature on the growth of railroads and their effect on the growth of the national economy, including Edward Chase Kirkland, *Men, Cities and Transportation,* 2 vols. (Cambridge, Mass., 1948); Albert Fishlow, *American Railroads;* Robert Fogel, *Railroads and American Economic Growth* (Baltimore, 1964); Stephen Salsbury, *The State, the Investor, and the Railroad* (Cambridge, Mass., 1967). Boston railroads were probably an unusual case since industrialization was already far advanced by the time of the building of the rail network and since the region was already very heavily settled.

18. See Fogel, *Railroads,* and Fishlow, *American Railroads.*

19. Original papers of chapter 26, 12 June 1829, of the General Laws of the Commonwealth of Massachusetts. (Hereafter cited as the General Laws.)

20. Original papers of chapter 4, 5 June 1830, of the General Laws.

21. Ibid.

22. Original papers of chapter 55, 22 June 1831, of the General Laws.

23. Ibid.

24. Original papers of chapter 95 of the General Laws of 1835. (Note that after the year 1833, legislative sessions of the general court were held within one calendar year and thus the date of the law is not necessary in the citation.)

25. Original papers of chapter 232 of the General Laws of 1836.

26. Ibid.

27. Original papers of chapter 150 of the General Laws of 1840.

28. Ibid.

29. Ibid.

30. Ibid.

31. Ibid.

32. *Report of the Committee Concerning the Route of the Old Colony Railroad* (Plymouth, 1844).

33. Original papers of chapter 84 of the General Laws of 1842 and the original papers of chapter 200 of the General Laws of 1847.

34. Original papers of chapter 116 of the General Laws of 1844.

35. Original papers of chapter 141 of the General Laws of 1844.

36. Ibid.

37. Original papers of chapter 226 of the General Laws of 1845.

38. Original papers of chapter 234 of the General Laws of 1845.

39. Original papers of chapter 79 of the General Laws of 1846.

40. Ibid. Towns petitioning for the railroad were Salem, Lynn, Danvers, Middleton, Marblehead, Gloucester, South Danvers, Rockport, Manchester, Beverly, Andover and Methuen.

41. Original papers of chapter 212 of the General Laws of 1846.

42. Original papers of chapter 255 of the General Laws of 1846.

43. Original papers of chapter 238 of the General Laws for 1847.

44. Original papers of chapter 276 of the General Laws for 1847.

45. Original papers of chapter 223 of the General Laws of 1848, and Thomas Hopkinson, "Argument . . . for a Railroad from Salem to Lowell" (Boston, 1848).

46. *Report of the President to the General Stockholders of the Boston and Maine Railroad* (Boston, 11 Sept. 1850), p. 12.

47. Bourne Spooner to Clapp & Co., Plymouth, 15 July 1846.

48. S. Melcher to P.T. Jackson and Kirk Boott, 13 Dec. 1842. BA119.

49. Silas Pierce & Co. to John Gates, 2 Sept. 1850. BA756.

50. Letter to Jenny, Rice and Gardner, Lowell, 12 Jan. 1846. Appleton Company Papers, MVT.

51. N.F. Cunningham to N.F. Ackley, 10 Apr. 1849. BA770.

52. John Fairfield to David Howe, Boston, 18 Mar. 1825. BA757. John Fairfield, a Boston wholesaler in 1825, had deliveries of shoes made to him regularly by a Mr. Howe of Haverhill at the rate of 5,000 per month.

53. Henry Hall to Robert Means, 27 Feb. 1833. BA164. See also Henry Hall to Israel Whitney, 26 Dec. 1833. BA164.

54. Wainwright and Tappan to Josh Shotswell, 20 Dec. 1842. BA769. See also Wainwright and Tappan to French and Horton of Newburyport, 13 Sept. 1844, and Wainwright and Tappan to A. W. Harris of Worcester, 23 May 1844. Wainwright and Tappan to Joseph S. Cabot, 16 Nov. 1847, talks of trucking goods from depot to depot in Boston, an especially lucrative business which emerged since each rail line had its own terminal in the city creating a demand for shuttles. All BA769.

55. H. Caldwell to William Richardson, 8 Apr. 1835. BA314.

56. Walter Baker to Grant and Stone, 4 Nov. 1848. BA142.

57. Bigelow Kenard to George F. Miller of Royalston, 12 Dec. 1840, and Bigelow Kenard to Dunbar and Story of Worcester, 10 Feb. 1841. BA1003.

58. C.W. Morgan to William C. Pickersgill, 7 May 1834. BA61.

59. Bourne Spooner to Caleb Loring, 9 Mar. 1833 and 22 June 1829. Spooner to Joseph Moore, 8 Dec. 1847. BA207.

60. Whittemore and Lovering to Kirk Boott, 10 Nov. 1836. BA119.

61. Haskel to William Richardson, 21 Aug. 1835. BA314.

62. Richard Borden to Tisdale and Borden, 16 Jan. 1850. BA241.

63. See BA163.

64. Reed and Barton to Edwin D. Godfrey, 15 Oct. 1842. BA284-5. See also Reed and Barton to Steinmetz and Justice, 18 May 1843. BA284-5.

65. Therson Duncan to Moses Plimpton, 3 July 1850. BA239.

66. [?] to Samuel Comly, 23 July 1827. BA159.

67. Wainwright and Tappan to Joseph S. Cabot, 25 Oct. 1847. BA769.

CHAPTER V

1. Banking Statistics taken from the Abstracts of Banks for the Commonwealth of Massachusetts for 1810, 1830 and 1850.

2. George D. Green, *Finance and Economic Development in the Old South* (Stanford, 1972) and Joseph Van Fenstermaker, *The Development of American Commercial Banking, 1782-1837* (Kent, 1965).

3. Boston Citizens "Exposition of Facts and Arguments in support of a memorial to the legislature of Massachusetts . . . in favor of a Bank of Ten Millions" (Boston, 1836), also Senate Doc. No. 30.

4. Spooner to Russell Thomas & Co., Plymouth, 12 Dec. 1837. BA207.

5. Ichabod Washburn, Daybook, vol. 2, 1833-1848. BA282A.

6. Reed and Barton to Fe–, Bass–dale & Cooper of Providence, 8 May 1843. BA285.

7. Nathaniel Stevens to B. Goodridge, 30 Mar. 1838. Stevens papers, MVT. See also Henry Oliver to Wm. Richardson, 26 Aug. 1811. BA314.

8. Henry Oliver to Wm. Richardson, 16 Aug. 1811. BA314; Jacob Peabody to Joseph S. Cabot (of Salem), 7 Nov. 1820. BA1024; Wainwright and Tappan to Messrs. D. & S. Jackson, Plymouth, 28 Jan. 1847. BA769; N.F. Cunningham to S. Shepherd & Son, Taunton. BA770.

9. B. Spooner to Wm. Lovering 1 Nov. 1825; B. Spooner to Caleb Loring, 11 May 1827; B. Spooner to Caleb Loring, 24 Apr. 1833; B. Spooner to Charles Tucker, Nov. ?, 1839. All BA207.

10. Wainwright and Tappan to N. Stevens of Andover, 18 Mar. 1843. BA769; Bigelow and Bigelow to Wm. Turner of Framingham, 26 Apr. 1841. BA1003; Caleb Loring to Daniel Deshon, 5 July 1827. BA207.

11. Samuel Allen to George A. Plimpton Jr., no date. BA239.

12. Charles Phelps to Wm. Belcher, 15 June 1820. BA751.

13. Charles W. Morgan to W.L. Fisher, 10 Nov. 1842. BA85.

14. Charles W. Morgan to W.L. Fisher, 17 Nov. 1842, and 8 Dec. 1842. BA85.

15. Charles W. Morgan to Thomas W. Morgan, 15 Dec. 1845. BA85. He still refers to banks with disdain: "The banks are so rascally that they take advantage of the least difficulty . . ." This particular comment was toward the banks in Philadelphia. See also Charles Morgan to Charles Hood, 6 Aug. 1834. BA61, and Charles Morgan to the Atlantic Bank of Boston, 2 Aug. 1836. BA61.

16. Nathan Appleton, *An Examination of the Banking System of Massachusetts, in Reference to the Renewal of the Bank Charters* (Boston, 1831), pp. 14-15.

17. Ibid., pp. 15-16.

18. Ibid., p. 16.

19. Ibid.

20. Ibid., pp. 20-21.

21. Ibid., p. 22.

22. A.A. Lawrence to Son, 4 Dec. 1830, Lawrence papers MHS.

23. Bray Hammond, *Banks and Politics in America* (Princeton, 1957), pp. 549-556. There is considerable debate over the significance of the activities of the Suffolk Bank. Hammond argues that the Suffolk acted much like a Federal Reserve—central Bank—in regulating the flow of credit. Others like Van Fenstermaker reject the model.

24. *Report from the Secretary of the Treasury in Obedience to a Resolution of the Senate with Returns of the Bank of the United States and the Deposit Banks,* 24th Congress, 1st Session, 14 Jan. 1836, Serial Set 282, p. 60.

25. *Letters from the Secretary of the Treasury Transmitting the Information Required by a Resolution of the House of Representatives of 10th July 1832, in Relation to the Condition of the State Banks etc.*, 25th Congress, 2nd Session, 8 Jan. 1838, Serial Set 324, p. 97.

26. Gerald T. White, *A History of the Massachusetts Hospital Life Insurance Co.* (Cambridge, Mass., 1955), p. 27.

27. Nathaniel Bowdich to Frederick Packard, Boston, 11 Dec. 1824. BA1086.

28. White, *Mass. Hosp. Life,* pp. 43, 46.

29. Ibid., pp. 47-51.

30. Wainwright and Tappan to William L. Boyce, (of Lynn), Boston, 18 Jan. 1844. BA769.

31. Wainwright and Tappan to Boynton and Whitcomb (of Templeton), Boston, 17 Aug. 1843. BA769.

32. Wainwright and Tappan to I. & C. Washburn (of Worcester), Boston. BA769.

33. For example, Wainwright and Tappan to Stephen C. Phillips (of Salem), Boston, 28 Sept. 1846.

34. For example, Caleb Loring to James Mansfield (of Gloucester), Boston, 9 Jan. 1829. BA207.

35. For example, R. Borden to W. & J. Renolds, 25 Mar. 1847. BA207.

36. Bigelow Brothers, letter book 1841-1844. BA1003.

37. Josiah Quincy to P.T. Jackson, Boston, 9 Nov. 1841. BA119.

38. Bigelow Brothers to George H. Brown (of E. Bridgewater), Boston, 15 Apr. 1842.

39. Bigelow Brothers to Dunbar and Story (of Worcester), Boston, 3 June 1840 and 17 Sept. 1840. BA1003.

40. Reed and Barton to Young Smith & Co. (of New York), Taunton, 11 May 1841. BA295.

41. Benjamin Loring to Samuel Veasie, Boston, 23 July 1827. BA207.

42. Silas Pierce to O.M. Donahoe (of Lowell), Boston, 19 Apr. 1848. BA756.

43. Benjamin Loring to Bourne Spooner, Boston, 13 Mar. 1828. BA207.

44. "Essay on the Manufacture of Straw Bonnets" (Providence, 1825), p. 14, in the Kress Library.

45. McLane Report.

46. "Straw Bonnets," *passim.*

47. James Whiton, *Diary,* p. 116 (1829). BA772.

48. Ibid., p. 126.

49. I. Howland to Caleb Loring, New Bedford, 29 May 1828. BA207.

50. Charles W. Morgan to William Fisher, 2 Mar. 1842, to Josiah Bradlee & Co. 24 Mar. 1842. BA85.

51. Charles W. Morgan to the Board of Investment, Fall River Institution for Savings, 1 July 1842. BA85.

52. Charles W. Morgan to William Fisher, 4 May 1846. BA85.

53. Charles W. Morgan to William Fisher, 26 Jan. 1842. BA85.

54. A. Lowell to Nathan Appleton, 15 Jan. 1833, MHS, Appleton Papers.

55. J.W. Paige to Nathan Appleton, 13 Aug. 1836, MHS, Appleton Papers.

56. The Thomas Lamb papers at MHS.

57. Thomas Dawes to Thomas Lamb, 1 June 1837, MHS, Lamb Papers.

58. Lawrence papers at MHS.

59. Lance E. Davis, "The New England Textile Mills and the Capital Markets: A Study of Industrial Borrowing, 1840-1860" in *Journal of Economic History,* vol. 20 (1960), pp. 1-30.

60. Lance Davis, "Stock Ownership in the Early New England Textile Industry" in *Business History Review,* vol. 32 (1958), pp. 204-222.

61. Henry B. Hough, *Wamsutta of New Bedford* (New Bedford, 1946).

CHAPTER VI

1. Glenn Porter and Harold Livesay, *Merchants and Manufacturers* (Baltimore, 1971), pp. 27-34.

2. A.A. Lawrence to William Stewart Esq., Boston, 2 Nov. 1850, MHS, Lawrence Papers.

3. Records of Waterson Pray & Co., BA762, used in conjunction with the Boston City Directory for 1832 in the Kress Library.

4. Records of Hatch and Fearing Co. BA767.

5. Records of the Boston Sugar Refinery. BA738.

6. Records of Burr and Pritchard. BA927.

7. See Account of Francis Coffin and John Derby 1816, MHS, Appleton Papers.

8. Porter and Livesay, *Merchants,* p. 78.

9. John H. Starr to William Richardson, 7 Apr. 1819. BA314.

10. Thomas With–?– to William Richardson, 26 Nov. 1817. BA314.

11. On the location of Richardson's agents, see Calvin Howe to William Richardson, 5 Aug. 1828, and Robinson and Olds to William Richardson, 9 Feb. 1829. BA314.

12. Nathan Lazell to John Hancock, 12 July 1811; D. & L. Laws to John Hancock, 7 May 1816; A. Hunting to John Hancock, 28 Jan. 1812. BA738.

13. F. Alger to P.T. Jackson, Boston, 26 July 1839. BA119.

14. Papers of C.W. Morgan, Receipt, 5 May 1836. BA61.

15. Thomas Dixon to Thomas Lamb, Boston, 20 Sept. 1824, MHS, Lamb Papers.

16. A.A. Lawrence to William Dwight, Boston, 11 June 1850, MHS, A.A. Lawrence Papers.

17. Dodd and Son to B. Spooner, Boston, 11 Mar. 1826. BA207.

18. Nichols and Folson to John Gates, Boston, 20 Dec. 1848. BA224.

19. Reed and Barton to W.N. Segmare & Co., Taunton, 5 Dec. 1846. BA285.

20. Silas Pierce & Co. to John Gates, Boston, 2 Sept. 1850. BA756. See also Acct. Book 1831-1833 and ledger 1845-1848. BA756.

21. Bigelow Brothers to Dunbar and Story (of Worcester), Boston, 14 Apr. 1840. BA1003.

22. Bigelow Brothers to J.C. Cole (of Rochester, N.H.), Boston, 15 May 1810; Bigelow Brothers to D. Goddard (of Worcester), Boston, 21 July 1842; Bigelow Brothers to S.H. Goodnow (of Fitchburgh), Boston, 18 May 1840; see also letter book 1841-1844. BA1003.

23. Wainwright and Tappan to Joseph Cabot, Boston, no date; Wainwright and Tappan to Samuel Lawrence, Boston, 12 Feb. 1847; Wainwright and Tappan to Waldo Higginson, Boston, 4 June 1844; Wainwright and Tappan to D.A. Neal, Boston, 2 Mar. 1846; Wainwright and Tappan to Daniel Knight, Boston, 29 June 1847; Wainwright and Tappan to Jeremiah Johnson, Boston, 26 July 1847; Wainwright and Tappan to William G. Appleton, Boston, 1 July 1842, 21 July 1842; Wainwright and Tappan to R.W. Roper (of Salem), Boston, 23 May 1845; Wainwright and Tappan to Horace Bradley, Boston, 22 Sept. 1842. BA769.

24. Wainwright and Tappan to William Appleton, Boston, 22 Apr. 1843. BA769.

25. Wainwright and Tappan to Hadden & Hall Co., Boston, 2 Nov. 1841. BA769.

26. W. Baker to James Brundage, 5 May 1840; W. Baker to Hussey & Mackay, 27 Sept. 1826, 25 Dec. 1822. BA142.

27. B. Spooner to Caleb Loring, 4 June 1830; B. Spooner to D.C. Nagoun Esq., 15 June 1837. BA207.

28. Nathaniel Stevens to Edward Lamb, Andover, 23 May 1840; Nathaniel Stevens to Clapp & Steele, Andover, 28 Feb. 1840, 6 Mar. 1840; Nathaniel Stevens to P.J. Farnum, Andover, 30 Jan. 1844, MVT, Stevens Papers.

29. McLane Report.

30. Papers of William Richardson, particularly general accounts and letter; E. Sansland (of Beverly) to William Richardson, 14 Oct. 1835. BA314.

31. Papers of the India Rubber Hat Co. BA216. Papers of John Goodwin, Reading Historical Society. Papers of the Boston and Lynn India Rubber Mfg. Co. of Lynn. BA300. Papers of I. & C. Washburn of Worcester, particularly letter of I. & C. Washburn to Joshua Schofield, 28 Feb. 1844. BA282c.

32. Papers of William Eddy & Son, vol. 2, Acct. Sheet, 24 Apr. 1844, and vol. 7, Misc. Bills 1837-1853. BA278. See also the papers of Lazelle Perkins Co. BA243.

33. Porter and Livesay, *Merchants*, p. 52.

34. Papers of Lazelle Perkins & Co., particularly Jon L. Milcher to Lazelle Perkins, 27 Aug. 1847. BA243.

35. "Catalogue of Boots and Shoes to be sold by Whitwell Bond & Co., August 29, 1828 . . . Faneuil Hall" (Boston, 1828). "Catalogue of Foreign and Domestic Wool sold at Auction

June 10, 1835" (Boston, 1835). "Oak Hall in 1850, Great Sale of the Season, G.W. Simmons" (Boston, 1850). All in the Kress Library, Harvard University.

36. J.L. Cunningham to Thomas Lamb, 14 Oct. 1825, and J.L. Cunningham to William Richardson, 19 July 1830, MHS, Lamb Papers.

37. Jacob Peabody to C. & J. Smith, Salem, 7 Jan. 1822; Jacob Peabody to William Bandlett, Salem, 24 May 1823; Jacob Peabody to J. Delano, Salem, 1 June 1820; Jacob Peabody to William King Esq., Salem, 12 June 1820; Jacob Peabody to Nathan Smith, Salem, 23 May 1821; Jacob Peabody to Nathaniel Stevens, Salem, 26 Aug. 1825; Jacob Peabody to Samuel Haskell, Salem, 16 Sept. 1822; Jacob Peabody to N. Bradley, Salem, 23 Dec. 1822. BA1024.

38. Jacob Peabody to Nathan Smith, Salem, 23 May 1821. BA1024.

39. Jacob Peabody to Nathaniel Stevens, Salem, 26 Aug. 1825. BA1024.

40. Jacob Peabody to Samuel Haskell, Salem, 16 Sept. 1822. BA1024.

41. Jacob Peabody to N. Bradley, Salem, 23 Dec. 1822. BA1024.

42. J.L. Cunningham to William Richardson, 19 July 1830. BA314.

43. Walter Baker to G. Vose, 5 Dec. 1826. BA142.

44. Isaac Howland & Co. to Bourne Spooner, 8 May 1827. BA207.

45. N.B. Gordon, Agent to Charles Bradley, 3 Feb. 1823. BA147.

46. Reed and Barton to Davis Palmer & Co., 31 Aug. 1840. BA285.

47. Blanche Hazard, *The Organization of the Boot and Shoe Industry in Massachusetts before 1875* (Cambridge, Mass., 1921), pp. 44-45.

48. Ibid., pp. 51-52.

49. Ibid., p. 50.

50. Census of manufactures, Massachusetts, Manuscript Returns, 1850.

51. Census (U.S.) for 1830 and for 1850.

52. W.H. Richardson, *Boot and Shoe Manufacture Assistant and Guide* (Boston, 1858), p. 16.

53. See Porter and Livesay, *Merchants,* pp. 13-61.

54. George S. Gibb, *The Saco Lowell Shops: Textile Machinery Building in New England* (New York, 1969), p. 127. See also C.J. Appleton to Nathan Appleton, 14 Dec. 1844, MHS, Appleton Papers.

55. Gibb, *Saco Lowell Shops,* p. 128. See also correspondence between Benjamin Loring and Bourne Spooner of the Plymouth Cordage Company, 2 Nov., 5 Nov., 12 Nov., and 20 June, 1827. BA202.

56. Gibb, *Saco Lowell Shops,* p. 219.

57. William Austin to ?, 8 Jan. 1833. BA163.

58. McLane Report, Lowell entry, pp. 340-344.

59. Manuscript returns of the Census of Manufacturers (U.S.) for Massachusetts, 1850.

60. Ibid.

61. C.W. Morgan to William Fisher, 21 Apr. 1843. BA61.

62. McLane Report, Collections in the Baker Library; see Lovett & Bishop, *List of Manuscripts at Baker Library* (Boston, 1969).

63. Papers of C.W. Morgan. BA61, and The Papers of Nathaniel Stevens, MVT, Stevens Papers.

BIBLIOGRAPHY

PRIMARY SOURCES

Government Documents

U.S. Census Office. Second Census (1800). *Return of the Whole Number of Persons Within the Several Districts of the United States, According to "An act providing for the second Census or Enumeration of the Inhabitants of the United States." Passed February the twenty eighth, one thousand eight hundred.* Washington: William Duane & Son, 1801.

U.S. Census Office. Third Census (1810). *Aggregate amount of each description of Persons within the United States of America, and the Territories thereof, agreeably to actual enumeration made according to law, in the year 1810.* [Washington: no publisher, 1811].

U.S. Census Office. Fourth Census (1820). *Census for 1820. Published by authority of an Act of Congress, under the direction of the Secretary of State.* Washington: Gales & Seaton, 1821.

U.S. Census Office. Fifth Census (1830). *Fifth Census; or, Enumeration of the Inhabitants of the United States, as Corrected at the Department of State, 1830. Published by authority of an Act of Congress, under the direction of the Secretary of State.* Washington: Duff Green, 1832.

U.S. Census Office. Sixth Census (1840). *Sixth Census or Enumeration of the Inhabitants of the United States, as Corrected at the Department of State, in 1840. Published, by Authority of an Act of Congress, Under the Direction of the Secretary of State.* Washington: Blair & Rives, 1841.

U.S. Census Office. Seventh Census (1850). *The Seventh Census of the United States: 1850. Embracing a Statistical View of Each of the States and Territories, Arranged by Counties, Towns, Etc., under the Following Divisions: . . . With an Introduction, Embracing the Aggregate Tables for the United States Compared with Every Previous Census Since 1790—Schedules and Laws of Congress Relating to the Census in the Same Period—Ratio Tables of Increase and Decrease of Cities and States, Etc., by Sex and Ages, and Color—Table of Population of Every County, Town, Township, Etc., in the United States, Alphabetically Arranged—Together with Some Explanatory Remarks, and an Appendix, Embracing Notes upon the Tables of Each of the States, Etc. J.D.B. DeBow, Superintendent of the United States Census.* Washington: Robert Armstrong, 1853.

U.S. *The Seventh Census. Report of the Superintendent of the Census for December 1, 1852; to Which is Appended the Report for December 1, 1851. Printed by Order of the House of Representatives of the United States.* Washington: Robert Armstrong, 1853.

U.S. Congress. House. 22nd Congress, 1st Session (1831-32). House Executive Document No. 308 (serial volumes 222 and 223). *Documents Relative to the Manufactures in the United States, Collected and Transmitted to the House of Representatives In compliance with a resolution of January 19, 1832, By the Secretary of the Treasury. In Two Volumes. Volume I. [II.] Printed by order of the House of Representatives.* 2 vols.; Washington: Duff Green, 1833. (Known as the "McLane Report.")

U.S. Congress. Senate. 24th Congress 1st Session 1836-37. *Report from the Secretary of the Treasury in Obedience to a Resolution of the Senate with Returns of the Bank of the United States and the Deposit Banks.* Jan. 14, 1836.

U.S. Congress. House. 25th Congress 2nd Session. 1837-38. *Letter from the Secretary of the Treasury Transmitting the Information Required by a Resolution of the House of Representatives of 10th July 1832, in Relation to the Condition of the State Banks, etc.* Jan. 8, 1838.

American State Papers, 32 vols., Washington, D.C., 1832-1861.

City Directories

Boston Directory 1810. Boston: Edward Cotton, 1810.

Boston Directory 1830. Boston: Charles Simpson, 1830.

Boston Directory 1849. Boston: George Adams, 1849.

Boston Almanac 1850. Boston: B.B. Mussey, 1850.

Cambridge Directory 1850. Cambridge: Chronicle Office, 1850.

Charlestown Directory 1848. Charlestown: E.P. Emmons, 1848.

Chelsea Directory 1847-48. Chelsea: Benj. Rivers, 1847.

Lowell Directory 1833, by Benj. Floyd. Lowell: Observer Press, 1833.

Lowell Directory 1849. Lowell: Oliver and Marsh, 1849.

New Bedford Directory 1849. New Bedford: C. & A. Taber, 1849.

Salem Directory and Almanac 1850. Salem: Henry Whipple, 1850.

Worcester Almanac Directory and Business Advertiser 1850. Worcester: Henry J. Howland, 1850.

Newspapers

Boston Commercial Gazette

Boston Daily Advertiser

Boston Independent Chronicle

The Boston Patriot and Mercantile Advertiser

Boston Shipping List

Boston Weekly Messenger

The Columbian Centinel

In the Massachusetts Historical Society

Appleton Family Papers

Lee Family Papers

Thomas Cushing Papers

Jacob & John Wendell Papers

Thomas Lamb Papers

Lamb Family Papers

Amos A. Lawrence Papers

Thomas H. Perkins Papers

Aaron Marble Family Papers

John Bromfield Papers

Rotch Family Papers

Daniel F. Child Diaries

"Letter to the Hon. Abbott Lawrence and the Hon. Robert G. Shaw on the present condition and future growth of Boston." Boston: John Wilson & Son, 1853.

In the Massachusetts State Library

"Of the Statement of the Several BANKS in the Commonwealth of Massachusetts, rendered in January 1811 . . ." Secretary of the Commonwealth, 1811.

"Abstract from the Returns of Banks in Massachusetts." Secretary of the Commonwealth, 1830.

"Abstract Exhibiting the Condition of the Banks in Massachusetts on the first Saturday of September, 1850." Boston: Dutton and Wentworth, 1850.

Manuscript Returns, Census of Manufactures, Census of Population and Census of Agriculture (U.S.) for 1850.

Manuscript compilation, "Valuation of the Commonwealth of Massachusetts for 1850."

Manuscript compilation, "1830 aggregate valuation."

In the New Hampshire State Library

Manuscript Returns, Census of Population, Census of Agriculture, and Census of Manufactures for Rockingham County, N.H. for 1850.

In the Massachusetts State Archives

Original papers of the General Laws of the Commonwealth of Massachusetts for the following years:
> (Dates follow earlier years since legislative sessions were held from March to March of the following year.) Numerals refer to chapters.

1829:   12 (11 June 29), 26 (12 June 29).

1830:   4 (June 30), 17 (7 June 30), 93 (10 March 30), 94 (12 March 30), 95 (12 March 30).

1831:   55 (22 June 31), 56 (22 June 31), 57 (22 June 31), 72 (23 June 31).

1833:   109 (15 March 33), 116 (15 March 33), 118 (15 March 33).

1834:   171.

1835:   95, 111, 131.

1836:   187, 232, 249, 264, 267, 269.

1837:   94, 113, 152.

1838:   96, 103, 195.

1841:   100.

1842:   84.

1844:   89, 100, 109, 116, 134, 141, 150, 172.

1845:   83, 109, 186, 226, 234, 246, 251.

1846:   15, 75, 79, 90, 152, 157, 158, 212, 239, 247, 255, 267.

1847:   70, 85, 146, 178, 187, 200, 204, 238, 243, 249, 250, 252, 253, 269, 276.

1848:   65, 107, 114, 152, 160, 180, 204, 207, 223, 231, 238, 264, 268, 275.

1849:   8, 55, 168, 170, 180, 183, 193, 199, 212.

1851:   107, 113, 125, 128, 221, 242, 245, 283.

In the Merrimack Valley Textile Museum

Appleton Company 1829-1859
Lowell Mass.
4 volumes

Blackstone Company 1828-1853
Blackstone, Mass.
2035 letters

Dudley Woolen Manufacturing Company 1824-1837
Webster, Mass.
5 volumes

New England Southern Mills 1838-1926
Boston, Mass.
2 volumes, 6 document cases

J.P. Stevens & Co. Inc. 1811-1961
New York, N.Y.
1210 vols., 477 document cases
(Includes Records of Nathaniel Stevens, Andover, Mass. 1813-1850)

Essex Company 1845-1948
Lawrence, Mass.
92 volumes, 26 document cases

In the Kress Library, Harvard University

"An Act for Incorporating Certain Persons for the purpose of laying out and making a
     Turnpike Road from Salem to Charles River Bridge." Salem: Joshua Cushing, 1813.

"Act of Incorporation Charlestown Wharf Co." Charlestown: Bunker Hill Press, 1836.

Boston Association of Master Tailors, *Price List.* Boston, 1811 (a broadside).

"Brief Statement of Facts in Relation to the Proposed Railroad from Boston to Plymouth."
     Plymouth: J. Thurber, 1844.

"Brief Statement of facts relative to the Proposed Railroad from Fitchburg to Brattleboro." Boston: Dutton & Wentworth, 1844.

Thomas G. Cary, Result of Manufactures at Lowell. Boston: Little, Brown & Co., 1845.

"Catalogues of Boots and Shoes to be sold by Whitwell Bond & Co., Aug. 29, 1828 . . . Faneuil Hall." Boston: Beals & Homer Co., 1828.

Committee on Boston and Roxbury Mill Corp., "Report." Boston, 1814.

"Catalogue of Foreign Domestic Wool Sold at Auction June 10, 1835." Boston: Livermore & Kendall, 1835.

Nathan T. Davis, Treatise on Tanning. Boston: Private Printing, 1836.

H.A.S. Dearborn, Letters on the Internal Improvements and Commerce of the West. Boston: Henry Lewis, 1839.

P.P.F. DeGrand, Tarriff of Duties on Importations into the United States and Revenue Laws and Custom House Regulations. Boston: P.P.F. DeGrand, 1828.

H.M. Dexter, Influence of Manufacturing Towns. Andover: Wm. H. Wardwell, 1848.

"Essay on the Manufacture of Straw Bonnets." Providence: Barnum Field & Co., 1825.

Boston Citizens "Exposition of Facts and Arguments in Support of a memorial to the Legislature of Mass. . . . in favor of a Bank of Ten Millions." Boston: Dutton & Wentworth, 1836.

Benjamin Foster, The Merchant's Manual. Boston: Perkins & Marvin, 1838.

N.L. Frothingham, The Duties of Hard Times. Boston: Munroe & Francis, 1837.

John Hayward, Gazeteer of Massachusetts 1847. Boston: John Hayward, 1847.

Thomas Hopkinson, "Agreement . . . for a Railroad from Salem to Lowell." Boston: Stacey Richardson, 1848.

James Montgomery, A Practical Detail of the Cotton Manufacture of the United States . . . compared with that of Great Britain. Glasgow: John Niven, Jr., 1840.

"Oak Hall in 1850, Great Sale of the Season, G.W. Simmons." Boston: Snow & Wilder, 1850.

"Proceedings of an Association of the Merchants of Boston for the Mutual Benefit of Creditor and Debtor March 11 1824." Boston: Private Printing, 1834.

"Proceedings of the Convention of the Manufacturers, Dealers, and Operators in the Shoe & Leather Trade." Boston: Saxon & Pierce, 1842.

"Remarks on the Project of Establishing a Line of Packets between Boston and Liverpool."
1822 (?).

"Reports of the Board of Directors of the Lewis Wharf Co. . . . Apr. 6, 1840." Boston:
Beals & Greene, 1840.

"Report of the Committee Appointed by the Stockholders of the Charlestown Wharf Co.
July 5, 1839." Boston: Sleeper, Dix & Rogers, 1839.

"Report of the Committee of Merchants . . . on the Tarriff." Boston: Wells & Tilly, 1820.

"Report of the Directors of the Boston Exchange Co. January 1843." Boston: S.N. Dickinson, 1843.

"Report of the Committee . . . to make sale of the Upland and Flats lying west of Charles
St." 1824.

Worcester Mining Co., *Coal and Articles of Agreement.* Worcester: Henry J. Howland, 1848.

In the Baker Library, Harvard University

(Note: Numbers assigned to each collection correspond to those used in the footnotes.)

BA23   Ebenezer Joy, 1807-1827
         Newmarket, New Hampshire
         1 ledger

BA24   Joseph Heald, Jr., 1808-1813
         Pepperell, Massachusetts
         1 account book

BA30   Dennis Northrup, 1825-1830
         Tyringham, Massachusetts
         1 account book

BA33   John Jones, 1826-1850
         Charlestown, Massachusetts
         1 account book

BA37   William Hosmer, 1842-1853
         Westfield, Massachusetts
         1 diary

BA45   S.K. Brooks, 1814
         Boston, Massachusetts
         1 volume

BA55   Thomas E. Oliver, 1809-1865
         Newcastle, New Hampshire
         32 volumes, 14 boxes (6 ft.)

BA61   Charles W. Morgan, 1820-1865
          New Bedford, Massachusetts
          5 volumes, 1 box

BA85   Duncannon Iron Works, 1841-1850
          Clark's Ferry, Pennsylvania
          2 letter books

BA119   Proprietors of Locks and Canals on Merrimack River, 1792-1947
          Lowell, Massachusetts
          355 volumes, 2 cases (13 ft.)

BA120   Essex Company, 1847-1860
          Lawrence, Massachusetts
          1 box

BA127   Mathew Noble, 1766-1840
          Westfield, Massachusetts
          1 ledger

BA139   Boston Sugar Refinery, 1837-1843
          (Appleton Collection)
          Boston, Massachusetts
          3 volumes, 1 box

BA142   Walter Baker Chocolate Company, 1812-1945
          Dorchester, Massachusetts
          147 volumes, 1 box (14 ft.)

BA146B   Slater and Tiffany, 1812-1847
          Oxford, Massachusetts
          101 volumes

BA147   N.B. Gordon, Agent, 1813-1846
          Various companies
          12 volumes

BA148   Boston Manufacturing Company, 1813-1930
          Waltham, Massachusetts
          182 volumes, 11 boxes, 15 envelopes, 1 case (22 ft.)

BA151   Merrimack Manufacturing Company, 1821-1946
          Lowell, Massachusetts
          114 volumes, 2 boxes, 3 cases (11 ft.)

BA154   Taunton Manufacturing Company, 1823-1844
          Taunton, Massachusetts
          2 volumes

BA157   Annawan Manufactory, 1825-1899
          (Fall River Iron Works Collection)

Fall River, Massachusetts
25 volumes (2 ft.)

BA158   Hamilton Manufacturing Company, 1825-1917
Lowell, Massachusetts
794 volumes, 15 boxes, 6 cases, 3 crates (93 ft.)

BA159   Newmarket Manufacturing Company, 1827-1830
Salem, Massachusetts, and Newmarket, New Hampshire
1 letter book

BA163   Lawrence Manufacturing Company, 1831-1926
Lowell, Massachusetts
924 volumes, 103 boxes, 3 crates (121 ft.)

BA164   Tremont and Suffolk Mills, 1831-1936
Lowell, Massachusetts
106 volumes, 8 boxes (12 ft.)

BA170   Lancaster Mills, 1844-1931
Clinton, Massachusetts
212 volumes, 6 boxes, 3 crates (31 ft.)

BA171   Naumkeag Steam Cotton Manufacturing Company, 1845 (1839)-1947
Salem, Massachusetts
411 volumes, 3 cases, 1 box (45 ft.)

BA186   Moses Holt, 1806-1849
Exeter and Derry, New Hampshire
1 ledger

BA187B   Dudley Manufacturing Company, 1827-1845
Dudley, Massachusetts
28 volumes, 1 box

BA187C   Webster Woolen Company, 1837-1866
Webster, Massachusetts
106 volumes, 19 boxes

BA189   Flannel Manufacturing Company, 1821-1852
Amesbury, Massachusetts
1 volume (8 pages)

BA192   Cordiss Mills, 1836-1887
Millbury, Massachusetts
4 account books

BA200   Bigelow-Sanford Carpet Company, 1828-1953
New York, New York
109 volumes, 1 box, 6 cases, 4 drawers (28 ft.)

BA205   Malden Dye House, 1830-1846
         Hingham and Boston, Massachusetts
         1 small account book

BA207   Plymouth Cordage Company, 1824-1966
         Plymouth, Massachusetts
         404 volumes, 5 boxes, 2 cases, 11 cabinets (58 ft.)

BA211   Endicott and Oliver, 1804-1833 (1810-1814)
         Boston, Massachusetts
         1 volume, 1 box

BA212   James Waldock, 1841-1843
         Boston, Massachusetts
         1 volume

BA216   India Rubber Hat Company, 1829-1857
         Lexington, Massachusetts
         2 account books, 1 folder

BA223   East Boston Timber Company, 1834-1840
         Boston, Massachusetts
         1 box

BA224   John Gates and Sons Company, 1835-1907
         Worcester, Massachusetts
         64 volumes, 2 boxes, 2 cases (12 ft.)

BA231   Edward Slead, 1797-1827
         Dartmouth, Massachusetts
         1 ledger

BA239   C.G. and H.M. Plimpton, 1811-1865
         Walpole, Massachusetts
         36 volumes, 5 boxes, 1 case (6 ft.)

BA241   Fall River Iron Works, 1821-1909
         Fall River, Massachusetts
         285 volumes, 4 cases (34 ft.)

BA243   Lazelle, Perkins and Company, 1828-1849
         South Bridgewater, Massachusetts
         Daybook, folder

BA244   J.C. Hobbs and Sons, 1840-1887
         Billerica, Massachusetts
         7 volumes, 1 box

BA245   Plymouth Mills, 1846-1910
         Plymouth, Massachusetts
         1 record book

BA254   Lowell Machine Shop, 1845-1912
          Lowell, Massachusetts
          447 volumes, 9 boxes, 5 cases (45 ft.)

BA255   Kilburn, Lincoln Machine Company, 1846-1869 (1931)
          Fall River, Massachusetts
          9 cases (9 ft.)

BA260   Thompson Weeks and Company, 1845-1847
          Boston and Charlestown, Massachusetts
          1 daybook

B262   Osgood Bradley Car Company, 1843-1890
          Worcester, Massachusetts
          3 volumes

BA263   Taunton Locomotive Manufacturing Company, 1847-1887
          Taunton, Massachusetts
          3 volumes

BA271   Pyam Cushing, 1837-1845
          Medford, Massachusetts
          1 ledger

BA272   Judah Loring, 1839-1852
          Medford, Massachusetts
          1 account book

BA278   William S. Eddy and Son, 1827-1873
          East Middleboro, Massachusetts
          1 volume, 13 boxes (3 ft.)

BA279   Kimball and Farwell, 1834-1839
          Fitchburg, Massachusetts
          1 volume

BA282   American Steel and Wire Companies, 1822-1936
          Massachusetts and other states
          271 volumes, 16 boxes, 10 cases (30 ft.)

BA282A   Washburn and Goddard, 1822-1848
          Worcester, Massachusetts
          4 volumes

BA282B   Ichabod Washburn, 1835-1842
          Worcester, Massachusetts
          4 volumes

BA282C   I. and C. Washburn, 1842-1849
          Worcester, Massachusetts
          1 ledger

BA282D   I. Washburn and Company, 1850-1861
         Worcester, Massachusetts
         4 volumes

BA284   Taunton Britannia Company, 1830-1844
         Taunton, Massachusetts
         1 volume

BA285   Reed and Barton, 1831-1931
         Taunton, Massachusetts
         218 volumes, 12 boxes, 1 case (25 ft.)

BA289   Samuel Capen, 1800-1817
         Dorchester, Massachusetts
         1 account book

BA297   Eliphalet Davis, 1820-1880
         Cambridgeport, Massachusetts
         34 volumes (3 ft.)

BA300   Boston and Lynn India Rubber Manufacturing Company, 1833-1843
         Lynn, Massachusetts
         1 case (1 ft.)

BA313   Ebenezer Belcher, 1808-1842
         Randolph, Massachusetts
         1 volume

BA314   William Richardson, 1811-1839
         Stoneham, Massachusetts
         1 box

BA315   Samuel R. Duren and Duren family, 1814-1869
         Woburn and Lexington, Massachusetts
         1 volume, 1 box

BA316   Hosea Hollis, 1816-1843
         Randolph, Massachusetts
         1 volume

BA318   No name given, 1823-1855
         New Bedford, Massachusetts
         1 ledger

BA320   John Pearson, 1830-1841
         Newbury, Massachusetts
         1 account book

BA321   Adoniram J. Dyer, 1832-1858
         Randolph, Massachusetts
         1 account book

BA322   Aaron Claflin, 1839-1845
         Milford, Massachusetts
         1 account book

BA324   Jeremiah Hunt, Jr., 1839-1873
         Northboro, Massachusetts
         2 account books

BA325   French, Howard and Company, 1842-1855
         Randolph, Massachusetts
         2 volumes

BA349   Houghton Mifflin Company, 1832- c.1920
         Boston, Massachusetts
         c. 300 volumes, 5 cabinets (in the Houghton Library, Harvard University)

BA395   Boston and Lowell Railroad, Woburn Branch, 1832-1834
         Woburn, Massachusetts
         2 volumes

BA398   Troy and Greenfield Railroad Company, 1844-1881
         Greenfield, Massachusetts
         3 boxes

BA438   New York, New Haven and Hartford Railroad, 1822-1927
         New Haven, Connecticut
         382 volumes, 5 boxes (66 ft.)

BA443   Boston and Albany Railroad Company, 1831-1898
         Boston, Massachusetts
         307 volumes, 28 cases (66 ft.)

BA498   Sloop *Mayflower,* 1824-1825
         Boston, Massachusetts
         1 memorandum book

BA505   Wendell family, 1722-1865
         Portsmouth, New Hampshire
         101 volumes, 7 boxes, 23 cases (39 ft.)

BA738   Hancock family papers, 1712-1854
         Boston, Massachusetts
         29 volumes, 53 boxes (13 ft.)

BA751   Phelps and Rand, 1800-1825
         Boston, Massachusetts
         12 volumes, 1 box (1 ft.)

BA756   Silas Pierce and Company, 1818-1914
         Boston, Massachusetts
         113 volumes, 2 boxes (12 ft.)

BA757   John Fairfield, 1822-1826
         Boston, Massachusetts
         1 letter book

BA758A   Joshua C. Oliver and Company, 1823-1831
         Location not certain
         1 day book

BA759   William Stearns and Company, 1827-1893
         Boston, Massachusetts
         4 volumes, 5 boxes (1 ft.)

BA762   Waterson, Pray and Company, 1832-1833
         Boston, Massachusetts
         1 sales book

BA764   Thompson and Morton, 1834-1861
         Boston, Massachusetts
         42 volumes, 12 boxes, 31 notebooks (10 ft.)

BA765   Griggs and Weld (Aaron D. Weld), 1835-1848
         Boston, Massachusetts
         2 boxes

BA767   Hatch and Fearing, 1838-1839
         Boston, Massachusetts
         2 volumes

BA769   Wainwright and Tappan, 1840-1871
         Boston, Massachusetts
         10 volumes, 2 cases, 1 box (4 ft.)

BA770   N.F. Cunningham and Company, 1841-1851
         Boston, Massachusetts
         8 volumes

BA772   James Morris Whiton, 1843-1857 (1795-1906)
         Boston, Massachusetts
         1 volume

BA774   Lawrence and Company, 1843-1920
         Boston, Massachusetts
         157 volumes, 42 boxes, 29 cases (43 ft.)

BA778   George Huseey, 1850-1871
         New Bedford, Massachusetts
         1 journal

BA837   Thomas Wigglesworth, 1806-1847
         Boston, Massachusetts
         12 volumes (2 ft.)

BA855   William Appleton and Company, 1840-1889
      Boston, Massachusetts
      87 volumes, 93 boxes (24 ft.)

BA905   Daniel Putnam, Jr.; Putnam and Perkins; Putnam and Whitney, 1798-1821
      Fitchburg and Lunenburg, Massachusetts
      5 account books

BA909   Whitney and Dorr, 1799-1813
      Boston, Massachusetts
      5 pamphlets in box

BA911   Robert P. Tolman, 1804-1840
      Dorchester, Massachusetts
      17 volumes (1 ft.)

BA914   Collamore family papers, 1807-1853
      Pembroke and Boston, Massachusetts
      16 volumes (2 ft.)

BA919   Nathan Sweetland, 1811-1816
      Pawtucket, Rhode Island
      1 ledger

BA927   Burr and Pritchard, 1813-1855
      Concord, Massachusetts
      1 box

BA928   David Fisher, Jr., 1815-1818
      Wrentham, Massachusetts
      1 ledger

BA931   Retail selling, 1818-1820
      Boston, Massachusetts
      1 ledger

BA932   M.B. Trundy, 1818-1842
      Portsmouth, New Hampshire
      19 account books (2 ft.)

BA934   John Osborn and Company, 1821-1825
      Boston, Massachusetts
      1 ledger

BA960   General store, 1833-1835
      Sutton, New Hampshire
      1 ledger

BA967   Morton Eddy and Fred K. Cushing, 1843-1845
      Bridgewater, Massachusetts
      1 ledger

BA969   R.W. Turner Company, 1843-1888
         Randolph, Massachusetts
         14 volumes (1 ft.)

BA972   Wyman family, 1845-1856
         Charlestown, Massachusetts
         1 account book and 4 small notebooks

BA978   Walcott and Holden, 1848-1875
         Concord, Massachusetts
         1 volume, 1 box

BA984   Solomon Perry, 1817-1878
         Perry and Sherman
         New Bedford, Massachusetts
         15 volumes, 6 boxes (3 ft.)

BA986   Thomas Austin, 1796-1814
         Boston, Massachusetts
         3 account books

BA987   Gamaliel Manning, 1796-1826
         Billerica, Massachusetts
         2 ledgers

BA988   No name given, 1816-1819
         Harwich, Massachusetts
         1 ledger

BA989   Edward F. Jacobs, 1821-1836
         South Scituate, Massachusetts
         1 day book

BA990   Z. Porter, 1824-1837
         Danvers, Massachusetts
         1 journal

BA991   A.G. Wyman, 1828-1831
         Boston, Massachusetts
         1 volume

BA992   Freeman C. Tobey, 1829-1830
         Barnstable, Massachusetts
         1 day book

BA993   Jonathan Ireland, 1829-1831
         Boston, Massachusetts
         1 volume

BA994   Robert Ingraham, 1829-1849
           New Bedford, Massachusetts
           2 volumes

BA995   Noah Coombs, 1835-1847
           Medway, Massachusetts
           2 volumes

BA998   John Hicks Rogers, 1830-1888
           Boston, Massachusetts
           1 sales book

BA1003   Bigelow, Kennard and Company, 1830-1925
           Boston, Massachusetts
           92 volumes, 2 boxes, and 40 cases (50 ft.)

BA1024   Jacob Peabody and Company, 1804-1826
           Salem, Massachusetts
           10 volumes, 2 boxes (1 ft.)

BA1086   Massachusetts Hospital Life Insurance Company, 1823-1956
           Boston, Massachusetts
           334 volumes, 58 boxes, 12 cases (57 ft.)

BA1107   Elizur Wright; Walter C. Wright, 1845-1916
           Boston, Massachusetts
           2 cases, 1 box (2 ft.)

BA1112   Massachusetts Mutual Fire Insurance Company, 1798-1876
           Boston, Massachusetts
           4 volumes

BA1114   Globe Fire and Marine Insurance Company, 1824-1838
           Boston, Massachusetts
           1 volume

BA1127   Mercantile Marine Insurance Company, 1823-1873
           Boston, Massachusetts
           2 volumes

BA1128   Ocean Insurance Company, 1826-1838
           Porland, Maine
           1 envelope

BA1233   Samuel Sheafe, 1835-1849
           Portsmouth, New Hampshire
           1 journal

SECONDARY SOURCES

Albion, Robert G., "New York and its Disappointed Rivals 1815-1860" in *Journal of Economic and Business History 1930-1931,* pp. 602-629.

Armstrong, John Borden, *Factory Under the Elms: A History of Harrisville New Hampshire 1774-1969.* Cambridge, Mass.: MIT Press, 1969.

Babson, John J., *History of the Town of Gloucester.* Gloucester: Procter Brothers, 1860.

Bacon, Oliver N., *History of Natick.* Boston: Damrell E. Moore, 1856.

Baldwin, R., "Patterns of Development in Newly Settled Regions" in *Manchester School of Economic and Social Studies,* XXIV, 1956, pp. 161-179.

Ballou, Adin, *History of the Town of Milford.* Boston: Rand, Avery & Co., 1882.

Barbour, Harriet B., *Sandwich: The Town that Glass Built.* Boston: Houghton Mifflin Co., 1948.

Barry, William, *History of Framingham Massachusetts.* Boston: James Munroe & Co., 1847.

Beckmann, Martin, *Location Theory.* New York: Random House, 1968.

Berry, Brian J.L., "City: Size Distribution and Economic Development" in *Economic Development and Cultural Change,* IX, 1961, pp. 573-588.

———, *Geography of Market Centers and Retail Distribution.* Englewood: Prentice Hall, 1967.

———, and Frank E. Horton (eds.), *Geographical Perspectives on Urban Systems.* Englewood: Prentice Hall, 1970.

Bidwell, Percy, "Agricultural Revolution in New England" in *American Historical Review,* XXVI, pp. 683-702.

Bigelow, E. Victor, *A Narrative History of the Town of Cohasset Massachusetts.* Cohasset: Private Printing, 1898.

Blumin, Stuart, *The Urban Threshold.* Chicago: University of Chicago Press, 1976.

Bolton History Committee, *History of Bolton 1738-1938.* Bolton: Private Printing, 1938.

Borchert, John R., "American Metropolitan Evolution" in *Geographical Review,* 1967, LVII, pp. 301-332.

Bradford, James, *History of Rowley.* Boston: Ferdinand Andrews, 1840.

Briggs, Asa, *Victorian Cities.* New York: Harper & Row, 1963.

Brigham, Clarence, *History and Bibliography of Early American Newspapers,* 2 vols. Worcester: American Antiquarian Society, 1947.

Brooks, Charles and Usher, James, *History of the Town of Medford.* Boston: Rand, Avery & Co., 1886.

Brown, Louise K., *Wilderness Town.* Bedford: Private Printing, 1968.

Bruchey, Stuart, *The Roots of American Economic Growth, 1607-1861.* New York: Harper & Row, 1968.

Butler, Caleb, *History of the Town of Groton.* Boston: T.R. Marvin, 1848.

Cabot, Mrs. Ropes, *Vanished Boston.* Boston: The Bostonian Society, 1968.

Chamberlain, Mellen, *A Documentary History of Chelsea 1624-1824.* Boston: Massachusetts Historical Society, 1908.

Chandler, Alfred D., "Anthracite Coal and the Beginnings of the Industrial Revolution in the United States" in *Business History Review,* XLVI, 1972, pp. 7-24.

———, "The Beginnings of 'Big Business' in American Industry" in *Business History Review,* XXXIII, 1959, pp. 1-30.

———, *Strategy and Structure.* Cambridge, Mass.: MIT Press, 1962.

———, *The Visible Hand: The Managerial Revolution in American Business.* Cambridge, Mass.: Harvard University Press, 1977.

Chase, George W., *The History of Haverhill Massachusetts.* Haverhill: Private Printing, 1861.

Chickering, Jessee, *A Statistical View of the Population of Massachusetts.* Boston: Little & Brown, 1840.

Christaller, Walter, *Central Places in Southern Germany.* Englewood: Prentice Hall, 1966.

Clarke, George K., *History of Needham Massachusetts.* Cambridge: Private Printing, 1912.

Coffin, Joshua, *A Sketch of the History of Newbury, Newburyport, and West Germany.* Boston: Samuel Drake, 1845.

Cole, Donald B., *Immigrant City: Lawrence Massachusetts 1845-1921.* Chapel Hill: University of North Carolina Press, 1963.

Coleman, Peter J., *The Transformation of Rhode Island.* Providence: Brown University Press, 1963.

Coolidge, John, *Mill and Mansion.* New York: Russell & Russell, 1967.

Cootner, Paul, "The Role of Railroads in the United States Economic Growth" in *Journal of Economic History,* XXIII, 1963, pp. 477-521.

Crowley, Charles, *History of Lowell.* Boston: Lee & Shepard, 1868.

Currier, John J., *History of Newburyport Massachusetts* 1764-1905, 2 volumes. Newburyport: Private Printing, 1906.

Curti, Merle, *The Making of An American Community.* Palo Alto: Stanford University Press, 1959.

Curtis, John Gould, *A History of the Town of Brookline.* Boston: Houghton Mifflin Co., 1933.

Daggett, John, *A Sketch of the History of Attleborough from its Settlement to the Division.* Boston: Samuel Usher, 1894.

Daniels, George F., *History of the Town of Oxford Massachusetts.* Oxford: Private Printing, 1892.

Darling, Arthur B., *Political Changes in Massachusetts 1824-1848.* New Haven: Yale University Press, 1925.

Davenport, Matthew, *Brief Historical Sketch of the Town of Boylston in the County of Worcester.* Lancaster: Carter, Andrews & Co., 1831.

David, Paul, "The Growth of Real Product in the United States before 1840" in *Journal of Economic History,* XXVII, January, 1967, pp. 151-194.

Davis, Lance E., "New England Textile Mills and the Capital Markets: A Study in Industrial Borrowing 1840-1860" in *Journal of Economic History,* XX, March, 1960, pp. 1-18.

———— , "Stock Ownership in the Early New England Textile Industry" in *Business History Review,* XXXII, 1958, pp. 204-222.

DeForest, H.P. and Bater, E.C., *The History of Westborough.* Westborough: Private Printing, 1891.

DeLue, Willard, *The Story of Walpole.* Norwood: Ambrose Press, 1925.

Dickinson, Robert E., *City and Region.* London: Routledge and Kegan Paul, 1964.

Dorchester Antiquarian and Historical Society, *A History of the Town of Dorchester.* Boston: Ebenezer Clapp Jr., 1859.

Dorgan, Maurice B., *History of Lawrence.* Lawrence: Private Printing, 1924.

Dow, George F., *History of Topsfield.* Topsfield: Topsfield Historical Society, 1940.

Duncan, Otis Dudley et al., *Metropolis and Region.* Baltimore: Johns Hopkins University Press, 1960.

Dwelley, Jedediah, and Simmons, John F., *History of Hanover Massachusetts.* Hanover: Private Printing, 1910.

Ellis, Leonard Bolles, *History of New Bedford 1602-1892.* Syracuse: D. Mason & Co., 1892.

Evans, George, "A Sketch of American Business Organization 1832-1900" in Journal of *Political Economy,* LX, December, 1952, pp. 475-486.

Ewell, John Louis, *The Story of Byfield.* Boston: George E. Littlefield, 1904.

Ewing, John S. and Norton, Nancy P., *Broadlooms and Businessmen*. Cambridge, Mass.: Harvard University Press, 1955.

Federal Writers Project, *History of Ashland*. Framingham, 1942.

Firey, Walter, *Land Use in Central Boston*. Cambridge, Mass.: Harvard University Press, 1948.

———, "Sentiment and Symbolism as Ecological Variables" in *American Sociological Review*, X, 1945, pp. 140-148.

Fishlow, Albert, *American Railroads and the Transformations of the Antebellum Economy*. Cambridge, Mass.: Harvard University Press, 1965.

Fogel, Robert W., "American Interregional Trade in the Nineteenth Century" in Andreano, Ralph (ed.), *New Views on American Economic History*. Cambridge, Mass.: Schenkman Publishing Co., 1965.

———, *Railroads and American Economic Growth*. Baltimore: Johns Hopkins University Press, 1964.

———, and Engerman, Stanley (eds.), *Reinterpretation of American Economic Growth*. New York: Harper & Row, 1971.

Ford, Andrew E., *History of the Origin of the Town of Clinton*. Clinton: W.J. Coulter, 1896.

Forrester, Jay W., *Urban Dynamics*. Cambridge, Mass.: MIT Press, 1969.

Friess, Claude M., *Andover: Symbol of New England*. Andover: Andover and North Andover Historical Societies, 1959.

Frisch, Michael, *Town into City: Springfield Massachusetts and the Meaning of Community 1840-1880*. Cambridge, Mass.: Harvard University Press, 1972.

Gibb, George S., *The Saco Lowell Shops*. Cambridge, Mass.: Harvard University Press, 1950.

———, *The Whitesmiths of Taunton: A History of Reed and Barton 1824-1943*. New York: Harper & Row, 1969.

Gilchrist, David T. (ed.), *The Growth of the Seaport Cities 1790-1825*. Charlottesville: University of Virginia Press, 1967.

Gilmour, James M., *The Spatial Evolution of Manufacturing Southern Ontario, 1851-1891*. Toronto: University of Toronto, 1972.

Glaab, Charles N. and Brown, A. Theodore, *A History of Urban America*. London: Collier & MacMillan Ltd., 1967.

Gottlieb, Manuel, *Estimates of Residential Building in the U.S. 1840-1939*. New York: National Bureau of Economic Research, 1964.

Gottmann, Jean, *Megalopolis*. New York: The Twentieth Century Fund, 1961.

Green, Constance M., *Holyoke, Massachusetts*. New Haven: Yale University Press, 1939.

———, *The Rise of Urban America*. New York: Harper & Row, 1965.

Gregory, Frances, *Nathan Appleton, Merchant and Entrepreneur 1779-1861*. Charlottesville: University of Virginia Press, 1975.

Habakkuk, H.J., *American and British Technology in the Nineteenth Century*. Cambridge, England: Cambridge University Press, 1967.

Hamilton, Edward P., *A History of Milton*. Milton: Milton Historical Society, 1957.

Hammond, Bray, *Banks and Politics in the United States*. Princeton: Princeton University Press, 1957.

Handlin, Oscar, *Boston's Immigrants*. Cambridge, Mass.: Harvard University Press, 1959.

———, *Commonwealth: Massachusetts 1774-1860*. Cambridge, Mass.: Harvard University Press, 1969.

———, and Burchard, John (eds.), *The Historian and the City*. Cambridge, Mass.: MIT Press, 1963.

Hayes, Lucie Caroline, *Boxborough: A New England Town and its People.* Philadelphia: J.W. Lewis & Co., 1891.

Hazard, Blanche E., *The Organization of the Boot and Shoe Industry in Massachusetts Before 1875.* Cambridge, Mass.: Harvard University Press, 1921.

Hazen, Henry A., *History of Billerica Massachusetts.* Boston: A. Williams & Co., 1883.

Henretta, James, "Economic Development and Social Structure in Colonial Boston" in *William and Mary Quarterly,* Ser. 3, XX, pp. 75-92.

Herrick, William D., *History of the Town of Gardner.* Gardner: Private Printing, 1878.

Higgs, Robert, *The Transformation of the American Economy.* New York: Wiley & Sons, 1971.

Hough, Henry B., *Wamsutta of New Bedford.* New Bedford: Private Printing, 1946.

Houghton, William A., *A History of the Town of Berlin 1874-1895.* Worcester: F.S. Blanchard & Co., 1895.

Hozelitz, B.F., "The City, The Factory and Economic Growth" in *American Economic Review,* XL, 1955, pp. 166-184.

Hudson, Charles, *History of the Town of Lexington.* Boston, Wiggin & Lunt, 1868.

Hunter, Louis, "Heavy Industries before 1860" in Harold Williamson (ed.), *Growth of the American Economy.* New York, 1951.

Huse, Charles P., *The Financial History of Boston 1822-1909.* Cambridge: Mass.: Harvard University Press, 1916.

Hutchinson, Ruth G., "A Study in Business Mortality" in *American Economic Review,* XXVIII, 1938.

Isard, Walter, *Location and Space Economy.* Cambridge, Mass.: MIT Press, 1956.

———, "Transport Developments and Building Cycles" in *Quarterly Journal of Economics,* LVII, 1947, pp. 90-112.

———, and Langford, Thomas, *Regional Input-Output Study: Recollections, Reflections, and Diverse Notes on the Philadelphia Experience.* Cambridge, Mass.: MIT Press, 1971.

Jaher, Frederic C., *The Age of Industrialism in America.* New York: The Free Press, 1968.

Jenkins, Charles W., *Facts Relating to the Early History of Falmouth, Massachusetts.* Private Printing.

Johnson, Arthur M., and Supple, Barry E., *Boston Capitalists and Western Railroads.* Cambridge, Mass.: Harvard University Press, 1967.

Kennedy, Charles J., "Commuter Services in the Boston Area" in *Business History Review,* XXXVI, 1962, pp. 153-170.

Kent, Josiah C., *Northborough History.* Newton: Garden City Press, 1921.

Kingman, Bradford, *History of North Bridgewater.* Boston: Private Printing, 1866.

Kirkland, Edward C., *Men, Cities and Transportation,* 2 volumes. Cambridge, Mass.: Harvard University Press, 1948.

Kirkpatrick, Doris, *The City and the River.* Fitchburg: Fitchburg Historical Society, 1971.

Knights, Peter, *The Plain People of Boston 1830-1860.* New York: Oxford University Press, 1971.

Krackhardt, Frederick A., *History of the Town of Berlin.* Berlin: Private Printing, 1962.

Labaree, Benjamin, *Patriots and Partisans.* Cambridge, Mass.: Harvard University Press, 1963.

Lamb, Robert, "The Entrepreneur and the Community" in Coben and Hill's *American Economic History.* New York, 1967, pp. 135-153.

Lampard, Eric, "The History of Cities in Economically Advanced Areas" in *Economic Development and Cultural Change III,* pp. 81-136.

Lamson, Darius, *History of the Town of Manchester, Massachusetts, 1645-1895.* Manchester: Private Printing, 1895.

Lane, Roger, *Policing the City 1822-1885.* Cambridge, Mass.: Harvard University Press, 1963.

Lebergott, Stanley, *Manpower and Economic Growth.* New York: McGraw Hill, 1964.

Le Blanc, Robert, *The Location of Manufacturing in New England in the Nineteenth Century.* Hanover: Dartmouth College, 1969.

Lincoln, George, *History of the Town of Hingham,* 2 volumes. Hingham: Private Printing, 1893.

Lindstrom, Diane, *Economic Development in the Philadelphia Region, 1810-1850.* New York: Columbia University Press, 1977.

Lockridge, Kenneth A., *A New England Town: The First Hundred Years.* New York: W.W. Norton, 1970.

Losch, August, "The Nature of Economic Regions" in *Southern Economic Journal,* V, July, 1938, pp. 71-78.

Lovett, Robert W. and Bishop, Eleanor C., *List of Manuscripts in Baker Library.* Boston: Baker Library, 1969.

Lukermann, F., "Empirical Expressions of Nodality and Hierarchy in a Circulation Manifold" in *East Lakes Geographer II,* 1966, pp. 17-44.

Mansfield, Edwin, *Microeconomics.* New York: Norton, 1970.

Marshfield Tercentenary Committee, *Marshfield . . . .* Marshfield: Private Printing, 1940.

Marvin, Abijah P., *History of the Town of Lancaster, Massachusetts.* Lancaster: Private Printing, 1879.

Mayer, Harold M. and Kohn, Clyde B. (eds.), *Headings in Urban Geography.* Chicago: University of Chicago Press, 1959.

Merrill, Joseph, *History of Amesbury . . . and Merrimac.* Haverhill: Franklin P. Stiles, 1880.

Millbury Historical Committee, *Centennial History of the Town of Millbury.* Millbury: Private Printing, 1915.

Miller, Roberta B., *City and Hinterland: A Case Study Of Urban Growth and Regional Development.* Westport: Greenwood Press, 1979.

Moore, Charles W., *Timing a Century: History of the Waltham Watch Company.* Cambridge, Mass.: Harvard University Press, 1945.

Moore, Esther G., *History of Gardner, Massachusetts.* Gardner. Private Printing, 1967.

Morgan, William C., *Beverly: Garden City by the Sea.* Beverly: Amos L. Odell, 1897.

Morison, Samuel E., *The Maritime History of Massachusetts.* Boston: Houghton Mifflin, 1961.

———, *The Ropemakers of Plymouth.* Boston: Houghton Mifflin, 1950.

National Bureau of Economic Research, *Demographic and Economic Change in Developed Countries.* Princeton: Princeton University Press, 1960.

Navin, Thomas R., *The Whitin Machine Works Since 1831.* Cambridge, Mass.: Harvard University Press, 1950.

North, Douglass C., *The Economic Growth of the United States.* New York: Norton, 1961.

———, *Growth and Welfare in the American Past.* Englewood: Prentice Hall, 1966.

Nourse, Henry S., *History of the Town of Harvard, Massachusetts 1732-1893.* Harvard: Warren Hopgood, 1894.

Nourse, Hugh O., *Regional Economics.* New York: McGraw Hill, 1968.

Nutt, Charles, *History of Worcester and its People.* 4 volumes. New York: Lewis Historical Publishing Company, 1919.

Parker, Margaret T., *Lowell, A Study in Industrial Development.* New York: Macmillan & Company, 1940.

Partridge, George F., *History of the Town of Bellingham, Massachusetts 1719-1919.* Bellingham: Private Printing, 1919.

Pattee, William S., *A History of Old Braintree and Quincy*. Quincy: Green & Prescott, 1878.

Perloff, Harvey and Wingo, Lowdon. *Issues in Urban Economics*. Baltimore: Johns Hopkins University Press, 1968.

———, and Dunn, Edgar, Lampard, Eric and Muth, Richard, *Regions, Resources and Economic Growth*. Lincoln: University of Nebraska Press, 1960.

Pierce, C.H. and Dean, H.J., *Surface Water of Massachusetts*. Washington: Gov't. Print Office, 1916.

Pierce, Frederick Clifton, *History of Grafton, Massachusetts*. Worcester: C. Hamilton, 1879.

Porter, Glenn (ed.), *Regional Economic History, the Mid-Atlantic Area Since 1700*. Greenville: Eleutherian Mills Hagley Foundation, 1976.

Porter, Glenn and Livesay, Harold, *Merchants and Manufacturers*. Baltimore: Johns Hopkins University Press, 1971.

Pred, Allan, *The Spatial Dynamics of Urban Industrial Growth, 1800-1914*. Cambridge, Mass.: MIT Press, 1966.

———, *Urban Growth and the Circulation of Information*. Cambridge, Mass.: Harvard University Press, 1973.

Purdue University, *Purdue Faculty Papers in Economic History 1956-1966*. Homewood: Irwin, 1967.

Roads, Samuel, *History and Traditions of Marblehead*. Marblehead: N.A. Lindsey, 1897.

Roberts, Christopher, *The Middlesex Canal, 1793-1860*. Cambridge, Mass.: Harvard University Press, 1938.

Rosen, Elliot, "Growth of the American City 1830-1860" in unpublished doctoral dissertation, New York University, 1953.

Rowe, Henry K., *Tercentenary History of Newton 1630-1930*. Newton: City of Newton, 1930.

Rozman, Gilbert, *Urban Networks in Ching China and Tokugawa Japan*. Princeton: Princeton University Press, 1974.

Russell, Josiah Cox, *Medieval Regions and their Cities*. London: David and Charles, 1972.

Salsbury, Stephen, *The State, The Investor and The Railroad*. Cambridge, Mass.: Harvard University Press, 1967.

Schlesinger, Arthur, *The Rise of the City 1878-1898*. New York: Macmillan, 1933.

Schnore, Leo and Hauser, Philip, *The Study of Urbanization*. New York: Wiley & Sons, 1965.

Seabury, Carl and Paterson, Stanley, *Merchant Prince of Boston: Colonel T.H. Perkins 1764-1854*. Cambridge, Mass.: Harvard University Press, 1971.

Sharpless, John B., *City Growth in the United States, England and Wales, 1820-1861: The Effects of Location Size and economic Structure on Inter-Urban Variations in Demographic Growth*. New York, Arno Press, 1976.

Skinner, G.W., "Marketing and Social Structure in Rural China" in *Journal of Asian Studies*, XXXIV, November, 1964.

Sly, John, *Town Government in Massachusetts*. Cambridge, Mass.: Harvard University Press, 1930.

Smith, Frank, *A History of Dedham, Massachusetts*. Dedham: Dedham Transcript Press, 1936.

Smith, Samuel L., *History of Newton*. Boston: American Logotype Company, 1880.

Smolensky E. and Ratejezak, D., "The Conception of Cities" in *Explorations in Entrepreneurial History*, 1965, pp. 90-131.

Stearns, Ezra, *History of Ashburnham Massachusetts*. Ashburnham: Published by the Town, 1887.

Stevens, William, *History of Stoneham*. Stoneham: F.L. and W.E. Whittier, 1891.

Stone, Edwin M., *History of Beverly 1630-1842*. Boston: James Munroe & Company, 1843.

Stone, Ora, *A History of Massachusetts Industries*, 4 volumes. Boston-Chicago: S.J. Clarke, 1930.

Summers, William, *A History of East Boston*. Boston: J.E. Tilton and Company, 1858.

Taylor, George R., "American Urban Growth Preceding the Railway Age" in *Journal of Economic History*, XXVII, 1967, pp. 309-339.

Temin, Peter, "Steam and Water Power in the Early Nineteenth Century" in *Journal of Economic History*, XXVI, June, 1966.

Temple, J.H., *A History of Framingham Massachusetts*. Framingham: Town of Framingham, 1887.

Thernstrom, Stephen and Sennett, Richard (eds.), *Nineteenth Century Cities*. New Haven: Yale University Press, 1969.

———, *The Other Bostonians*. Cambridge, Mass.: Harvard University Press, 1973.

———, *Poverty and Progress: Social Mobility in a Nineteenth Century City*. Cambridge, Mass.: Harvard University Press, 1964.

Thompson, Wilbur, *A Preface to Urban Economics*. Baltimore: Johns Hopkins University Press, 1968.

Tilton, George H., *History of Rehoboth*, Massachusetts. Boston: Private Printing, 1918.

Trayser, Donald G., *Barnstable: Three Centuries of a Cape Cod Town*. Hyannis: F.B. and F.P. Goss, 1939.

Vinovskis, Maris, "Mortality Rates and Trends in Massachusetts before 1860" in *Journal of Economic History*, XXXII, 1972, pp. 184-213.

Wade, Richard C., *The Urban Frontier*. Chicago: University of Chicago Press, 1964.

Walsh, Margaret, *The Manufacturing Frontier: Pioneer Industry in Antebellum Wisconsin, 1830-1860*. Madison: State Historical Society of Wisconsin, 1972.

Ward, David, *Cities and Immigrants*. New York: Oxford University Press, 1971.

Ware, Caroline, *Early New England Cotton Manufacture*. Boston: Houghton Mifflin, 1931.

Warner, Sam Bass, Jr., "If all the World were Philadelphia: A Scaffolding for Urban History 1774-1930" in *American Historical Review*, LXXIV, October 1968, pp. 26-43.

———, *The Private City: Philadelphia in Three Periods of its Growth*. Philadelphia: University of Pennsylvania Press, 1968.

———, *Streetcar Suburbs: The Process of Growth in Boston 1870-1900*. Cambridge: Mass.: Harvard & MIT, 1962.

———, *The Urban Wilderness*. New York: Harper & Row, 1972.

Waters, Thomas F., *Ipswich in the Massachusetts Bay Colony*, 2 volumes. Ipswich: Ipswich Historical Society, 1917.

Waters, Wilson, *A History of Chelmsford, Massachusetts*. Lowell: Courier Citizen Company, 1917.

Weber, Adna Ferrin, *The Growth of Cities in the Nineteenth Century: A Study in Statistics*. New York: Macmillan Company, 1899 (Ithaca: Cornell University Press, 1963, reprint).

Wells, John A., *The Peabody Story*. Salem: Essex Institute, 1972.

Westminster Historical Society, *A History of Westminster*. Peterborough: Private Printing, 1961.

Weston, Thomas, *History of the Town of Middleboro*. Boston: Houghton Mifflin Company, 1906.

White, Gerald T., *A History of the Massachusetts Hospital Life Insurance Company*. Cambridge, Mass.: Harvard University Press, 1955.

White, Kevin, *Historical Data on Mass Cities and Towns*. Boston: Massachusetts Secretary of State, 1966.

Whitehall, Walter M., *Boston: A Topographical History*. Cambridge, Mass.: Harvard University Press, 1963.

Wilkinson, Thomas O., *The Urbanization of the Japanese Labor Force*. Amherst: University of Massachusetts, 1965.

Williamson, Jeffrey, "AnteBellum Urbanization in the American Northeast" in *Journal of Economic History*, XXV.

———— , and Swanson, J., "Growth of Cities in the American Northeast" in *Explorations in Entrepreneurial History*, 2nd Ser., 1965, volume 4 supplement.

Windsor, Justin (ed.), *The Memorial History of Boston*, 4 volumes. Boston: Ticknor and Company, 1881.

Wiswall, Clarence A., and Crafts, Eleanor Boit, *One Hundred Years of Paper Making*. Reading: Private Printing, 1938.

Wrigley, E. A., *Population and History*. New York: McGraw Hill, 1969.

Yazaki, Takeo, *The Japanese City*. Tokyo: Japan Publications Trading Company, 1963.

INDEX